PSYCHOTHERAPY REVISED:

New Frontiers in Research and Practice

PSYCHOTHERAPY REVISED:

New Frontiers in Research and Practice

E. Lakin Phillips
The George Washington University

In Collaboration With
Peter J. Fagan
Michael D. Kaiser
Diane M. DePalma
Theodore J.C. Heavner

LEA LAWRENCE ERLBAUM ASSOCIATES, PUBLISHERS
1985   Hillsdale, New Jersey   London

Lawrence Erlbaum Associates, Inc., Publishers
365 Broadway
Hillsdale, New Jersey 07642

Library of Congress Cataloging-in-Publication Data

Phillips, E. Lakin (Ewing Lakin), 1915–
   Psychotherapy revised.

   Bibliography: p.
   Includes index.
   1. Psychotherapy.   I. Title. [DNLM: 1. Psycho-
therapy. WM 420 P558pb]
RC480.5.P49   1985   616.89′14   85-13149
ISBN 0-89859-571-1

Printed in the United States of America
10   9   8   7   6   5   4   3   2   1

Contents

Preface

This book is the product of many minds, many hands, and many hours at the computer. I would have to write another book of the same size to express my indebtedness to all those who have stimulated me, worked with me, criticized, and enlarged upon my ideas and practices. For many years I have tried out the ideas of others as well as some of my own, among my colleagues at the Counseling Center, members of the Psychology Department, and friends.

One's distillation is never final; that is a good thing. But one must find occasional quiet places, plateaus if you will, lagoons for resting after strenuous effort. I am at such a juncture now.

Writing this book and sharing ideas with peers and students probably has been the most exciting intellectual time of my life. I only hope it can excite similar interest and challenge among others. I am grateful for the stimulation and help afforded by those cooperating with me in writing this book and in much of the research preliminary to the writing: Peter J. Fagan, Diane M. DePalma, Michael B. Kaiser, Theodore Heavner, to my secretary, May Nakamura, to my research assistant, Renee Pettis, to Ed Trenn, graphic artist, and to all other members of my staff at the Counseling Center. Over the years I have discussed many of the issues addressed in this book with colleagues who have been of inestimable value: Arthur J. Bachrach, James N. Mosel, Charles E. Rice, John J. Sullivan, and Daniel N. Wiener. To try to name even the outstanding members of my seminars over the years would take a long time; suffice it to say I have found such time highly provocative and rewarding. My remaining hope is that others will find my particular distillation useful, productive, and rewarding; that is all one can ask from friendship or science.

1 Attrition: The Number One Problem of Psychotherapy Practice and Research

Over the past several decades psychotherapy has evidenced enormous activity without demonstrating much change. The proliferation of theories of psychotherapy has grown to staggering proportions (Corsini, 1981; Garfield, Herink, 1980; 1981 Patterson). Given this much activity, there should have been a greater distillation of ideas; not a rigid prescription of what is, or how to do, psychotherapy, but a settling in on basic concepts and some unification delimiting of practice.

The reason for this proliferation of theories is more understandable than its consequences. On the one hand, the "talking cure" has stimulated a lot of thinking, guesswork, and some theorizing of value—thus accounting for many therapists/theorists throwing their hats in the ring—but has resulted in a corresponding lack of appropriate research addressing salient issues. Most research has been on very narrow problems of technique, important in some problem areas and apparently without much value in other areas (Bergin & Lambert, 1978; Glass & Miller, 1980; Garfield, 1978; Landman & Dawes, 1982; Smith, Glass, & Miller, 1980)—and much has been left dangling among studies of therapy evaluation and outcome. The matter of outcome is still an important issue in psychotherapy. How are we to judge the value of something unless we can study its consequences? The opinion that the outcome problem has been left hanging is a judgment supported throughout this book; but for the now, suffice it to say that the reason the outcome problem is so hazy, ill-studied, and lacking in generalizability leads us precisely to the main issue of the book: attrition.

Attrition has lamed or even killed off much outcome research that was testing hypotheses about psychotherapy practice, technique, diagnosis, presenting problems, and the like. The weak offerings it has rendered have pointed to issues inherent in generalizing results to other populations. If one were to transport our culture to a different land, and were obliged to select from the vast psychotherapy literature practices and validations that would put the new society in good stead for dealing with its problems there would be a great clamor by present-day therapists/theorists to be represented, but few substantial criteria on which to base a decision. (One possible outcome of such a hypothetical challenge might be that there were no winners and everybody's notions would be up for grabs in the new land.)

The literature on psychotherapy research contains infrequent and unsystematic references to the impact of attrition. Herein lies a serious problem, open to study.

LITERATURE REVIEW ON ATTRITION

Few of the Annual Reviews of Psychology (published since 1950) contain references to attrition. Most reviews cover studies that concern themselves primarily with internal processes among various viewpoints, and some report outcome results. However, some reviews of attrition (also called "dropping out") have been comprehensive and informative. The main review studies follow.

Luborsky and Associates.   Luborsky, Chandler, Auerbach, Cohen, and Bachrach (1971) and Luborsky, Singer, and Luborsky (1975) reviewed 166 studies of outpatient psychotherapy among individual adult cases. They studied predictors of outcome from psychotherapy based on patient, therapist, and treatment factors. Most studies dealt with client or patient predictors, far fewer with therapist or treatment variables. The psychological status of clients — the healthier the better — their motivation for treatment, the presence of some anxiety or discomfort, and intellectual/educational/social characteristics that bode well for gainful therapeutic outcome have been more fully addressed. Few lower class or uneducated persons have been studied. That most psychotherapy has been addressed to the young, attractive, verbal, intelligent, and stable (the so-called YAVIS characteristics) began to be recognized about this time. The Luborsky et al. review defined psychotherapy as distinct from information giving, educational or occupational guidance, shock-chemotherapy treatments, laboratory analogues (more recently a common development), or behavior therapy (also more common since the 1971 Luborsky et al. review). Zax and Klein (1960) and Snyder (1947) also offered definitions of psychotherapy.

Although there are many variables reported on in the Luborsky et al. review (1971; Table I, p. 148), the portion of the review concerning this book revolves around the "drop-out versus stay-in psychotherapy phenomenon" (pp. 154–157). These reviewers assert that "there is some indirect evidence . . . that *length of treatment* is positively related to gain from psychotherapy" but they did not elect to review the dropout problem as thoroughly as some other variables because they averred there was "no *explicit* evidence that this variable was consistently related to the amount of gain a patient makes" (p. 154). Despite this disclaimer — one to be challenged here — Luborsky et al. did turn up some interesting information on dropouts from psychotherapy. Although these reviewers report on 20 studies of length of sessions (Table I, p. 148) that were significantly related to outcome, two studies were unrelated to outcome, but the number-of-sessions variable did not usually include dropout figures, nor comparisons with "stayers" at the end of the therapy series. The burden of staying or dropping out fell on the descriptive or predictive power of *client* variables and included characteristics previously cited. The motivation-for-treatment variable added the most to the terminator-remainer battery that attempted to predict outcome from psychotherapy (p. 155). An interesting final remark in this section of the paper was, "Therapists have some influence, but not a large one, on the proportions of both populations (remainers and terminators) they can hold in treatment" (p. 155) Data are presented later to question this generalization.

Other generalizations from the Luborsky et al. review (1971) addressed are the following: Most research conclusions about the clients stem from studies of how they were *before* treatment; little data support generalizations about therapist characteristics or theoretical orientation; the most used criterion measure of outcome was therapists' gross improvement ratings of clients; clients who drop out are seen as not improving, or as failures; and of the 166 studies reviewed only a few meet wide-ranging criteria or predictive research adequacy in the matter of outcome: Rogers and Dymond (1954); Fiske, Cartwright and Kirtner (1964); Frank, Gliedman, Imber, Stone, and Nash (1959); Gottschalk, Mayerson, and Gottlieb (1967); Rogers, Gendlin, Kiesler, and Truax (1967); Wallerstein, Robbins, Sargent, and Luborsky (1956).

Brandt's Review. Brandt (1965) reviewed 25 specific studies of factors promoting client dropouts among individual adult patients. Among 29 variables investigated in 18 research reports, there was no differentiation found between stayers and dropouts in regard to sex, age, and marital status; the only differentiation pivoted on personality characteristics. Higher client educational attainment was related to staying in therapy, congruent with Luborsky et al. (1971).

Brandt's (1965) review places the cause of dropping out mainly on the patient's initiative, although allowing for some "guidance" in the matter by therapists (p. 6). Some research reported in the Brandt review allows for unsystematically explored differences in attrition among long-term and private practice therapy cases compared to short-term cases, but no review of factors related to client or therapist behavior is identified. Sometimes therapists are said to discharge allegedly unsuccessful cases (Myers & Auld, 1955). The generality of any possibly progressive attritional pattern was unknown. The range in the number of therapy treatments in the Brandt review is extremely large — from a few sessions to years (Burnham, 1951). Sometimes the attrition issue was rendered unclear by reference to a "trial period" of 3 to 6 months before therapy evolved. In the Burnham report, even the trial period of 3 to 6 months (three to five interviews per week) would suggest a total of 35 to 120 sessions, a period several times longer than brief therapy. Attrition in short-term therapy would therefore appear to be much more definitive and observably related to other variables. Against this longer range period of therapy sessions, Brandt's Table 1 (p. 7) nonetheless identifies 25 studies that vary in the mean number of sessions from 5.6 for the shorter therapies to 12.6 sessions for the longer ones. Despite references to long-term psychotherapy, Brandt concentrates on studies in which short-term therapy (whether time-limited or not) was the prevailing model of treatment. Apropos of the importance of the *pattern* of attrition, which will be addressed more fully later, Brandt's Fig. 1 (p. 8) (possibly the first report of this kind in the literature) shows the percentage of clients dropping out after one or more sessions, study by study, for a total of 20 sessions. This figure shows that only five studies afforded a proper data base (Affleck & Medwick, 1959 Hiler, 1958; Kadushin, 1969; Kurland, 1956; and Rogers, 1951) on client loss to attrition (about 50% by the third or fourth session). Brandt's figure showed that the *first* therapy session saw a termination of about 35% of the clientele. Studies in the Brandt review that followed attrition from intake to the end of therapy, session-by-session, were rare.

Brandt reviewed factors related to pre-therapy or intake dropouts. (This topic is treated systematically below.) Suffice it to say now that the "rejection of treatment . . . by patients . . . at intake" led Brandt to state that from 3% to 35% of the clients dropped out at intake, in the seven studies surveyed that reported on this particular statistic (Table I, p. 7). However interesting this statistic appears, it seems to have been abandoned, even in research reviews as late as 1983; and Brandt observed that "an extensive literature search did not reveal a single follow-up study of pre-therapy dropout" (Brandt, 1965, p. 10). This situation about pre-therapy (or intake) attrition appears to be the same today inasmuch as few of the recent reviews of attrition or follow-up evaluation have even noted the problem, much less studied it (Garfield, 1978, 1981; Gelso & Johnson, 1983; Smith, Glass, & Miller, 1980).

Miscellaneous Reviews.   In the comprehensive *Handbook* (Garfield & Bergin, 1978), there are only two index references to attrition and none to dropout. Despite this indexed lack there are, nonetheless, some informative discussions of attrition. Bergin and Lambert (1978) discuss issues raised by Eysenck (1952, 1960, 1965, 1966, 1967) and Rachman (1971), and Rachman and Wilson (1980), who agree with Eysenck about the success rate of psychotherapy compared to people who appear to get better on their own. The voluminous reporting of pro and con opinions on this subject cannot be addressed in detail here. However, the systematic study of attrition affords the opportunity to reanalyze data presented by Bergin and Lambert concerning therapeutic outcome research, for example, from the Berlin Psychoanalytic Institute about 1930 (Bergin & Lambert, 1978, pp. 141–144; Knight 1941). During its first 10 years of operation, the BPI had 1955 "consultations" (called "ostensible therapy applicants" here) from which population 721 analyses were begun. These two figures give us an intake or "pre-therapy" figure of a 64% loss. Thus about two thirds of the potential analysands were screened out or eliminated on some therapist-determined grounds at the outset. Further, of the 721 cases beginning psychoanalysis, 361, or 50% had "concluded treatment at the time of the report" (Bergin & Lambert, 1978, p. 141). Of the 721 beginning treatment, 241 cases, or 33%, had terminated prematurely (due to patient, therapist, or mutual decision), with 117 patients still in treatment at the time of the report. Of the 363 patients completing treatment, 47 (13%) were considered "uncured," and 116, 89, and 111 cases were judged, respectively, improved in increasing amounts (total = 316, or 87%). If one takes as the basis for deciding on outcome (the 316 cases completing treatment) then 87% of the 363 "concluding treatment" would be successful or highly so; but when one considers that the figures begin with *commencement* of therapy (721 cases of psychoanalysis netting 316 successful cases), the percentage shrinks to 44%; and, when the 316 successful cases are seen as a percentage of the ostensible therapy cases (N = 1955), the percentage shrinks to *16%* (the 117 patients remaining in treatment would have to be properly apportioned upon termination).

Data are presented later showing that in short-term, outpatient, individual psychotherapy, reported success ratings range from 15% to 25% of the original (ostenstible therapy) population, a figure closely similar to that of the Berlin Psychoanalytic Institute over a 10-year period. Two issues derive from the BPI data: First, *all* cases must be considered in arriving at evaluations of outcome, from pre-therapy (or intake) onward; and, second, the role of screening out, judging satisfactory or not for treatment—largely if not wholly in the clinician's hands—must be questioned more thoroughly if the delivery of mental health services to the populace is to remain an important issue.

In the Bergin and Lambert article (1978), their summary data (Table 5.1, pp. 142–143)—in disputation over the Eysenck issue—become moot. That is, the differing criteria offered by various interpreters of the BPI data fail to show an agreed-upon attritional base. Whether people get better "on their own" significantly often, as Eysenck and Rachman and others allege, is important in its own right, but within the context of the reporting clinics, the attritional issue cuts through the Eysenck dispute and enlarges the problem of outcome evaluations. Nearly all clinics have been somewhat superficial in reporting on various types of outcome data inasmuch as they have concentrated on data at what is often some arbitrary beginning point (not from intake) and calculated successes and failures therefrom. For the same reason – the neglect of attrition – the Bergin and Lambert Table 5.2 and Table 5.3 (pp. 146–147), regarding the percentages of "remission rates" from a variety of studies, are also moot, because one seldom knows from their review what juncture – from the intake interview onward – is the basic one. The subtleties of eliminating patients/clients from psychotherapy, and the attendant reasons, are often beyond the comprehension of the reader of research reports.

The Role of Controls. The obfuscation of outcome research and conclusions from psychotherapy is contributed to not only by the attritional problem. Frank (1973) has shown that controls are not put "on ice," awaiting the opportunity for therapy, but up to 50% seek other therapy or informal contacts, a fact that confronts the Eysenck and Rachman contentions. Information is needed on controls in studies more widely dispersed than Frank's report elucidating their informal attempts to gain help and how these gains would compare with formal therapy efforts (see discussion of the Di Loreto study following). Bergin and Lambert end a section on the role of informal or "spontaneous" help by saying, "Perhaps selected helping persons in the 'natural' social environment provide adequate or better coping conditions for neurosis than do trained mental health experts" (p. 149). In this connection it is well known that minimally trained persons can have a salutary effect on helping emotionally disturbed people (Carkhuff & Truax, 1965; Emrick & Lassen, 1977; Gruver, 1971; Johnson & Katz, 1973; Poser, 1966; Siegel, 1973; Strupp, Hadley, & Gomes-Schwartz, 1977). Adding together nonspecific factors in mental health/psychotherapy change (Frank et al., 1959; Garfield, 1980, pp. 126–133), and the possibility that attrition from psychotherapy does not necessarily bode failure, we are forced to considerably enlarge our notions of therapeutic change and how it may be brought about.

Length of Treatment. Of value regarding psychotherapy outcome is the length-of-treatment variable often considered as the main therapeutic variable. In Table 5.4 (Bergin & Lambert, 1978, p. 155), studies are cited that illustrate both deteriorating and positive change from both short- and long-term therapy. Of nine studies cited, one is of short-term duration (4 months) among 96 junior high school students; one of 3–5 months duration with 72 short- and longer term psychotics; one study reports on 80 eclectically treated college students (3 therapy sessions) involving anxiety complaints; and in the six other studies cited psychotherapy lasted from 24 sessions to six years. There is no decisiveness favoring long-term therapy in this summary. With short-term therapy, "deterioratng" cases can be noted early with possible correction following. If long-term therapy produced no clearly better follow-up results than short-term therapy (Luborsky et al., 1971), then the early detection of possibly untoward results from therapy would seem to be very important and should not wait on lengthy time periods for evidence. However, conclusions from the Bergin and Lambert summary are hard to come by, because the important issue of attrition has been neglected in all of the reported studies.

Garfield (1978) discusses the problem of premature dropout from therapy before a mutual client-therapist agreement has been reached (by definition *dropout* implies non-mutual decisions). Garfield offers a summary of some findings on length of treatment (Table 6.1, p. 195), which showed how 560 patients seen at a VA clinic (Garfield & Kurz, 1952) were distributed over a number of psychotherapy sessions. The mean number of therapy sessions was about 6, and 67% had left therapy by the tenth interview. Only 9% of the 560 patients came for more than 25 interviews in an open-ended therapy regimen.

REPLOTTING DATA

Replotting the Garfield Table 6.1 (p. 195), the present Table 1.1 was derived from the earlier Garfield and Kurz article (1952) by adding a fourth column, "Percentage of Accumulative Attritional Loss." Table 1.1 shows what Fig. 1.1 displays graphically to be a characteristic attritional curve, a negatively

TABLE 1.1

Replotting Garfield Data (Garfield & Bergen, 1978, Table 6.1, p. 195) Regarding Length Of Treatment; Total $N = 560$

Number Interviews	No. Cases	Percent of Cases	/ /	% Remaining[a]
Less than 5	239	42.7		57.3
5–9	134	23.9		33.4
10–14	73	13.0		20.4
15–19	41	7.3		13.1
20–25	24	4.3		8.8
25 & Over	40	8.8	/ /	00.0

[a]Calculations showing attritional loss; added by present author.

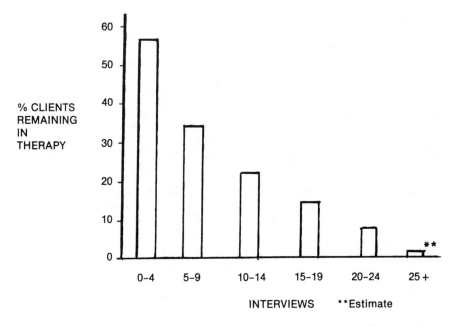

FIG. 1.1   Showing attritional curve (% remaining after each session interval); replotted from Garfield and Bergen, 1978 (See Table 1.1).

accelerating declining ("decay") curve. This curve has been found repeatedly in psychotherapy research reports, as will be shown, but was brought into focus by rearranging the data to show declining numbers of participants (vertical axis) over the series of therapy sessions (horizontal axis).

This curve suggests that most people get help (or not) in a very short period of time; a few seem to require more time. What the various portions of the attritional curve are related to in terms of client, therapist, and clinic variables is not readily available in the literature; in fact, the nature of this attritional curve has not been noted before, except in a somewhat different way in the Brandt review (1965). The central place of the attritional curve is beginning to show significance and is elaborated on further.

Garfield's Table 6.2 (p. 196) summarizes the length of treatment over a number of VA, university, and psychiatric clinics, from data reported from 1948 to 1970. In this summary the mean number of interviews was about six; and one-half the therapy clients were lost by the eighth interview (unrelated to the number lost at intake). We are not told whether these were from time-limited or time-unlimited settings. Large-scale figures are offered by the National Center for Health Statistics (1966), which show that among 979,000 patients of consulting psychiatrists, in 1963–1964, the average number of therapy sessions was 4.7. Eiduson (1968) found in a review of attrition and length of therapy that 30% to 65% of all kinds of psychiatric patients drop out from therapy before mutual termination occurs.

Garfield, Eiduson, and others fail to report the number of dropouts at the *intake* point. In the Baekeland and Lundwall (1975) review, about 50% drop out at intake (data presented later concerning present research confirm this figure). Thus, the attrition rate *during* therapy — shown in the Garfield and Kurz (1952) report and in the Eiduson (1968) report — represents only a part of the problem; the equally large issue, or possibly larger for a number of reasons, is the dropping out at intake (Baekeland & Lundwall, 1975; Phillips & Fagan, 1982a, 1982b).

Although it is not the main purpose here to discuss research on patient characteristics that favor staying in therapy — this may no longer be a fruitful topic for research — it should be noted most such research fails to find characteristics in patient populations that detect the potential for early termination (Garfield, 1978, pp. 202-206). It appears to some that staying in therapy is not so much one of client characteristics (although, to be sure, some of the variance may be so related), but is more likely one of how the therapeutic situation adapts to the client's needs and perspective, and how the delivery system, qua system, operates overall in the clinic. If more study focuses on the attrition curve, therapists could *then* look at the curve and find therapist, client, policy, and system variables that might relate to greater therapeutic flexibility, and thereby improve service delivery.

The delineation of therapist variables related to process and outcome (Parloff, Waskow, & Wolfe, 1978) nets about the same results as does the delineation of client variables related to attrition from therapy. These authors state, in concluding their review of therapist variables, "The therapist variables most frequently selected by the researcher for study are, unfortunately, such simplistic, global concepts as to cause this field to suffer from possible terminal vagueness" (p. 272). The finding from the Baekeland and Lundwall (1975) and Luborsky et al. reviews (1971, 1975) end on similar notes (also, see Garfield, 1982, pp. 239-266).

Psychoanalytic Patients. Some research on therapeutic outcome has been done on psychoanalytic therapy patients (Luborsky & Spence, 1978). These reviewers found five quantitative studies of psychoanalytic patients wherein initial and final status of the patients was interrelated. The number of patients in these studies was small: 30 patients (Klein, 1960); 27 patients (Knapp et al. 1960); 21 patients, each, in two groups, one psychoanalytic psychotherapy and one group psychoanalytically oriented psychotherapy (Kernberg et al., 1972; Wallerstein et al., 1956); 183 patients in a retrospective study (Sashin, Eldred & Van Amerongen, 1975); and a survey of about 3,000 patients on whom therapists filled out initial and final questionnaires (Hamburg et al., 1967). Although patients with the best initial personality functioning tend to show the best outcomes (Luborsky et al., 1971), their review of 26 studies showed that 13 studies revealed no relationship between initial and end-of-treatment status, and 13 studies showed, as stated, that the better initial status predicted better final status. The five quantitative research reports cited by Luborsky and Spence (1978) fit this generalizaion. The Menninger Foundation study (Kernberg et al., 1972) found a correlation of .50 between patient anxiety at the outset and therapist-rated global improvement at the end of therapy. However, none of these studies dealt systematically with the problem of attrition, and none began with the number of patients originally applying for psychoanalytic therapy (ostensible therapy cases) from which the final patient population was selected. Hence, research on predictor variables relating the beginning of therapy to the termination (completion) is greatly vitiated in effectiveness due to considerable patient selection.

Long-term therapy, which appears in some quarters to be on the increase rather than decreasing as a result of knowledge distillation (Garfield, 1980, p. 278), also complicates the study of attrition and evaluation of outcome. One study reports psychoanalysis/psychodynamic therapy to take an average of 835 hours (Bergin & Lambert, 1978), and longer periods — up to 20 years — are reported (Zilbergeld, 1983). What the attrition curve would look like in these settings would be interesting to know.

Drugs.   Sometimes the use of drugs in psychotherapy, as an explicit decision at the start of a project, in combination or not with psychotherapy, encourages early assessment and keeping track of patients. However, the lengthy report by Hollon and Beck (1978) in which 33 studies are summarized (Table 12.1, pp. 446–459) does not account for attrition. They do, however, discuss the attrition problem generally and suggest some remedies (p. 443), including replacing dropouts from experimental and control populations (not very satisfactory), doing assessments earlier and more often, examining reasons for dropping out, and multiple data analysis. This discussion is one offering the most discernment of the problem of attrition in the Garfield and Bergin book (1978), albeit very brief and not directly applied to the research studies. Hollon and Beck have more to say about attrition: In the Johns Hopkins Group (see Covi, Lipman, Drogatis, 1974), where 218 depressed females between ages 20 and 50 were assigned to one of six cells in a 3 × 2 factorial design, various combinations of therapy and medication were employed. Hollon and Beck (1978) say, "Overall attrition was high. Twenty percent of the initial sample failed to survive the placebo 'washout' period, while another 32 percent of those surviving did not complete the 16 weeks of active treatment. Overall, 47 percent of the sample screened into the study failed to complete the treatment protocol" (p. 461). The dropouts were not studied further for whatever enlightenment they might provide. The authors say it remained in doubt whether the members of this population constituted treatment failure or remission, or suffered possible side effects.

Further evidence of attrition in drug-and-psychotherapy studies, reviewed by Hollon and Beck in regard to attrition, netted the following results: 278 females were the patients for a 4- to 6-week trial period; of these, 150 (54%) showed a reduction in symptomatology and were screened into the study. Of these 150, 106 (70%) survived the full treatment without relapse (106 survivors equals 38% of the original 278 patient population). We do not know from the report whether the 278 patients given the 4 to 6-week trial period were, as a group, screened in from a large group of applicants. The attrition may have been greater than reported figures state.

CRISIS THERAPY

Crisis-oriented brief psychotherapy may yield lower attritional rates, owing in part to the brevity of the therapeutic contacts and to the foci of intervention being manifestly salient to the patient (Avnet, 1965a, 1965b; Malan, 1973; McNair, Lorr, & Callahan, 1963; Sifneos, 1972, 1979). Success figures ("improvement," a global rating) as a generalization appear to hover around the 70% mark (Butcher & Koss, 1978) for crisis-oriented or very brief therapy. The Butcher and Koss review (1978, Table 19.3, pp. 751–753) covers 41 research reports, between 1956 and 1976, and shows a follow-up improvement rate (various measures, self-reports, etc.) in the vicinity of 70%. This figure, however, cannot be taken at face value because the percentage of returns at follow-up is not related, in many cases, to the original number treated, or to the total number of applications or ostensibly therapy cases. As to the differences between brief therapy and long-term (or psychoanalytic) therapy candidates, the Wallerstein et al. (1956) finding may be of some value. Wallerstein et al. used a 100-point Health-Sickness Rating Scale; it was found at the Menninger Clinic that among the initial state of patients receiving various forms of psychotherapy, those in psychoanalysis rated higher on this scale (51.4) than patients receiving expressive psychotherapy (38.2 rating), or those receiving supportive psychotherapy (36.7 rating). Thus, in this population – and we must take into consideration the population of patients likely to be at the Menninger Clinic in the 1950s – the more strictly psychoanalytic patients were the "healthier," which seems on the surface to be a contradiction. Why, then, would less healthy patients be relegated to less intensive treatment? There may be a good deal of therapist bias in choosing patients with whom one prefers to work, especially if the therapeutic work runs into the hundreds of hours. Health-Sickness or other ratings at a pre-therapy or beginning therapy juncture are not available for direct comparison among different lengths or types of therapy, or in relation to attrition.

Baekeland and Lundwall Review.   The summary in the Baekeland and Lundwall review (1975) points up the attrition problem in outpatient psychotherapy to an extent not matched in other literature reviews. Some summary statements from their review are salient: "In general psychiatric clinics, 20–57% of the patients fail to return after the first visit" and "31–56% attend no more than four times" (p. 738). Many of these dropouts will, however, return later or go elsewhere to treatment within a short period of time (Baekeland & Lundwall, 1975, p. 743). It is not known from present reviews of the literature whether these "returnees" will again follow a similar dropout pattern (data are presented later on this issue), the issue of dropping out and returning not having been systematically studied. These authors point up that attritional loss does not mean no gain for these patients, differing with Eysenck and Rachman. However, these authors suggest ways to curb attrition: Eliminate waiting lists; offer a wider range of ancillary services and better explanations of therapy as a process; and determine if a patient has dropped out of therapy before—among other suggestions.

Gelso (1979) offers a general discussion of counseling and psychotherapy issues of a methodological and professional nature. Gelso covers many issues relating to process and outcome but leaves out attrition altogether. The seemingly temporary interest in attrition during the decade between 1965 (Brandt, 1965) and 1975 (Baekland & Lundwall, 1975) appears to have pointed to a problem that has had too little study since (except for very recent analogue/meta-analysis research, see Chapter 3).

TIME-LIMITED CONDITIONS

Gelso and Johnson (1983) have reported on systematic studies of time-limited and time-unlimited therapy, which has raised interesting points concerning attrition. They do not bring forth the attrition problem but they do offer data on dropping out of very brief, time-limited therapy. They report that 79 students from the University of Maryland Counseling Center sought personal counseling or psychotherapy during a 6-week period in 1973. Twenty-two of them (28%) were screened out via MMPI selection procedures, and 15 (19%) were lost for other reasons. Beginning with 79 cases, they ended with a study population of 42, a loss of 37/79 of 47% at the outset. The researchers' contribution to this loss, via selection, however, was only 28%; the remaining loss came from clients not showing for the first session, not taking the tests, or cancelling. This order of attrition is typical (Baekeland & Lundwall, 1975; Brandt, 1965; Garfield, 1978; Luborsky et al., 1971). Add to this attrition the fact that 18 of 42 clients were available for follow-up 2.5 years later (i.e., 43% of the study population or 18/79 of the original ostensible therapy population [23%], showing attrition of 77%).

This figure (23%) is slightly better than figures previously presented for the Berlin Psychoanalytic Institute, but equal to the figures presented in Chapter 2. Follow-up data from the Gelso and Johnson study have to be considered in the light of the attritional figures presented. For example, the statistics at the time of the 2 1/2-year follow-up revealed that of the 18 clients in both time-limited (8 and 16 session limits) and time-unlimited therapy "all three groups improved over time" (p. 9). The three groups were time-limited, time-unlimited, and controls; where the controls (N = 13 at start of study) numbered 5 at follow-up. The two time-limited conditions netted a mean of 6.9 sessions (range = 1 to 12 sessions) and 8.61, respectively, for the 8 sessions and 16 sessions time-limited conditions (p. 51). These mean figures are strikingly close to those presented by Brandt (1965), Garfield (1978), the National Center for Health Statistics (1966) without the possible benefit of contrasting time-limited conditions, and in data reported in Chapter 2. Time-unlimited therapy in the Gelso and Johnson study was said to be in the vicinity of 20 sessions (p. 51).

Gelso, Spiegel, and Mills (1983) studied 87 clients at the same Counseling Center (over a 28-month period, beginning November 1973), by giving them a battery of tests. Follow-up times were 1 and 18 months later. At the initial follow-up, 41 of 87 clients (47%) responded (loss of 53%); later, through intensive phoning, the attrition rate was dropped to about 10% (78 of 87 responding to the call for a completed Counseling Center Follow-Up Questionnaire), a remarkably good return. Following this information, the authors say, "It should also be noted that 21 client applicants were assigned to therapists but failed to attend any sessions, and are not included in any of the analyses" (p. 24). These 21 clients either did not show or openly declined counseling. Is the 21-client loss, then, 24% of 87 clients pool, or a 27% loss from 78 clients?

The 18-month follow-up reveals that the researchers were able to obtain usable results from 67 of the original clients (87%), or 67 of the 71 clients who could be located (p. 24). The original plan, however, was for 90 clients, 30 each for three conditions, 8 session (time-limited), the 16 session (time-limited) and the time-unlimited session. Table 2.1 (p. 25) reveals how close the groups were to the originally planned figures, with Ns of 27, 28, and 23, respectively, at the 1-month follow-up, and Ns of 21, 24, and 22, respectively, for the 18-month follow-up; a good record. Significant for the problem of attrition is the reported attitudes of therapists about short-term psychotherapy wherein therapists are said to prefer working with the better adjusted clients and to feel that time-limited therapy (especially 8-session) would probably be inimical to good therapeutic progress. This therapist bias was challenged in the Gelso and Johnson research yet obtains in much published research. The issue of therapist preferences and/or satisfaction in therapy can often influence the choice of clients for therapy (Beuter, Johnson,

Newell, Warburn, & Elkins, 1973; Burton, 1975) and thereby influence attrition.

Miscellaneous Psychoanalytic-Oriented Studies. Strupp, Fox, and Lessler (1969) were able to study a sample of private patients seen by 11 psychiatrists and psychologists (p. 12). In a comprehensive questionnaire, they posed questions about therapist-patient relationships to 76 former patients; forty-four (58%) responded with usable data, a 42% loss. The nature of the 42 nonresponding cases was not reported on. Quite unlike short-term psychotherapy in duration, the Strupp et al. study reported an average of 166 interviews for this young (median age 31–32 years), male, upper middle-class, educated clientele. Strupp et al. (1969) noted a substantial therapist-patient concordance in attitudes toward the therapy offered, an intensive, psychoanalytically oriented one; patients reported improvement in general well-being as well as disappearance in specific complaints (p. 14). However, the more favorable ratings of their therapy experience by patients came from those receiving less intensive therapy (p. 15), suggesting evidence for the value of brief therapy, even in the face of study attrition. We do not know what hidden attrition may have resulted in the selection of the 76 patients identified at the beginning of this study. The authors say, in corroboration of this point, "In addition to the differences attributable to the form of psychotherapy, we discerned the existence of an important selection factor . . . [where] . . . patients were selected for intensive psychotherapy mainly on the basis of age (young patients were preferred), sex (male patients were preferred), and education (more highly educated patients were preferred), although other factors appeared to be involved as well: motivation to enter a prolonged therapeutic relationship, degree of disturbance, level of anxiety and discomfort, defensiveness, and other clinical considerations" (Strupp et al., 1969, p. 16). With this much subtle selection going on at the hands of the 11 psychotherapists involved, it is difficult to ascertain how representative these patients were of even intensive psychotherapy, not to mention the attritional impact.

In the second study reported on by Strupp et al. (1969) — in contrast to the first study where ratings were made *ex post facto* — ratings were obtained from clinical records before and after the therapy (p. 46), as well as ratings via questionnaires completed by the patients. The second study was on patients seen in a hospital outpatient clinic. The basis of the study was 696 completed cases, from which pool 91 cases had been seen for 20 interviews or more. Of the pool of 696 patients, 257 had been referred for therapy, the others primarily for diagnostic purposes, allowing us to take now as the "ostensible therapy cases" the 257 cases specifically referred to this clinic for therapy. The basis for deciding on elements of attrition is further complicated by the authors asserting that of 450 patients seen in one year, a large number terminated within a year, indicated in a quotation from Pfouts, Wallach, and Jenkins (1963) that "Too often policies and procedures are set up as if the clinic were almost exclusively a long-term intensive treatment center, when in reality it is for the majority of patients a diagnostic and brief therapy center" (p. 48). Strupp et al. continue "For these reasons, patients selected for our sample cannot be regarded as a cross-section of all patients seen at the clinic" (p. 48). The clientele, then, consisted of 244 patients seen for more than 25 interviews by psychiatric residents, advanced graduate students in clinical psychology, or staff members of the clinic. They add: "The requirement of 25 interviews was imposed because we wished to concentrate on individuals who had remained in therapy for a reasonable period and for whom therapy might be presumed to have been a significant experience. *By eliminating early dropouts we also hoped to obtain a more homogeneous sample of stayers*" (italics added p. 28). Thus, 244 questionnaires were mailed to former patients, yielding at first 92 returns, followed a month later with a mailing that yielded an additional 39 questionnaires, providing a total of 131 returns, showing an attritional figure of 113/244 (46%). These 244 cases were apparently selected from the 257 cases (ostensible therapy?) referred for treatment (p. 47), the basis for which we are not told. The rate of return — 54% — represents a commendable effort. In selecting only clients with 25 or more interviews, they limited their coverage considerably. What of the clients who had less than 25 interviews and the benefits they received? These are important lost data. Although researchers have the right to choose a study population — if this is done objectively via replicable criteria — the interposition of other subtle, often subjective factors muddies the research waters. The 131 questionnaire returns were reduced to 122, due to 9 incomplete replies, yielding an attritional loss of 122/244 (50%): or 122/257 (47% retained, or 53% attritional loss) based on the total population from which the study population of 244 cases was derived. The mean number of interviews per week for this population of 122 cases was 1.4 and the average number of interviews was 70.4. Most were seen for 26 to 49 hours of therapy, much longer than short-term therapy, but far less than intensive therapy cases. Recomputing Table 3, p. 54 (Strupp et al., 1969) allows for a rough table of progressive attrition by subtracting the number of cases left in the therapy population after each stated interview limit, resulting in a negatively accelerating declining curve similar to that found elsewhere (see Fig. 1.2). There is more descriptive value in viewing in a whole cloth manner the attritional decline curve compared to many other statistics. The declining (or "decay") nature of the attritional curve raises questions about the cases dropping out early and those taking more time or whatever benefits they obtain. The literature on outcome from psychotherapy has allowed to lie fallow the nature of the attritional curve phenomenon and has thereby lost much valuable information and prematurely forfeited heuristic problems.

Looking further at the Strupp et al. data (1969), we note on p. 64 that of the 122 cases reporting benefits — the average number of visits was

TABLE 1.2
Repeating and Extending Strupp et al., Table 3, p. 54 (1969); N = 122

Total Treatment Hrs.	N	/ /	Attritional Decline (N)	Attrition (%)
25–49	54		(122–54 = 68)	55.7
50–74	26		(122–80 = 42)	34.4
75–99	14		(122–94 = 28)	23.0
100–124	10		(122–104 = 18)	15.0
125–149	05		(122–109 = 13)	10.0
150–174	02		(122–111 = 11)	09.0
175–199	02		(122–113 = 09)	07.4
200 +	04		(122–117 = 05)	04.1
Unknown	05	/ /	(122–122 = 00)	00.0

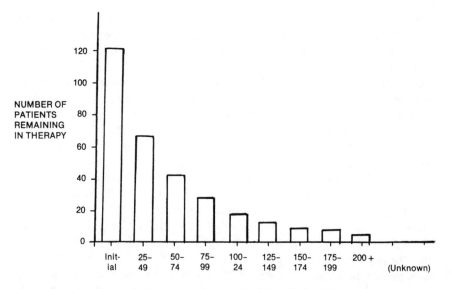

FIG. 1.2   Replotting, added attritional data (from Strupp et al. 1969, 54, Table 3)
N = 122 (See Table 1.2).

70.4 – 27% reported "marked change" after 1–3 months (mean = 1.4 visits
per week), or 7 to 21 visits, a figure closely similar to short-term therapy results in different settings. Moreover, another 18% report the next category of
time – 4–6 months of therapy – as the time interval within which they noted
"marked change." Is it possible that the entire study of intensive psychotherapy in this report is a lost opportunity to set up a firmer structure of short-

term therapy? The attritional curve suggests the possibility of this hypothesis, that is, that psychotherapy may be more beneficial than we have recognized from our data, that early dropping out may more often signal "success" than we have allowed, and that patients/clients are telling us in repeated ways that they can early on get help from brief support. If these notions turn out to be true in additional research — see below for further elaboration on this point — then a firming up of short-term psychotherapy may become the most important and urgent matter in all of psychotherapy; and the study of attrition may be the most cogent way of bringing this question to bear on our data bases, inasmuch as attrition curves expose the whole course of therapy, for better or worse, and provide the background for almost any other conceivable type of study of psychotherapy process or outcome.

VERY BRIEF THERAPY

Several chapters in the Budman (1981) volume on short-term psychotherapy bear directly on how attritional data have affected thinking about short-term psychotherapy (Bloom, 1981; Gustafson, 1981; Wilson, 1981). Gustafson speculates somewhat about why psychoanalysis or psychodynamically oriented psychotherapy had to become so long-term in the first place. Malan (1963) also raised this question a number of years ago and suggested that such concepts as resistance, working through negative transference and other transference, positing the roots of neurosis in early childhood, and so on, contributed to the lengthening of intensive treatment over the past 5 or 6 decades. It is the guarded opinion of Gustafson that short-term psychotherapy may be as effective in bringing about change as is long-term therapy (Gustafson, 1981, pp. 90–95).

Wilson (1981), in the same volume, reports on behavioral short-term therapy. He points out that Beck's (1976) study showed cognitive therapy to be more effective than drug treatment (imipramine) and also occasioned a lower dropout rate. However, Wilson (p. 137) adds, "This is an important finding . . . [that is, the lower dropout rate] . . . since there is good evidence that clients who drop out of treatment are almost inevitably treatment failures." This is a surprising statement but one often encountered in the literature (Eysenck, 1960; Rachman & Wilson, 1980). Wilson, however, does a good job of presenting the evidence that short-term (behavioral) therapy does not necessarily occasion symptom substitution, limit itself to unusually narrow focus in treatment, or remain limited in applicability to a wide range of problems (pp. 151–152). Whereas more traditional psychodynamic psychotherapy presented in a short-term context seems still to center much on problems related to transference, unconscious motivation, and childhood experiences as generic problem areas (Sifneos, 1972), briefer behaviorally oriented therapy eschews these postulates and centers, instead, on setting limited goals with the client, focusing an attack on problems, emphasizing the present context of life, and showing greater therapist activity along with recommending outside assignments or "behavioral practice" on the part of the client.

Bloom's chapter (1981) focuses on single-session therapy. He says that because such a high percentage of the American population — 10%–15% — need some kind of psychological assistance for emotional problems during their lives, the potential value of very brief treatment may be highly salutary and should not be dismissed lightly. Bloom's (1981) viewpoint is clearly stated: "While advocacy for planned short-term treatment flies in the face of a deeply ingrained mental health professional value system it is remarkably syntonic with the results of evaluation studies" (p. 168). Bloom cites a number of instances where single-session therapy is effective, where it is the *only* professional therapeutic contact many clients have, and where the characteristic (modal) number of client contacts with a mental health clinic is *one* (pp. 169–171). Similar to findings to be reported in Chapter 2, client satisfaction with brief contacts is noticeable in the Bloom report (pp. 171–180). Consonant with the quotation above from Wilson, Bloom states that there is "no question but that mental health professionals tend to view early and unilateral termination by clients as a sign of therapeutic failure and client dissatisfaction" (p. 171). He adds further, "Follow-up interviews with . . . single-session clients revealed that reality-based factors preventing continuance and improvements in the problem situations may have accounted for a substantial proportion of these unplanned closings" (p. 171). Here, again, is evidence that the mental health profession not only sets up a complex set of expectations that treatment will be more than short-term but that brief help signals poor results, client dissatisfaction, and waste of therapist time. But the evidence is strong that attrition is more than simply dropping out for negative reasons; it may signal a large number of "satisfactions" with therapy and a revelation that attrition follows a predictable course that may include factors of both a positive and negative nature.

Garfield points out in this connection that "early or premature termination on the part of the client is frequently viewed as a failure in psychotherapy, *even though there has been practically no systematic research evaluating the outcome of therapy in such cases"* (Garfield, 1978, p. 210) (emphasis added). To confuse further, the case for dropouts being treated one or another way, Sloane, Staples, Cristol, Yorkston, and Whipple (1975) say "dropouts are counted as failures by Eysenck, eliminated by Bergin, and might be more properly assigned by a third to success or failure, depending on their status at reassessment" (p. 16).

Bloom reviews other studies where the number of outpatients engaging in only one interview ranges from 32% to 45% (Bloom, 1981, pp. 170–171), and even on second admissions the number is 20%. Sarvis et al. (1958) reported on over 800 clients seen in a university mental health setting where 10% were seen only once; they were not rejected for treatment but seemed to get what was appropriate at the time. Sometimes, rather than either client or therapist rejecting short-term cases, reality situations prevent the client returning and prompt unplanned or not-agreed-upon closings of cases (Bloom, 1981, p. 171; Ewing, 1978; Kogan, 1957). Planned-for or unplanned closings seem to make no difference in the number of cases reporting satisfaction with therapeutic results; and therapists consistently underestimate the help the client receives and credits positively (Bloom, 1981, p. 172), with satisfactions running as high as 70% (as previously stated), often unrelated to the number of therapy sessions. In the more doctrinaire clinical settings, dropout rates appear to be more related to therapist characteristics than to client variables (Bloom, 1981, p. 173; Fiester & Rudestam, 1975). Summarizing single-session therapy results, Bloom demonstrates that such brief contacts are not only common and beneficial, but that clinicians characteristically underestimate their worth. If appropriately implemented, single-session therapy contacts may become the norm for much outpatient work and offer appropriate assistance in cost-effective ways (Bloom, 1981, p. 180). If this be the case, then dropping out of therapy becomes much less important and it behooves therapists to gear themselves more adroitly to short-term, even one-session, therapy, and learn how to focus, deal with the present, be judiciously active, help the client express feelings, keep structure by noting the time limits involved, try not to cover too much ground, avoid concentrating on presumed causes especially "first causes," and keep to the salient issues at hand (Bloom, 1980, 1981; Phillips & Wiener, 1966) as an alternative to time-limited dynamic psychotherapy (Strupp, 1981). Strupp's selection of patients for psychodynamic short-term therapy revolves around high patient motivation, ability to relate to the therapist, a history of satisfactory adjustment, and the selection of cases where the problem appears to be acute (p. 221). However useful such criteria might be, by the time a therapist was convinced that the potential client fit all these criteria and it was well to go on with brief therapy, the very brief type of contact would be over and past. It may be more heuristic to simply take people as they come — in outpatient settings, at least — and proceed as efficaciously as possible, *then* survey the results to see how, when, and where brief therapy works. Strupp and Hadley (1979) and Gomes-Schwartz (1978), in the Vanderbilt Project, identified a number of contra-indications for short-term therapy including such patient characteristics as rigidity, self-centeredness, masochism, self-destructiveness, profound negativism, and characterological disturbances. It could be, however, that too much analysis of the patient characteristics early on may contribute to excessive therapist efforts to screen out potential patients; how therapist selection processes can be objectively reported and independently assessed by other researchers remains an important and refractory problem. We know, too, that attempts to relate the presenting status of clients to later therapeutic outcome remain vague and inconclusive (Garfield, 1978; Gurman & Razin, 1977), although the "client variables" literature is extensive. Because attrition appears to be so powerful, most studies of client attitudes represent not a cross-section of *all* who apply for therapy (ostensible therapy cases), but only those who are somehow selected (self-selected, selected by the therapist, or by the policy of the clinic).

INTERRELATIONSHIPS

There have been some attempts to view the therapist-patient relationship as an "alliance," rather than concentrating so exclusively and separately on client variables and therapist variables (Kernberg et al., 1972; Malan, 1976; Sloane et al., 1975; Strupp, 1981, pp. 228–229; Strupp & Hadley, 1979). After reviewing somewhat the notion of the therapeutic alliance, Strupp (1981) states, "I base my adoption of this position (the importance of the therapeutic alliance) on accumulating research evidence . . . which has shown that the patient-therapist interaction represents the fulcrum upon which therapeutic progress turns" (p. 1229). However important this observation may seem to be, it is vitiated by the old bugaboo that the alliance does not properly take into account the selection (early dropping out and early selection out of cases, and attrition as a progressive in-therapy matter) of clients and, of course, important features of the client-therapist dyads that survive the attritional impact. It may simply be that what we observe in the dyads — the client-therapist interactions — are but creations of the workability of client and therapist with each other at a particular time and in a particular setting, and that this condition addresses hardly at all the more basic problem of how therapy works (or doesn't work) for the vast range of clients who do not become part of the enduring dyad. It would be more illuminating if the alliance were studied in those dyads that were one-session-only versus dyads that typified short-term therapy interventions (5–7 visits) versus those lasting for dozens of sessions. It may be suspected that in one-session-only or in very brief therapy, the dyadic features are hardly discernible and, at best, harbor none of the features stressed by Sifneos (1972, 1979) such as Oedipal conflicts, or Malan's (1976) notion that therapist-client conflicts mirror client-parent conflicts, and so on.

COMPARATIVE STUDIES

In a systematic study comparing behavioral and psychodynamic psychotherapy in an outpatient setting, with a beginning treatment N of 94, Sloane et al. (1975) found a number of interesting results from short-term psychotherapy (4 months duration). Regarding attrition, it was difficult to determine how many completed therapy over the 4 months (behavioral, psychodynamic, and control cases), or what the average number of interviews was for each viewpoint; but at a 1-year follow-up, 48.9% of the original population was available for study (p. 120). These data occurred in the context of the number of clients, each viewpoint, engaging in therapy *between* the 4 months' ending point and the 1-year follow-up ($N = 46$ or 48.9% of the original 94 clients entering therapy). However, because the number of clients in each therapeutic persuasion receiving psychotherapy differed, it is difficult to evaluate what the final results mean, due to missing attritional data in relation to the various therapeutic efforts. On page 203, we learn that of the 94 originally selected patients, 60 were treated and of these, 48 (80%, one-half, each, to behavior therapy and psychodynamic therapy) returned follow-up questionnaires "one to two years after completing therapy" (p. 202). Thus, looking at the attrition figures at the end point (follow-up) in the light of the starting population, we find 49/84 or 58% lost somewhere along the line. The picture is somewhat more clouded in the "Summary" section (pp. 215–226) when we learn that 126 people applying for psychotherapy were first considered ("interviewed at length by an experienced psychiatrist" and "ninety-four were accepted for treatment" p. 215). Thus, the attrition figures look somewhat differently than before: The number offered treatment, 94/126, equals 74.6% (or a loss at outset of 25.4%); followed by 60 cases actually treated, which shows further attritional data to be 60/126 or 48%, giving a 52% loss; followed by a follow-up return of 48/126 or approximately 30% (the reciprocal of which is a 70% attritional loss from the starting point to the follow-up more than a year later). Although the conclusions are fairly strong — "On a rating of overall improvement, 93% of the behavior therapy patients contrasted to 77% of the psychotherapy and wait-list patients were considered either improved or recovered ($X = 3.98$; $p < .05$)" (p. 218) — we do not know how many patients had how many interviews during the course of therapy, how the attritional loss during therapy was brought about, and any other data on loss of clientele. In mentioning the original population of 126 clients, the authors say: "We excluded those who were considered too disturbed to be assigned to a four-month wait-list control group, those whose disturbance seemed so minor that therapy was not indicated, and those who seemed more likely to respond to some other treatment (for example, antidepressant medication) than to any kind of psychotherapy" (p. 215). The overall evaluations in the light of attritional data show up in the following statement: "Unfortunately, the psychotherapy patients who could be reassessed at two years proved to be those who had already shown most improvement at one year. Because of this sample bias, a comparison with the behavior therapy and wait-list patients, who were representative of their original samples, was not feasible" (p. 220). Although it is admirable to want to assess the stability of personality and/or behavior change over time, it may be uneconomical to try locating clientele after a period of 2 or more years; further, the attritional features might make the available client data hard to interpret or highly redundant with earlier evaluations. As some of the researchers dealing with very brief or one-session therapy have remarked, there is nothing wrong with returning for additional therapy, and no compelling reason to assume that once improved, life circumstances will remain so constant as not to challenge earlier gains. The more economical and feasible route might be to make therapy as brief and effective as is consonant with strong consumer interests and look later at data that show some require a longer time (Gelso & Johnson, 1983; also see Chapter 2 of this volume.)

Recomputing the Sloane et al. data, it is apparent that some attritional features found earlier (see Figs. 1.3 and 1.3-continued) are present. One difficulty with their reporting is that it is hard to keep track of the patient population and what happened at various junctures along the treatment path. Figure 1.3 shows the reconstructed attritional curve in the same form as previously presented.

Figure 1.3 requires some explanation. The "ostensible therapy cases" ($N = 126$) are followed through the process of attempting delivery of treatment to some ($N = 94$) judged acceptable for treatment. Sixty of them were treated, and 48 returned follow-up questionnaires. Additional therapy was available to the study population—see Table 14, p. 120—entitled, "Patients Receiving Treatment Between Four-Month and One-Year Assessments"—and is broken down here in Fig. 1.3-continued in terms of the number of cases engaging in 3–5, 6–10, 11–26, and 26+ sessions.

This last set of follow-up data ($N = 46$), then, divide themselves as shown in Fig. 1.3-continued in a way that is not similar to the basic attrition curve (starting with an N of 126 cases) and is also atypical of other attrition curves provided in this paper. Moreover, even the additional treatment cases cannot be fully plotted by the data provided since of the 46 cases reported on in Table 15, 11 cases (24% of the 46 cases) are not identified as to the number of therapy visits they had beyond 26 sessions. There must have been an asymptote, but it is not possible to identify it. The main attrition curve derived from this study is consonant with other attritional curves; the "added-on" therapy phenomena provide some disclaimer of the common attritional curves cited above. The overall value of the Sloane et al. (1975) study is vitiated somewhat not only by the attritional data cited but by the meaning of the additional therapy sessions and their distribution at the end of the main study period.

The Di Loreto Study.   More care in reporting and dealing with loss of clientele is seen in the Di Loreto study (1971). In comparing the effectiveness of several types of psychotherapy—20 cases, each, for systematic desens-

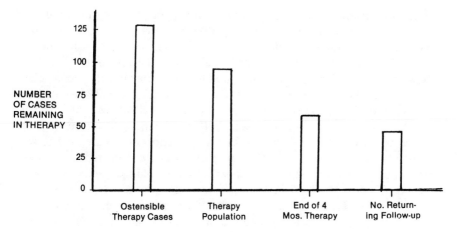

FIG. 1.3   Based on replotted data from Sloane et al. (1975, pp. 64, 76, & 120). N = 126

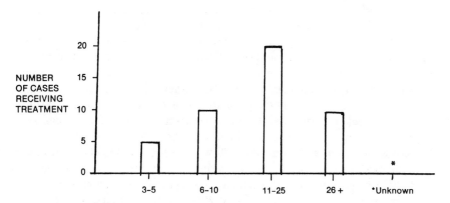

FIG. 1.3, continued. Additional therapy, 4–12 Mos. N = 46. See Sloane et al., 1975, p. 120, Table 14, "Patients receiving treatment between four months and one-year assessments."

itization, client-centered and rationale-emotive therapy — the author reports explicitly on beginning with a psychology class of 600 students, from which population 217 students volunteered and took the pre-test battery. Criteria were set in terms of cutoff scores on the tests and the resulting population (N = 100) was assigned randomly to the three treatment modes and to two control groups, with stratified subdivisions of these cases into male/female and introvert/extrovert categories of equal numbers (p. 36). Nine sessions were provided; post-treatment followed upon completion of the therapy regimen, and follow-up evaluations 13 weeks later. A type of flow chart is provided (Table 2.1, pp. 40–41) to show how the experimental regimen worked, a very useful inspectional aid to one wanting to replicate Di Loreto's research. The clear presentation of data from the outset suggests there was only slight experimenter-initiated selection of cases, and that on objective, replicable bases. The number of sessions missed by clients in each type of treatment are shown in Table 3.5 (p. 108) and appeared to constitute the only uncontrolled client attritional feature of this research. A total of 35 client-sessions were missed, a negligible figure (there are 9 × 60 or 540 client-sessions in the research plan, thus showing an "internal attrition" among client/sessions attended of only 6.5%). Seldom do researchers report on the number of sessions missed by clients: It is then difficult to know what to expect upon replication of a study, to know whether the number of scheduled sessions and the mean number of client-session attendance figures are comparable, whether fewer sessions would accomplish the same purpose, and so on.

Researchers seldom know — and seldom inquire — about client participation in therapy prior to a given research occasion, and researchers cannot control whether clients obtain therapy during or after a study (as between termination and follow-up, for example), but Di Loreto made an effort to come to grips with this set of problems. If people can get help in short periods of time, what is to stop clients from obtaining informal (or even formal) help while participating in a study and should not this "extracurricular therapy" be as influential as the formal attempt? We simply do not recognize such exigencies in research plans, but Di Loreto's study does identify the occurrence of "unofficial" help. On p. 109, he presents Table 3.6, which refers to "Additional treatment received by each S prior to treatment, during treatment, and during follow-up." There were 69 client-sessions prior to Di Loreto's study, 33 during the study, and 14 during follow-up, a total of 116 client-sessions. Comparing this to the 540 client-sessions in the main study, this "extracurricular" therapy amounts to a supplement, a distraction, a vitiation (or what?) to the main effort of 116/540 or about 20%. Informal intersession therapy added to the main effort will require more research; it certainly issues an admonition to researchers to be cognizant of the role of extra sessions (see Gelso & Johnson, 1983, in this regard). Also, in the Di Loreto study, although it appears that the N's for the end-of-therapy and post-therapy follow-up figures are the same as the beginning figures (no attrition!), this is not explicitly evident. It is remarkable, then, if true, that this is an exception to the usual instances of considerable attrition between start of therapy and later follow-up, making this study strong on generalizability and replicability.

Paul's Study. Paul (1966) studied a population of 96 subjects (students) selected from a total number of 710 in a speech class (p. 33). Through administering several tests relating to speech and other anxiety conditions, 96 subjects met the criteria for inclusion in the study: 15 subjects, each, for three treatment groups (desensitization, insight-oriented therapy, and placebo-attention), and 22 subjects for the no-contact control group with 29 other subjects, the no-treatment classroom control group (the latter group was not a complete control group inasmuch as these students engaged in some reading and classroom activities related to speaking anxiety and emotional problems). Of the 96 subjects, 74 survived the final screening, which was based on individual interviews where "screening for motivation was provided by dropping those students who did not appear for the scheduled evaluation speech" (p. 25). And: "Final screening of the subjects took place in an individual interview with the investigator; at this point those students who had received previous psychological treatment, and those who reported a reduction in anxiety during the required classroom speechs completed prior to the treatment, were to have been dropped; however, no subjects needed to be excluded for these reasons" (p. 25). Thus, there was a loss of subjects from 96 to 74 (23% attrition) due to these investigator-determined procedures and due to potential clients not appearing for scheduled evaluations. Following this loss there appears to have been no further loss of clientele except for 7 controls from the Palmar Sweat Index (PSI) and the Physiological Composite (p. 33). The main attritional question revolves around the possible subjectivity of the decision to drop subjects in the study population, the 23% cited above; thereafter, the three clinical populations of 15 subjects each, and the 22 controls remained intact for follow-up evaluations (see Appendices F, G, and H, pp. 127–132). The portion of the proposed typical attrition curve cited above in several studies (and following in Chapters 2 and 3) extended to only two points and did not include the in-study process, the end-of-treatment findings or the follow-up findings.

Questions can always be raised whether populations studied by Paul (1966) or by Di Loreto (1971) are "real patients," because they are chosen by invitation or similar means. Self-initiated clientele may be a somewhat different clinical population (more varied?), may show a different gender ratio (e.g., Paul's study population was 68 males and 28 females, a 2.5:1 ratio, whereas counseling centers report a 60/40 female/male proportion), and may relate to no particular extant circumstance like public speaking anxiety, snake or spider phobia, and so on. Studies of the Paul and Di Loreto type are known as "analogue studies" (Kazdin, 1982; Landman & Dawes, 1982; Smith et al., 1980). More research will be needed before it is known whether self-selected versus volunteer clinical groups are different, whether the ensuing attritional patterns are different and whether observed differences bode well or poorly for subsequent change. The attritional course appears similar in the two types of studies, but the amount of attrition appears to be less in the analogue methodology (see Chapter 3).

INTENSIVE THERAPY ATTRITION

The study of patient dropping out from various types of intensive psychotherapy is found in the Reder and Tyson report (1980). They surveyed four
types of therapeutic outcome cases: long-term therapy ($N = 47$ studies);
long-term therapy measured in months of treatment (12 studies); brief psychotherapy (10 studies); and psychoanalysis distributed over months (9 studies). Data collection is faulted on several counts, yet the resulting attrition
curves are similar in some respects to those previously reported and following
in Chapter 2 (see Figs. 1.4, 1.5, 1.6, and 1.7).

Figure 1.4 replots the Reder and Tyson data (1980, Table 1, p. 232) based
on the percentages of clients having 2–5, 6–10, and so forth, interviews, out
to an upper limit of 31–35 interviews; the last category of the number of sessions contains only one study (of 47) and no data on an asymptote are presented. Further, no data on intake-only and/or the number having only one
therapy session are reported, leaving the attrition curve truncated on both
ends. Further, only one study includes data for 26–30 therapy sessions, hence
both final categories of number of sessions lack sample adequacy. Despite
these lacks, the attrition curve from these 47 studies is similar to other
attritional data, where the number of sessions begins with intake and ends
with the final number of interviews.

Figure 1.5 reports on 12 studies of a long-term nature (*months* of treatment) (Table 2, p. 234), and displays the same methodological lacks. Figure
1.5 shows only 1 study, each, for clients having 9 and 15 months of treatment; yet the attrition curve is close to those offered above. No studies occur
for the 18 months period of treatment. Smoothing the curve in Fig. 1.5 by an
alternate column from 6 months to 12 to 24 months, despite the absence of

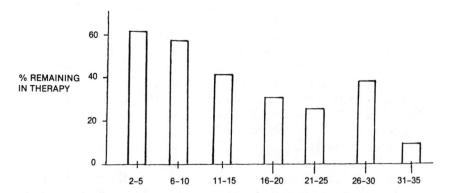

FIG. 1.4   Replotting Reder & Tyson data (1980, Table 1, p. 232) regarding No. Sessions, Long-Term Psychotherapy. $N = 47$ Studies; abscissa is summary of number of
sessions across all studies.

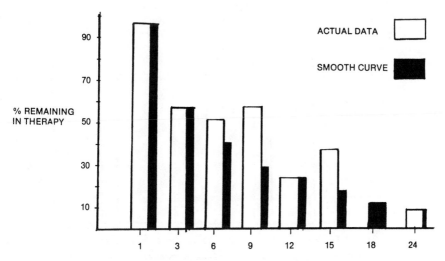

FIG. 1.5   Replotting Reder & Tyson data (1980, Table 2, p. 234) regarding No. Months, Long-Term Psychotherapy. N = 12 Studies; abscissa is summary of number of months across all studies.

data on the asymptote, suggests its similarity to attritional curves already presented. The assumption is that if the data points were complete, the attrition curve would resemble the "standard" one.

Reder and Tyson (Table 3, p. 234) also report on brief therapy measured in terms of number of sessions. These data likewise lack intake, first-session, and asymptote data but the resulting curve, as far as it can be plotted, shows an attritional feature similar to other curves. Unlike the long-term psychotherapy data — Table 2 from Reder and Tyson — which is presented in terms of months (the actual number of sessions likely varies between three and six per week), Fig. 1.6 presents data in regard to the actual number of therapy sessions. Presenting data in terms of months of treatment makes the data base even more vague — did the patient attend every session for the periods of time reported?

The last Reder and Tyson Table (Table 4, p. 235) covers nine studies of psychoanalysis by number of months of treatment, from 6 months to 36 months, with no data on the early sessions nor on the 36 months-plus sessions (see Fig. 1.7). Data are very sparse; no studies appear that terminated after 15 or 21 months, and only one study reported data on 36 months of treatment. The resulting curve resembles hardly at all the other attritional curves. To correct this situation, one would need data on the early selection process, on the number of sessions from the very inception of therapy out to the asymptote.

Seldom is a clinic likely to experiment with shorter or longer term psychotherapy. Although selection procedures are often fuzzily reported on, and

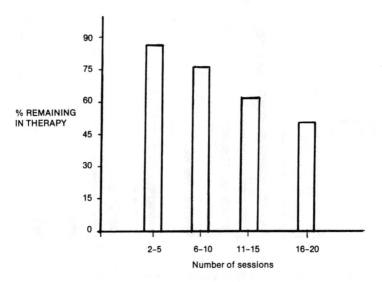

FIG. 1.6   Replotting Reder & Tyson (1980, Table 3, p. 234), referring to a summary of 10 studies on brief therapy, per number of sessions.

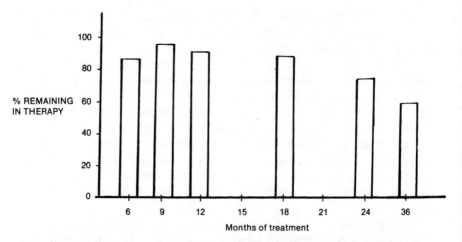

FIG. 1.7   Replotting Reder & Tyson data (1980, Table 4, p. 234), summarizing 9 studies of psychoanalysis, in months of treatment, across studies.

are often highly subjective in nature, Straker (1968) reported on these two contrasting time limits related to a policy change in an outpatient clinic. Although Straker reports that "brief psychotherapy is seen as a treatment technique particularly suitable for selected patients" (1968, p. 1221), the basis for selection are more clinician's impressions – the notion that the client is in a transitory state and is not psychotic. Comparing the clinic longer-term "preorganizational" status with later short-term therapy, Straker reports that the dropout rate was 32% for 220 short-term patients in 1964, compared to 62% (from an earlier sample of 220 cases) among long-term cases. The average number of visits was 8.1, for 822 short-term (new) patients and 8.9 visits for 90 patients before the change in policy. No other data were presented on the dropout features from intake onward, save for the 62% versus 32% overall figures cited above. Straker reports that only about 11% of his clinic's clientele went beyond 11 visits (p. 1221). The most useful data—the full attritional curve—were unreported. In spite of these data lacks, Straker's clinic apparently solved the issue of clinician attitudes toward brief therapy. This result brings to mind the Ursano and Dressler (1974) study of clinician attitudes toward brief therapy: it was considered "second best" (p. 55), and/or as suitable for a very limited range of patients. Yet Bennett and Wisneski (1979) showed that only 1%–2% of HMO outpatients, within a broad range of services, required long-term, continuous psychotherapy (p. 1283). Although the conclusions from the Bennett and Wisnecki report are interesting, data relevant to the actual number of patients per session from intake onward were not reported.

OTHER IMPLICATIONS OF THERAPY

Cummings and Follette (1976) and Follette and Cummings (1967) reported on some interesting aspects of short-term and long-term psychotherapy in relation to utilizing medical services other than psychiatric services, in an outpatient prepaid health plan setting. Although their reporting does not include the range of sessions from intake onward, they do present data on brief versus long-term therapy (Follette & Cummings, 1967, Tables 3 and 4, p. 29, 30, respectively). All three psychotherapy groups—one-session, brief therapy, and long-term therapy($N = 152$ cases)—evidenced a lower utilization of medical services for a period of up to 5 years, post-psychotherapy-treatment time (Follette & Cummings, Table 4, p. 30) than controls. The one-session and brief psychotherapy groups ($N = 80$ and 41, respectively) showed statistically significant lesser usage of medical services than 152 comparable controls not receiving any form of psychotherapy. This finding was related, in turn, to somewhat better results for one-session-only and brief therapy (mean visits = 6.2 sessions)(p. 27) compared to long-term psychotherapy (mean number sessions = 33.9). Further, the experimental subjects for this investigation were selected systematically by including every fifth psychiatric patient whose initial interview took place between January 1 and December 21, 1960. Of the 152 patients thus selected, 80 were seen for one interview only, 41 were seen for two to eight interviews (mean of 6.2) and were defined as "brief therapy"; and 31 were seen for nine or more interviews (mean of

33.9) and were defined as "long-term therapy" (p. 27). These are the only attrition-related data. This study is a good example of taking advantage of an attritional event to subdivide the population and ascertain the effect of given numbers of therapy sessions on some dependent variable (subsequent medical services utilization).

Elsewhere, Cummings (1977) studied further data based on the two above-referenced studies and found that patients seen 2 years or longer in psychotherapy — compared to brief therapy cases — " demonstrated no overall decline in total outpatient utilization, inasmuch as psychotherapy visits tended to supplant medical visits" (p. 495). Further research into brief psychotherapy and the related utilization of other medical services in a prepaid medical service delivery system led Cummings to say that longer-term psychotherapy — the "interminable" patient — " rarely supplanted frequent outpatient medical visits with weekly psychotherapy, resulting in a cost-therapeutic-effectiveness ratio not significantly better than that of the control group" (p. 498). In Cummings' report, very brief therapy netted a mean of 3.8 visits, brief therapy a mean of 8.6 visits, long-term therapy (only 10% of the patients) a mean of 19.2 sessions and the so-called interminable cases took 47.9 sessions per year. Study of the whole attritional process, then, promises some important, cost-benefit-related data, and may highlight further the usefulness and economy of short-term therapeutic work.

CASE SELECTION AND OUTCOME RATINGS

Although it is difficult to know in many cases how the self-selection of clients determines who continues in therapy beyond a session or two, the chances that therapist selection — as we have seen — influences attrition are great. If therapists subtly, or otherwise, choose whom they wish to work with, and the basis of the choosing is not objectively determined, hence not replicable, we can expect the attritional curve to reflect this fact. In the matter of evaluation, clients are known to rate their progress and outcome higher than clinicians (Kissel, 1974; Luborsky et al., 1971; Parlof et al., 1978). Therapists also tend to rate clients more successful in positive relationship to the number of sessions held (Luborsky et al., 1971). These points are corroborated in a report on mothers' and therapists' evaluations of brief therapy among children (Kissel, 1974), as well as showing a typical attrition curve in the selection of clients. Based on a total study group of 813 cases, 323 cases (representing a loss of 60.3%) were considered appropriate and were mailed questionnaires; of this group, 168 replies were received (a 48% loss) from the mailing list, identifying a 20.8% resulant study population from the 813 originally identified for study. Although the mean number of sessions for this study population of 168 cases was 13.15 sessions, the trailing off of some cases to over 2 years in therapy was noted. The attritional results are shown in Fig. 1.8. (See, also, Phillips & Johnston, 1954).

The redrawing of the Kissel data leaves something to be desired (in Fig. 1.8), owing to the lack of data on the number of interviews for long-term and short-term cases. The long-term cases could have been plotted at the extreme right of the horizontal axis to show (or imply) the trailing off of the asymptote, but the short-term cases were plotted in the extreme right owing to their numbers being smaller than the long-term cases (94 long-term cases vs. 74 short-term ones). Since we are not given the exact number of long-term case interviews — even though they trailed off beyond a 2-year period — we cannot be fully accurate in translating Kissel's data into this figure. Kissel's data plotted another way (see Fig. 1.9) may only highlight the matter further.

In the second replotting of the Kissel data (Fig. 1.9) the absence of an asymptote (beyond 2 years) leaves us in a quandary, but the general shape of the attritional curve is evident. If each time interval — "less 6 months," "6 to 12 months," and so on — had been broken down further, the attritional curve may have been more consonant with above attritional curves. The importance of attritional data, then, seems incontestable. Moreover, the very detailed summary of patient and client factors influencing the outcome of psychotherapy (Luborsky et al., 1971, Appendix, pp. 162–179) suggests that few if any pre-therapy conditions describing either client or therapist bode particularly well or poorly for outcome evaluation. The Kissel study illustrates this matter somewhat by revealing that mothers of children in short-term psychotherapy rated their children gaining (rating was "improvement," p. 297)

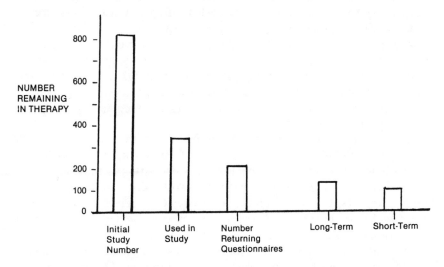

FIG. 1.8   Replotting data from Kissel (1974), showing long- and short-term cases, population characteristics. $N = 813$

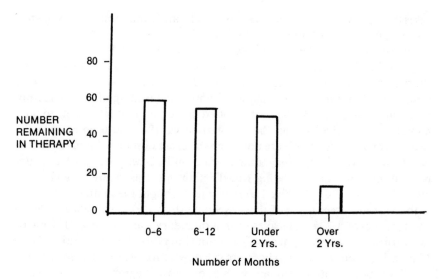

FIG. 1.9   Second replotting of Kissel data (1974), showing number months cases seen. (N = 323 cases appropriate for study among 813.)

nearly 21/2 times as frequently as therapists, and parents rated children "worse" 3 times to therapist zero cases, in the short-term framework. In the long-term therapy framework, therapists rated children "improved" somewhat more frequently than did mothers (75 vs. 67 cases, respectively), and therapists rated children "slightly better" 21 to 13 times compared to mothers. The bias at both ends of the evaluation spectrum add to the lack of correspondence in therapist/client ratings of outcome. If attrition is viewed, as it seems to be, by therapists in one light – dropping out being negatively evaluated by clinicians – then staying in therapy is likely to produce systematically higher clinician ratings. Clients, on the other hand, seem to get (and know) what they want in a shorter period of time. Attrition, then, favors client ratings and disfavors therapists, as to outcome, especially in a short-term framework.

Part of the problem of ratings of client outcome by therapists is seen in the Strupp et al. (1977) study of negative effects from psychotherapy. Primarily based on opinions of therapists regarding unsuccessful cases in their knowledge or among their clientele, these authors concluded that negative effects were an important clinical problem. They cite 46 references from the literature in which negative effects in therapeutic outcome were reported but were not attributed to any particular set of conditions and often not even discussed. The point of the Strupp et al. report was that negative effects are noticeably present but have not been properly addressed. The one major descriptive statistic missing is that there is no distribution of successful cases forming a backdrop and no accounting for attrition against which conditions negative effects could be discussed or interpreted. Are the negative effects likely to arise from those clients who remain in therapy for a long time and become inured to change? Or do they arise from clients—in the clinician's judgment—who terminate early on? Until a larger perspective is forthcoming, it is very difficult to know what therapeutic failures and negative effects mean. Because much of the literature supports the observation that clients and therapists disagree on outcome ratings, that therapists tend to rate higher those clients who stay in therapy longer, and that clinicians tend to play down the significance of short-term frameworks, then the presence of rated negative effects and the attribution of causes remains unclear.

ALCOHOLICS AND ATTRITION

Baekeland, Lundwall, and Shanahan (1973) studied dropouts from therapy among outpatient alcoholics. Starting with an N of 143 cases, selected from 190 cases (47 clients failed to complete all data on the assessment battery), there emerges an attrition curve as follows: 190 ostensible therapy cases, less 47 (24.7%) lost from incomplete assessment, followed by 25 immediate dropouts (no therapy sessions) (13%), followed by 37 "rapid dropouts" (20%), and 43 "slow dropouts" (22.6%), with 38 (20%) remaining for a mean of 46 weeks. Basing figures upon the number actually making appointments—143—the resulting figures for attrition are, successively, 18%, 26%, 30%, and 26.6%. The last figures represent a mean of 46 weeks of treatment, the distribution of which, and the asymptote, are missing from the data reported. Figures 1.10 and 1.11 (pp. 102 and 103, respectively) show a fairly

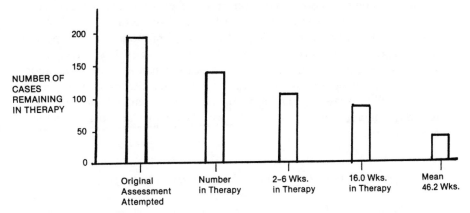

FIG. 1.10   Baekeland et al. (1973) showing attrition from initial assessment group ($N = 190$ cases).

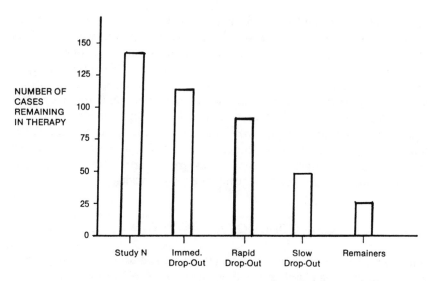

FIG. 1.11   Showing conditions of dropping-out of therapy per Baekeland et al. (1973); $N = 143$ cases.

typical attrition curve. Because the asymptote is missing from their data, it is possible to report only that the longest remaining patients ($N = 38$, or 26.6% of the 143 studied, or 20% of the total 38/190) fall into this category; how long these patients remained in therapy is not known. In summary (p. 105), these authors state that two fifths of the patients dropped out within 1 month and over three quarters within 6 months. The lengthy assessment battery and patient unwillingness to fill out forms, they aver, accounted for some of the early dropouts. Further, the "immediate dropouts" were better educated and of higher income and presented a longer period of prior abstinence (2 years) before admission (comparable to the "stayers" in therapy). Further discussion by these authors of the "rapid" and "slow" dropouts would appear to offer suggestions for other studies of attrition, inasmuch as the position where clients appear on the attrition curve may signal other matters of importance in the delivery of psychotherapy services. New research on outpatient alcoholic clinic treatment in relation to attrition is presented in the next chapter. (See Chapter 7 by Kaiser on a study of Alcoholic Clinic delivery system characteristics.)

COMMUNITY CLINICS AND COUNSELING CENTER DATA

Barten (1971) edited a book on brief methods of psychotherapy in which two groups of authors (Sarvis, Dewees, & Johnson, 1971, and Jacobson et al., 1965) offered some quantitative data on the number receiving outpatient therapy. The first authors (Sarvis et al., 1971) reported on p. 103 a table based on 824 outpatient psychotherapy cases from a mental health unit, 1955. Their data indicate that 10.1% had just one interview (presumably after intake), and 3.5% came for over 25 sessions. Rearranging the data from their Table 1 (p. 103) allows the computation of Fig. 1.12.

Recomputation of the Sarvis et al. table leaves something to be desired, yet the slope of the resulting attrition curve is evident. Missing are data on intake and on the distribution of the final 3.5% of cases at the 25 + number of therapy interviews, a matter represented in Fig. 1.12.

In the same book by Barten (1971), Jacobson et al. (1971) also reported in Table 2 (p. 143) figures that required replotting in order to study attrition. Replotting their Table 2 is shown in Fig. 1.13. Data are likewise missing on the intake procedures and on the number of cases seen for more than six interviews. Figure 1.13 is drawn to reflect the incompleteness of the asymptotic data; nonetheless the attrition curve for these 735 cases shows the characteristic pattern. Neither of these sets of authors gives the mean number of sessions, but the data suggest a mean of four or five visits, comparable to other outpatient statistics (also see Jacobson, Wilner, Marley, Schneider, Strickler, & Sommer, 1965 for similar finding).

It was previously noted that the Brandt (1965) review of attrition netted a curve (although differently plotted) similar to the reworked data reported on from a variety of sources in this report. There are some other research reports on university counseling center data that come closer to the present interest in exploring new ways of looking at attrition. One study (Leventhal, 1964) sought to predict the number of interviews incoming clients would engage in

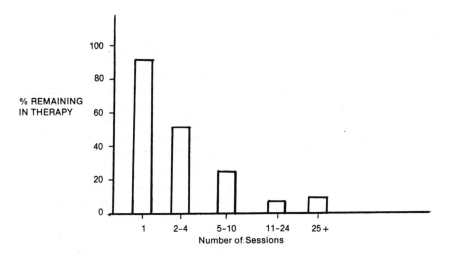

FIG. 1.12   Replotting Sarvis et al. data (1971, Table 1, p. 103) concerning attribution loss among 824 cases.

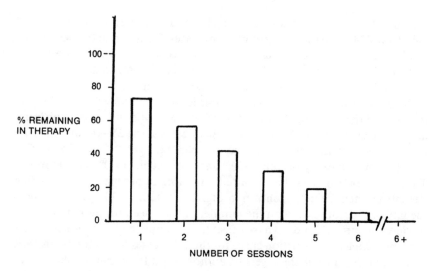

FIG. 1.13   Jacobson et al. (1971, Table 2, p. 143) data on 735 short-term psychotherapy cases, replotted.

where counselor and intake interview ratings served as predictors, compared with a base rate already observed of 88% short-term and 12% long-term cases. Ten interviews or less was defined as short-term, over 10 as long-term. Counselors' ratings were compared to intake screeners' in predicting who would fall into the long- or short-term series. Intake interviewer (not necessarily the subsequent counselor) predicted correctly 93% of the short-term cases, and 49% of the longer term cases. Counselors did as well: 92% accuracy for the short-term group and 43% for the longer term group. Leventhal concludes: "Thus a rater who was not the counselor, on the basis of a more brief interview, could as accurately predict number of interviews (as categorized here) as the counselor himself" (p. 106). What Leventhal did not know—or report—was that the attrition curve (the 92% short-termers and 8% long-termers) would make the predictions highly likely and might not represent any particularly acute judgment of later client behavior. Had Leventhal observed the attritional decline in the number of clients (285 in the first set of ratings, 344 in the second set) having one or more interviews, he might have focused more on the particulars of the screeners' and counselors' ratings; the accuracy of the ratings of short- and long-termers might have been redundantly built into the already observed base rates of client dropping out behaviors. Phillips, Raiford, & Batrawi (1965) went at the attrition problem somewhat differently by noting the number of clients in three 3-month segments in a university counseling center who applied for help, began and finished evaluations, and started therapy. Summing their data for a 1-year period, 205 cases of undergraduate applications to a counseling center showed that 115 cases (56.1%) actually got into therapy (hence a 43.9% attrition at intake) over the 1-year span. The number engaging in from 1 to 10 interviews (under a 10-session limit) was not reported, hence the full data on the attrition curve were not available. Both studies were based on the unrecognized attrition curve thereby limiting the value of the reported studies.

PSYCHOTHERAPY PRIVATE PRACTICE DATA

Data among private practice psychotherapists are hard to come by (Walberg, 1980). One effort to study private psychotherapy practices, along the lines reported on here, failed to gain enough responses to warrant publication. Koss (1979) does present data on 100 cases (See Fig. 1.14) to warrant tentative generalizations concerning her results. Although her data are from only 7 psychotherapists, 100 cases, over a 1-year span, it is highly suggestive that private practice efforts, properly documented, would show about the

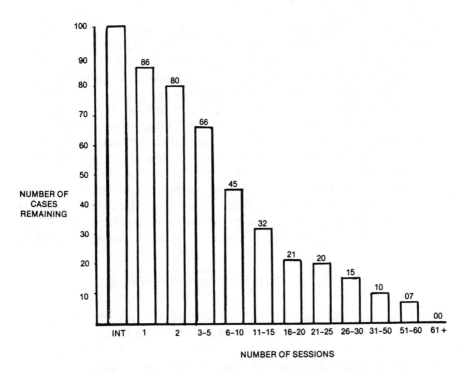

FIG. 1.14   Showing attrition curve, private practice psychological clinic, 7 psychotherapists, one year (1975); $N = 100$; Median = 8 Interviews. Adapted from Koss, 1979.

same attrition curve as public mental health and counseling center facilities. As with other data collation, it was necessary to replot the Koss data to reflect the number of cases remaining after each number of sessions of therapy reported on the horizontal axis. The aggregation of data in gross number of sessions categories fails to show the finer grained details of attrition, but the resultant curve nonetheless supports to a considerable degree the attritional matters studied herein. Further tests of this phenomenon among private practitioners are sorely needed, especially if data collation begins with intake, presents the flow in closer detail, and fills out the asymptote to the end.

TIME IN THERAPY AND OUTCOME

In a number of studies, the relationship between time in therapy and outcome ratings (and/or satisfaction with therapy on the part of the client) is moot. Some data showed that length of therapy in time-unlimited settings yields low positive correlations with outcome (Cooley & Lejoy, 1980; Edwards, Yarvis, Mueller, & Langsley, 1978; Fiester & Rudestam, 1975; Flynn, Balch, Lewis, & Katz, 1981; Leve, 1974; Mintz, Luborsky, & Christoph, 1979) but the evidence is not strong. In time-limited settings, outcome seems essentially unrelated to the number of sessions (many studies report the mean number of interviews to be about 4 to 5 [Budman, 1981; Garfield, 1978]), and there is apparently more openness in judging both satisfaction and outcome levels by therapists and by clients in the shorter framework (Pardes & Pincus, 1981). Very long therapy may encourage an attitude of inurement by both client and therapist, hence reducing a possible relationship between number of sessions and reported satisfaction by the client (Phillips, 1960; Stieper & Wiener, 1965). In view of the importance of attritional features of all therapies in a variety of settings, the judging of outcome and/or satisfaction by client — and outcome by therapist — should be referred to the points on the attritional curve from which the clientele are drawn. The larger picture, the base rates attritional data, appears to be fundamental enough to refer all other outcome data to this characteristic curve.

SUMMARY

The review of attritional studies of psychotherapy reveals some characteristics across service delivery settings (community mental health clinics, counseling centers, outpatient centers associated with hospitals), across types of patients, among both short- and long-term treatment regimens and from time-limited and time-unlimited settings. Data have been presented from the literature showing that attrition has been a neglected issue in most reports on psychotherapy. The research literature lacks a breakdown for the actual number of cases being served one, two, three . . . sessions, out to an asymptote. Few studies have given full data on the number and characteristics of cases chosen for therapy and the selection criteria used. Accepting the therapists'/researchers' rights to select cases for a given treatment project or regimen is one thing and expecting, in turn, explicit criteria for inclusion in a therapeutic offering is quite often another matter. The latter instance is where most research reports fail; this lack stems from a neglect of the problem of attrition.

When the existing literature on attrition and related topics — mean number of interviews, range of interviews, people available for follow-up, and so on — is examined and when the reported data are replotted, a "characteristic attritional curve" (Poisson distribution)[1] results. It is observable when the number of cases served begins with intake interviews (or screening interviews) and covers all therapy sessions. Relevant, also, are the number of cases in follow-up research. When all these data points are included, a negatively accelerated declining curve results.

The potential value of a characteristic attritional curve is sizable. Studies reporting on outcome research are dependent upon client reports throughout therapy and including follow-up data. The larger context of attritional effects would seem to be basic to all related selection, process, product and evaluation research, yet this possibility has never been explicitly studied and has seldom even been mentioned. It is likely that the Poisson distribution of infrequently occurring events is the basic phenomenon underlying the attrition data. It is further likely that a mathematical/conceptual base such as is suggested by the Poisson distribution could provide important leads for further research on the nature of the attritional curve and suggest heuristic points of intervention in the delivery and evaluation of therapeutic services.

The matter must be raised in regard to the delivery of services to the consuming public. The research review shows the modal number of interviews to be one; the modal number of client contacts at the intake interview

---

[1]The Poisson distribution is a derivative of the binomial expansion, where N is large, p is less than .50 and the events are independent. Kennedy, J. J. (1983). *Analyzing qualitative data*. New York: Praeger. Lewis, D. (1960). *Quantitative methods in psychology*. New York: McGraw-Hill. This distribution is said to characterize the decay of atoms, some aspects of the behavior of light, etc. (Massaro, D. W. (1975). *Experimental psychology and information processing*. Chicago: Rand-McNally.) The presented attrition curve may better fit a negative exponential "decay" curve (Lewis, 1960); or simply a learning curve where the number "learning" what possible solutions they can in one session ("trial") (about 50%), with others requiring more time, and so on down to an asymptote. Research might study the cost-effectiveness in relation to the number of sessions required for X number of clients to learn what they needed to know, comparing different therapeutic techniques; this would afford a more rigorous comparison of therapies or techniques than presently conducted studies lacking the baseline of the attrition curve.

(ostensible therapy cases) is one. The median number of contacts is in the three-to-five sessions range and the mean varies from five to eight sessions. Thus the delivery of apparently appropriate therapeutic services calls for a "rapid response" type of focus, not an intensive one, and it remains moot at this juncture in our research base whether intensive treatment serves as useful a purpose or is as necessary, as many clinicians think. Experimenting more on the appropriate number of sessions as an outer limit (10, 15, 20, etc., sessions) might become an important empirical problem, and cutting off service when clients reach a given number of sessions—once reported as unharmful by Stieper and Wiener (1965), and subsequently neglected as a useful clinical practice—may have to be revived. Further, clinics that deviate much from the characteristic attritional curve might be questioned whether their service delivery is appropriate, or whether other interests are being primarily served. Still further considerations of the attrition curve bear on psychotherapy theory. There are few references to attrition and its impact on theory and practice in the numerous books on psychotherapy and counseling theory (Corsini, 1981; Herink, 1980; Patterson, 1980). It is almost as if theory were part of one world and practice another. Reference to the basic attritional curve will doubtless surface as the appropriate backdrop for examining questions related to high volume, short-term help, as contrasted with intensive, long-range help for a few; with comparisons between therapeutic persuasions, and with the setting of appropriate limits on the number of sessions with proper attention to proven exceptions. All psychotherapy theory will have to address the attrition phenomenon. Further, evaluations as to what dropouts mean (Brandt, 1964, 1965; Garfield & Afflek, 1959; Gundlach & Geller, 1958; Silverman & Beech, 1979) will need to be done. Studies of differences in therapeutic theory and practice will be referred for greater understanding to the attritional phenomena described.

Given the nature of the findings in this review of the literature on attrition, attention is now turned to the collection of further data from several outpatient settings in order to examine the presence or not of the characteristic attritional curve. Chapter 2 reports on new research data among walk-in, self-initiated clientele in counseling center and community mental health settings. This research on new clinical populations and service delivery systems affords the opportunity to exert relatively greater care in accounting for ostensible therapy cases (intake), the drop in therapy attendance and the length of the asymptote, as well as accounting for the means and SDs in the distributions.

2

Data Bases on Attrition Across Newly Researched Psychotherapy Delivery Systems

Given the nature of the attrition curve described in Chapter 1, it is incumbent on us to look at new data bases for possible confirmation of these findings. Several settings have been examined: a university counseling center covering a 7-year period; a community, outpatient alcoholic clinic with data over a 2.5-year span on first and second admissions; an HMO outpatiennt setting in a metropolitan area covering 1 year; reports on NIMH nationwide data published on "free standing" clinics; a 9-year data base from NIMH on community mental health centers as to base rates on number of interviews; and other data from a counseling center regarding client and therapist attitudes toward therapeutic help centered mainly on the intake process.

RECENT COUNSELING CENTER DATA

Table 2.1 presents data spanning a 7-year period from a metropolitan university counseling center, with over 3,000 cases. In regard to attrition, it is evident from Table 2.1 that the dropout rate for the entire period is 45% to 55%, with some variation year by year. A policy change in 1978 tightened up on the number of cases going beyond a 10-session limit, thereby influencing the asymptote.

Despite these changes the mean number of sessions stayed around 4 to 6. The cases going beyond the 10-time limit for the 7-year period averaged 14 sessions; earlier data (pre-1980) on details of the asymptote are not known. With the availability of computer help in 1980, the record keeping improved

TABLE 2.1
Summary Data, 1975–1982, Incl.: Intake, Dropout, Therapy and Follow-up Data[a]
The George Washington University

	1975–76 N	1975–76 %	1976–77 N	1976–77 %	1977–78 N	1977–78 %	1978–79 N	1978–79 %	1979–80 N	1979–80 %	1980–81 N	1980–81 %	1981–82 N	1981–82 %	1975–82 N	1975–82 %
Males	210	45.36	162	45.64	133	41.56	202	40.00	260	42.55	135	35.16	165	40.00	1267	41.65
Females	253	54.64	193	54.37	187	54.88	303	60.00	351	57.45	249	64.86	247	60.00	1783	58.45
Totals	463		355		320		505		611		384		412		3050	
1–3 Int.	125		25		70		184		122		68		72		666	42.68
4–10 Int.	14 } 216		25 } 165		51 } 193		97 } 334		98 } 277		101 } 189		139 } 247		525	30.30
11+ Int.	77		115		72		53		57		20		36		430	26.96
Tot./Therapy	216	45.65	165	46.48	193	60.31	334	66.14	277	45.33	189	49.22	247	60.00	1621	53.15
Drop (Int.)	247	53.35	190	53.52	127	39.69	171	33.86	334	54.67	195	50.78	165	40.00	1429	46.85
Follow-up No. versus All Applic.	80	17.24	110	30.09	116	36.22	72	14.26	84	12.11	65	17.00	412	15.05	589	19.31
Ther. Partic. (In Drop)	190	76.92	101	53.16	92	72.44	125	73.10	237	70.96	131	50.78	125	50.60	1002	61.81
Hold	60		16		30		05		14		00		20			
Refer	52 } 190		30 } 101		24 } 92		28 } 125		77 } 237		43 } 131		29 } 125		1002	61.81
Termin.	78		55		38		92		126		88		76			
Follow-up No. versus No. Therapy	216	37.03	165	66.67	193	60.10	334	66.14	277	30.32	189	34.39	247	39.83	1621	36.34

[a]Cases were "technically closed" at end of year plus summer term (July 31st); total number of sessions were counted when such cases actually terminated; cases re-admitted — very few in number — were counted as new cases.

and the two subsequent years of data — 1980 to 1982 — are provided in Fig. 2.1 showing the full therapy session range for these years.

Returning to a fuller consideration of Table 2.1 on the 7-year data span, it is clear that a number of important data bear on client and therapist/clinic behavior in the delivery of therapeutic services. The ratio of women to men remained close to 60/40. Equally important data show the number of cases responding to follow-up, 3–5 months after termination of therapy, is about 20% of the total intake population. The number of cases followed up on relative to the number in therapy for at least one interview was about 36%. These figures on follow-up are highly selective, suggesting skepticism about reports on various types of therapy and their effectiveness in the literature.

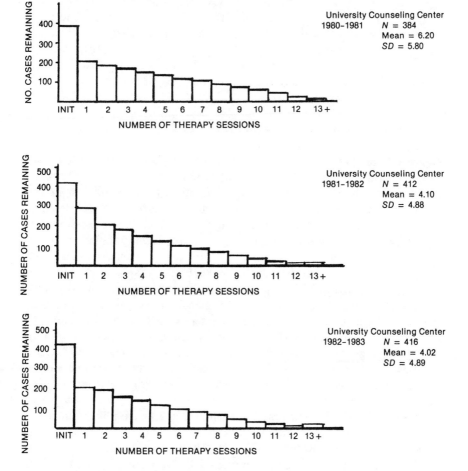

FIG. 2.1   Showing attrition curve, University Counseling Center Data, 1980–1983.

Interesting, also, are the data on therapist participation in client leaving therapy. The figures from Table 2.1 indicate that nearly 60% of clients leaving therapy — put on hold, referred out, or terminated — were partially influenced to do so by the therapist (at intake, mostly, but also later in therapy). Further studies are reported later that confirm these figures, which were thought to be somewhat unreliable inasmuch as they were arrived at in the 1975–1980 period via monthly staff résumés of the client load. Now that accountability looms larger, older methods have been called into question, and new data supplied. However, the relatively high incidence of therapist collaboration in client termination raises a number of additional issues: Is this encouragement by the therapist due to feeling the client is not very "workable"? Is it due to the possibility that the client has already gotten what he or she wants and is ready to move on? Is it due to some mismatch between client and therapist? Or is attrition independent of these matters? And so on. The literature shows that client and therapist do not agree on the matter of client improvement in therapy to a very great extent; possibly, too, in-therapy judgments are also askew, and the notion of mutuality in client-therapist decisions regarding termination may be more a myth than heretofore supposed (Posin, 1963; Small, 1971).

More Detailed Counseling Center Data, 1980–1983

Figure 2.1 presents more detailed data on attrition in the same clinic for the 1980–83 period, respectively, with Ns of 384, 412, and 416 "ostensible therapy" cases. Of the 384 applying for therapy, 1980–81, 191 (almost 50%) continued into the first interview and 50% failed to return; data are presented showing the number of clients continuing through each therapy session, and data on cases of 11 or more sessions (the asymptote in this population continued to 15 sessions, with a mean of 13 sessions for the extended cases only). This figure shows a larger drop at the intake, by far, than at any other point in the treatment series. The steepness of the negatively accelerating declining curve speaks either to efficiency or inefficiency in bringing psychotherapy services to the clientele. Within the therapy series, also, the modal number of sessions is one. The mean of the 1980–1981 sample is 6.2 sessions ($SD = 5.8$), close to that reported by a number of other researchers (Garfield, 1978; Gelso & Johnson, 1983; National Center for Health Statistics, 1966; and Rosenstein & Milazzo-Sayer, 1981), and also showing similarity between the mean and the standard deviation.

Data for 1981–1982, same outpatient clinic (Fig. 2.1), gave like results. The number of clients not returning for therapy after the intake was 165 and the number going beyond 10 sessions was 36. The mean of the total population was 4.10 sessions ($SD = 4.88$); steepness of the drop from the number at intake session to the number beginning therapy was somewhat less than for the

1980–81 data, and the asymptote in the latter year extended about 5 standard deviations. Whether there is any relationship between the number entering therapy in relation to the number applying to the clinic for therapy (those called "ostensible therapy cases") and the length of the asymptote (possibly implying greater selection at the outset) remains moot. This conjecture is, however, only one of several possibilities.

The 1982–83 data (Fig. 2.1) are close to the 1980–81 and 1981–82 data bases. The 1982–83 mean and standard deviation are similar (4.02 and 4.89, respectively) and the asymptote includes about 8%–9% of the total intake population, showing the general stability over these 3 years of the means and standard deviations and asymptotes. What it would take — if alteration were possible — to change these general "decay" curves remains moot at this time. We take up this problem later (see Chapter 5).

ATTRITION IN OTHER OUTPATIENT SETTINGS

Outpatient Alcoholic Treatment

An outpatient alcoholic clinic study (Kaiser, 1982)[1] was based on an N of 345 first admissions and a second admissions (repeaters) of 55 cases, during a 2½-year period, 1979–1981; total $N = 400$ cases.[2] The attrition curves for both populations are found in Figs. 2.2 and 2.3.

Figure 2.2, $N = 345$, shows the "typical" attrition curve except that the drop from intake to the first interview is not as steep as some. Also, the asymptote, going out to 59 visits, is longer than many other attrition curves. The *unlimited* time conditions in this clinic, however, appear not to affect the general slope of the curve. In the Poisson distribution, the mean is equal to the variance; in this population, the mean was 8.13 and the standard deviation 8.50, with the asymptote extending about 6.5 standard deviations. If the asymptote is very lengthy (say, more than 3 standard deviations), one would then want to know more about the delivery of services policies, the nature of the clinical population, the types of therapies offered, whether certain therapists tended to accumulate longer term cases, and whether the long-term cases were validly in need. All of these are empirical questions for further research, questions that may be more heuristic than trying to identify (before therapy) very specific variables characteristic of the client population. Once

---

[1] We are indebted to Sharon Migliore, Chief, Division of Program Monitoring, Pennsylvania; and Alden Small, Ph.D., Chief, Statistical and Analysis Unit; both of the Department of Health for these data; conclusions drawn are the responsibility of the present authors and do not reflect policies or opinions of the Commission.

[2] A more comprehensive report on this population, by M. J. Kaiser, is found in Chapter 7.

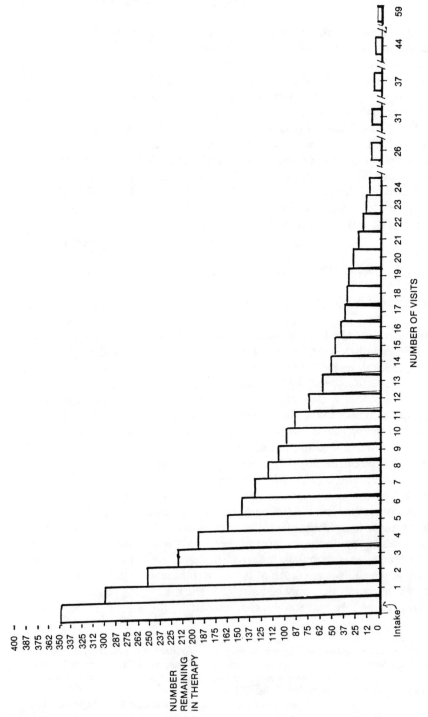

FIG. 2.2   First admissions, Alcoholic Out-Patient Clinic, 2½ Years. *N* = 345 Cases; Mean = 8.13; *SD* = 8.50 Sessions.

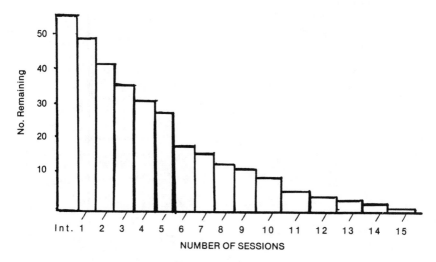

FIG. 2.3   Second admissions, Alcoholic Out-Patient Clinic, 2½ Years. $N = 55$, Mean = 5.15, SD = 5.04 Sessions.

the lengthier cases are properly identified, then patient, therapist, and clinic-related variables become more heuristically available for study.

The second admissions population ($N = 55$) in this clinic showed an attrition curve closely similar to the first admissions curve but with a mean of 5.64 visits and a standard deviation of 5.04 visits. Note, too, that the asymptote leans out to an end-point of 25 visits, approximately 4 standard deviations from the mean. In these data when people return for a second series of visits, they tend to go a shorter length of time but to show the same general attritional characteristics. Would it, then, be fair and economical to limit the number of sessions in the first admission, knowing that some (in this case, 16%) will likely return for more help? Because 72% of the first admission cases left (finished?) therapy by the tenth interview, and 89% of the readmissions cases by the tenth interview, would not a time limit serve to increase focus and perhaps net a less varied outcome? Because outcome evaluations are lacking from these alcoholic populations, there is no way to relate length of therapy to satisfaction or sobriety outcomes. Future research will have to be more consistent on this important point; the usual case of about one sixth to one fourth being followed up as to client ratings of outcome will, somehow, have to be considerably improved if we are to have greater confidence in the outcome from service delivery systems.

HMO Outpatient Data

The next study comes from a time-limited ($N = 20$ sessions), outpatient HMO center (see Fig. 2.4).

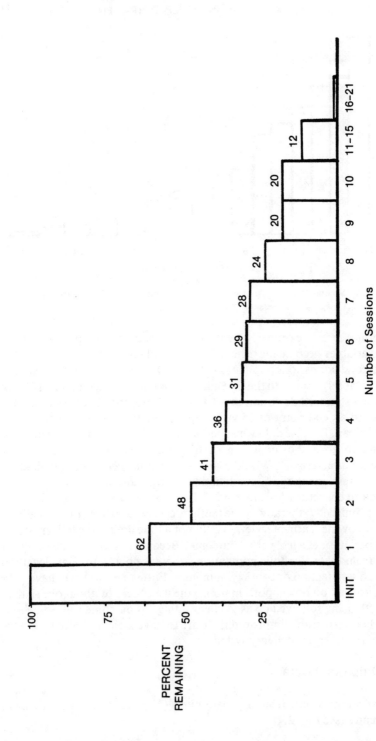

FIG. 2.4 Showing attritional curve, HMO, 1 Year, 1981; 20% Sample. N = 148; Mean = 5.58; SD = 5.13.

In this study (Stone, personal communication, May 1, 1983), a 20% sample of the 1981 outpatient population was obtained (N = 153 sample cases) by taking from the intake records every fifth case. The mean number of sessions was 5.27 and the standard deviation was 5.08. The asymptote ended with two cases going the limit of 20 sessions and two cases for 21 sessions, about three standard deviations beyond the mean, a figure perhaps closer to the "ideal" attrition curve, and one suggesting a firmer grasp on the clientele receiving help. The drop in the curve between intake and one-session-only cases was very steep, suggesting that the intake is either a very efficient or inefficient interaction; because either possibility is reasonable from what we know about the delivery of psychotherapy services, further empirical study of the cases leaving therapy at intake becomes imperative. Client and therapist interactional characteristics and clinic policies should derive from empirical findings; the attrition curve is an appropriate way of determining base rate considerations that may lead to improved efficiency and effectiveness in psychotherapy.

The mean of from four to about eight visits appears to be a fairly stable range within which most outpatient populations receiving psychotherapy fall (Brandt, 1965; Garfield & Kurz, 1952; Bennett & Wisnecki, 1979, and the findings reviewed here.)

National Figures

To test further the notion of the mean number of sessions among outpatient psychotherapy clientele, national statistics have been consulted. Figure 2.5 shows the distribution of 1,406,065 cases from a publication, *Characteristics of Admissions to Selected Mental Health Facilities,* 1975 (Rosenstein & Milazzo-Sayer, 1981), for white/nonwhite M/F outpatients from free-standing clinics. The range of visits is from 1 to 31 + with the asymptote not broken down, but comprising only 1.4% of the total number of visits. The mean number of visits is 3.7 (3.7 for males, 3.6 for females) comprising, respectively, 634,355 and 772,710 cases for the 1-year period (Rosenstein & Milazzo-Sayer, 1981, Table 11a, pp. 103–104). The present figure is replotted to follow the original authors' numeration – 1, 2, 3/4, 5/6 . . . 11/15, etc. visits. The standard deviation was calculated by the present writer by rounding off the one hundred thousand figures to one thousand as a base, and averaging the number of cases found in each session-interval; this netted a standard deviation of 4.0, a likely figure. Thus the asymptote stretched out in these data to 7-plus standard deviations, a fairly long tail compared to other data offered here. However, the survey data (Rosenstein & Milazzo-Sayer, 1981), coming from over 1.4 million cases nationally, are likely to show maximal variation and also may represent reporting errors.

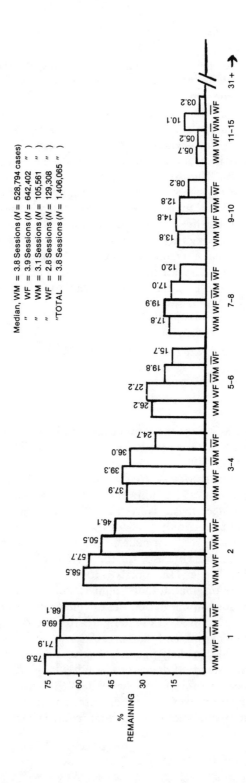

FIG. 2.5 Showing breakdown for White/Non-White M/F; 1.4 + Million Cases, 1 Year. (From Rosenstein, M. J. & Milazzo-Sayre, 1981; p. 104, Table 11a)

Median, WM = 3.8 Sessions (N = 528,794 cases)
"   WF = 3.9 Sessions (N = 642,402   ")
"   WM = 3.1 Sessions (N = 105,561   ")
"   WF = 2.8 Sessions (N = 129,308   ")
"TOTAL = 3.8 Sessions (N = 1,406,065   ")

50

Additional data (Federally Funded Community Mental Health Centers, 1981) covered annually from 205 to 600 community mental health outpatient clinics, and from 2.8 to 9.7 million cases, 1970–1978. These data show the mean number of psychotherapy visits nationally (individual, group, and family cases) to be as follows: 1970 (5.3); 1971 (5.4); 1972 (5.6); 1973 (5.3); 1974 (5.1); 1975 (4.8); 1976 (4.8); 1977 (5.1); and 1978 (5.0). The overall mean for the 9-year period was 5.16, surely a stable baseline against which to compare almost any other psychotherapy service delivery system. Data were not presented allowing the calculations of standard deviations. These large community mental health clinic data bases do not state the number of intake interviews. The incompleteness of the NIMH data is expected to be overcome in time. Reporting errors or inconsistencies may also be present.

Additional NIMH Data

Recent data on service history and termination information from a sample of federally funded community mental health centers (Windle, 1983) allowed for further tests of the attrition phenomenon. It was shown previously that between 1970 and 1978, some 45 to 50 million client-contacts showed an average of about five visits for psychotherapy, this being considered a more than adequate baseline for one important aspect of psychotherapy service delivery. Data to follow are based on a more recent sample of the CMHC data and allow for the plotting of attrition curves for several clinics (Windle, 1983).

Combining data from the cited report (Windle, 1983), 33,391 sample cases are plotted in Fig. 2.6a. The number of sessions begins with zero on the abscissa and goes out to a value of 21 + sessions. Because intake and the first therapy session are often not separated by clinics reporting on their cases, the data base in Figure 2.6a begins with the first therapy session following intake (90% returning). All data in the following figures on the NIMH community clinics follow this pattern.

It is evident from Fig. 2.5 that the steepest drop in the number of clients remaining occurs in the first to second session and in the interval of the second to the third-to-fifth sessions. Combining the number of sessions into intervals (3–5, 6–8, etc.) is unnecessarily gross and destroys somewhat the symmetry of the declining attrition curve. However, the curve of attrition in Fig. 2.6a shows the same features as those previously cited from the literature and from the more recent studies found in this chapter. The grossness of reporting on data relating to number of therapy sessions shows how important it is to depict the flow of cases from the intake onward to the end of the asymptote. We do not know, of course, in this figure how far out the asymptote extends as the end-point — 21 + sessions — aggregates the remaining number of sessions into this one final interval. It is important to know how far out the asymptote extends as it is one basis for comparing the behavior of delivery

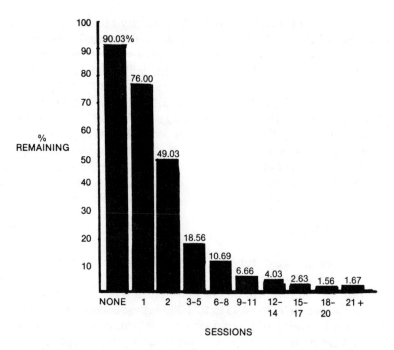

FIG. 2.6a   NIMH Data from C. Wendle (1983, pp. 68–70) N = 33, 391

systems—did cases extend out beyond three standard deviations? Are they contributed to by unusually "difficult" cases? Are the extended cases the work primarily of a few therapists or are they spread among the entire staff? And so on. (See also Fig. 2.6b—"outpatient hours"—in this same connection.)

To further illustrate individual differences in particular clinic delivery systems, Figs. 2.7a, 2.7b, 2.7c, and 2.7d combine the attritional patterns for four clinics from the same data set (Windle, 1983, pp. 68–73).

It is evident from Figs. 2.7a and 2.7b that clinic #9 has a large drop between intake (the zero number of previous sessions to the one-session interval) and the first inverview—over 50%; whereas the drop for clinic #8 is far more gradual with nearly equal percentage drops between intake and the second therapy session, followed by a relatively larger drop in the 3–5 session interval. Just how clinics differ in policies (time-limited or not, the number of intake session before therapy formally begins, and so forth) may be the pivotal consideration in these two comparisons; or they may simply represent small individual differences in clientele and related matters.

The contrast is further illustrated by comparing clinic #36 with clinics #8 and #9 (pp. 69–70). With clinic #36 the steeper drop is with session interval 3–5 and again with 6–8, followed by about equal numbers of people re-

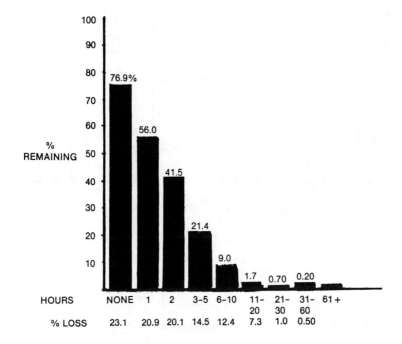

FIG. 2.6b NIMH Data-"No. Outpatient Hours," C. Wendle (1983, page 71); $N = 24,979$

maining for session numbers 9-11, 12-14, 15-17, and 18-20; the number remaining at the 21 + suggesting a long asymptote. Because the mean number
of sessions and the standard deviations for each clinic in the number of sessions are not reported in these data, more detailed comparisons are not
possible.

Clinic #10 (p. 21) illustrates a still different aspect of clinic functioning.
This clinic has been reported on in terms of the number of *hours* and extends
out to an asymptote of 61 + , a remarkable and comparatively longer term delivery system if we are able to equate the number of hours with the number of
sessions. The generally smooth nature of the attrition curve (yet allowing for
a small blip at extended interval 31-60), however, is noticeable in comparison
to other attrition curves offered above.

It would be possible to report on the various attrition curve features of a
large number of clinics but this effort would be uneconomical in this context.
Suffice it to say that we learn a number of things from these data displays: the
importance of a flow system by which to report on clinic policies and delivery
system features, beginning with intake and going out to a fully broken-down
asymptote; to have means and standard deviations reported on for each facility and for any aggregates of clinics such as might accompany those with

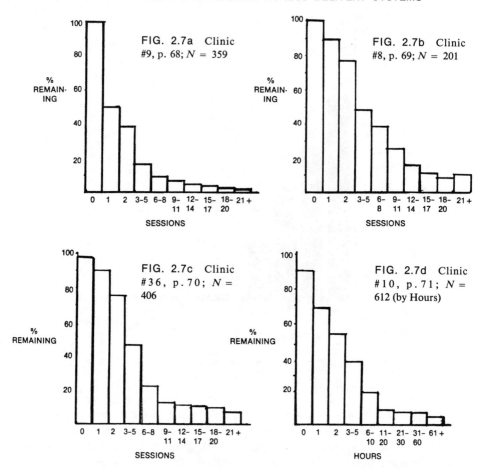

FIG. 2.7,a,b,c,d   Showing slightly different attrition curves for CMHC, by sessions/ hours, Wendle, 1983, pp. 68–71.

time-limited (or not) practices; and, of course, any special features of clinic practice such as specializing in one type of clientele (e.g., alcoholics, parent-child cases, etc.) compared to a general practice of psychotherapy with all incoming clients. Greater care in keeping statistical records would allow probing further into a very interesting array of problems such as those related to the time-honored characteristics of clients, therapists, diagnosis, client presenting complaints, and so forth. With an improved baseline on clinic delivery system features, older and previously unproductive questions could be reexamined if there appeared any likelihood that they could be gainfully revived; if not, they could be laid to rest and time better spent on a fascinating array of new questions.

ATTRITION FROM SEVERAL CLINICS, SAME AREA

After showing the attrition curve in a number of clinics, viewed separately, it now becomes possible to view a collection of clinics within the same geographic area, united under one administrative head, as these clinics serve alcoholic and drug abuse outpatients. The N for this population was 3,063, covering an 18-months period of time, 1979–1981.

Data were aggregated for Fig. 2.8 to show the total number of treatments from one to eight. All treatments — Detoxification, Counseling/Therapy, Vocational Rehabilitation — are combined in these percentage figures as are the various diagnostic categories (opiates, alcohol, amphetamines, marijuana, and others).

Figure 2.8 shows percentage of cases remaining after each numbered treatment, based on an intake N of 3,063; it displays a steep drop after the first interview. The total number referred for help was 3,063 and, although most (76%) came for one session of some kind of treatment, very few (15.54%) returned for a second interview; thus the drop-off was most pronounced after the first treatment session, not after intake. This condition may have arisen because there was often a legal sanction or some pressure for the clients to present themselves as a token of cooperation for at least one session. The drop-off after one session is remarkable, followed by more gradual drops, down to an asymptote beginning with the fourth or fifth session. Separate data — not presented here — showed that specific treatment regimens had only one to four sessions and dropped off markedly after the first or second treatment session. The asymptotes were reached among the various diagnostic groups after three or four sessions and only a few individuals among the more than three thousand received more than three or four treatment sessions (Fig. 2.8).

The meaning of these data is that extending the service delivery system from one clinic to a group of clinics in the same geographic area shows the attrition curve to be closely similar to that found for any one of several individual clinic data systems. The utilization of more than one clinic in a geographic area may accommodate people who are moving or changing jobs or are otherwise inclined to go from one clinic to another; the waiting list may also figure in the choice. There may be additional reasons not pursued in connection with the accumulation of this data register.

Some treatment regimens use up, so to say, their treatment possibilities quickly. For example, only 9 of 1,822 Detox treatment episodes (referrals, Detox cases) lasted as long as six sessions in treatment. Comparable figures for other treatment are as follows: Rehabilitation efforts netted only 49 of 2,796 treatment episodes (referral) cases having a second treatment session and only 2 additional episodes having a third treatment session; outpatient therapy produced only 14 treatment episodes (referrals) among 2,328 cases

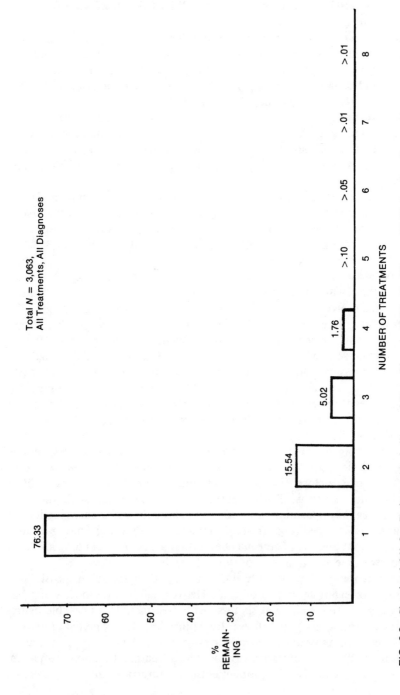

FIG. 2.8   Showing 3,063 Out-Patients, Alcoholics, and Drug Abusers, 18 Months History, 37 Clinics, One Geographic Area. (Adapted from Kaiser, 1984)

going for as many as six sessions and only 2 episodes lasted eight sessions. Outpatient or inpatient programs that attempt to remediate these alcoholic/drug abuse patients either will have to mobilize more highly effective treatments if they are to attract and hold patients, or they will need to develop other treatment systems if they are to be more effective. What happens in one or two treatment sessions of any type with any of these diagnostic categories will have to show a difference between zero and some treatment if the latter is to be worth its cost, insofar as these data go.

Even though there is attritional similarity between these alcoholic/drug abuse cases and outpatient mental health cases, the former groups often present more social, economic, and even legal problems. The former groups are likely to have longer and more formidable histories of drinking and drug abuse problems, compared to the percentage of serious mental health cases of a chronic nature in outpatient care. Treatment delivery systems for the alcoholic and drug abuse cases, then, have a more serious problem on their hands as they attempt rehabilitation of their clientele, compared to mental health practitioners. Sometimes the two groups overlap, of course, but no data were available to pursue this issues.

The nature of help seeking as described and discussed here ramifies considerably. It now appears likely that not only are individual clinics — private and public mental health centers, counseling centers and alcoholic clinics — very similar insofar as the attritional curve describing the delivery system is concerned, but the same curve holds up pretty consistently when one looks at a group of clinics, in a limited geographic area performing about the same services for a special group of diagnostically similar cases, viz., alcoholic and drug abuse cases. Research, training of clinicians, educating the public, and dealing productively with the flow of help-seeking clientele, as well as judging the effectiveness and efficiency of clinics of all types, are strongly affected by these attritional matters. The attritional features of clinics, offering help-seeking needs among the populace, and the number of sessions engaged in by the clientele, are bottom line considerations for any discussion of service delivery systems.

SUMMARY

It is clear from the aforementioned review of the literature and the presentation of new data on a variety of clinics, covering a variety of settings, both time-limited and not, that the attrition curve as a negatively accelerating declining ("decay") curve is a heretofore unrecognized but nonetheless important description of delivery systems covering the complex behavior called psychotherapy. But the curve is more than a descriptive one; it signals a number of questions regarding the delivery of services, the meaning of various aspects of the curve (intake, percentage drop from intake to one or more therapy sessions, the length of the asymptote, the mean and standard deviation of the number of sessions, and so on). The curve also seems to obtain, despite diagnostic categories, types of presenting complaints, theoretical predilections of therapists (although not explicitly studied herein), techniques used, and perhaps most other issues characterizing psychotherapy theory, research and practice. The described attrition curve may obtain despite any of the usual topics characterizing psychotherapy research. It may well be a new baseline, a starting point for almost any kind of research on psychotherapy.

The descriptive data offered in Chapters 1 and 2 related almost entirely to self-initiated, walk-in psychotherapy. This kind of service delivery system, although the most common by far, is not the only psychotherapy/behavior change modality. Recent work in the area termed analogue studies appears to show a growing presence in the literature and particularly now that meta-analysis research and evaluation have become prominent for a number of reasons. Chapter 3 concerns analogue studies and meta-analysis research with respect to attrition problems similar to — and somewhat different from — those considered above relating to walk-in, self-initiated therapy.

3 Analogue Studies and Attrition: Special Challenge

Chapters 1 and 2 data derive from outpatient, self-initiated therapy. It is unknown whether analogue studies might comprise a different set of problems. This chapter examines some problems related to attrition in analogue research.

Having examined the main features in regard to attrition in the literature on outpatient psychotherapy and several recently available original sources of data, it now becomes important to study the problem of attrition in the analogue type of research. Analogue studies (Kazdin, 1982) are types of studies wherein populations of people are invited, or solicited, for a very specific and limited behavior change purpose, often relating to specific fears or phobias, anxieties, underachievement problems, smoking cessation, weight loss, and the like. Usually, the analogue research is carried out where large populations of people with commonly shared characteristics exist (schools and hospitals) and wherein people share common complaints (test anxiety, for example). These populations are often screened via school classes or extant groups (speech, psychology, etc.) on one or more questionnaires so markedly deviate persons, or those showing no symptomatology at all, may be eliminated. Within a screened-in (or screened-out) population, further selection might occur on the basis of additional data, interviewing, subject willingness to participate, schedules, and so forth. A researcher might start with a population of hundreds of potential cases of a given complaint and end with a few dozen randomly assigned experimental cases receiving the major treatment thrust (and/or a similar number of contrasting treatment cases); matched controls measured only on questionnaires but receiving no treatment and who may not know at all of the treatment regimen; and placebo cases who receive some palliative effort but not one on the mark of the main experimental problem. A number of variations may exist on this general research theme.

The general schema of the analogue study appears at first to have less attrition than the self-initiated type of case, but there are still many slips along the way. Analogue studies have been covered well in the meta-analysis literature (*Journal of Counseling and Clinical Psychology,* Vol. 51, 1983, whole issue; Landman & Dawes, 1982; Smith & Glass, 1977; Smith, Glass, & Miller, 1980), although self-initiated clientele do occur to some extent in the cases studied in these references. Because analogue studies rely more openly, objectively, and pointedly on control and/or contrasting therapy treatment groups, they are ideal for meta-analysis. Implicit, also, in much analogue research is that the statement of a focal problem is a heuristic way to bring about general change as well. In such cases, the researcher/therapist is starting the client off with a specific problem in the attempt to reach first specific, then more general, change; in psychotherapy, the clinician (researcher or not) may begin with the general (presented) problem and try to work first to general and then specific changes (Phillips, 1984).

Landman and Dawes (1982) provide a summary of meta-analysis by referencing about a 14% sample from the larger Smith et al. (1980) volume on meta-analysis of psychotherapy outcome. This chapter examines the 65 studies in the Landman and Dawes synopsis looking for possible attrition problems. In the original work by Smith, Glass, and Miller, there appeared to be no sizable attrition problem. They state in several places (pp. 63, 64, and 123, as well as referring to their Table 5.10, p. 101) that attrition was not a major problem in their studies of the effects of psychotherapy. Attrition was referred to as "mortality" in experimental and control groups (Table 5.10, p. 101) and correlated .05 and .04, respectively, with over 1,500 ES measures. But their position does not remain consistent: On p. 123 they assert that the majority of studies they collated employed random assignments of clients to groups, and that 66% were rated high in internal validity (referring to random assignment of cases with low controlled mortality rates); but this still leaves 34% lacking in these controlled assignment and attritional respects, a figure close to that we have shown in Table 3.1.

Table 3.1 offers a general summary of attrition in the Landman and Dawes review.

Reexamining the Landman and Dawes Studies. The Landman and Dawes (1982) studies were rearranged topically: population (college, high school, children, adults) and types of problems (anxiety, phobia, etc.) (Phillips, Kaiser, & Heavner, 1983). Data were further broken down according to their original bibliographic number, the number of cases the experimenter contacted, the number/percent of subjects the experimenter rejected or selected out, the number lost through self-elimination, the within-study at-

TABLE 3.1
Summary of Research Junctures from 65 Study Sample of Analogue Research
(Landman & Dawes, 1982)

	Reporting		Not Reporting	
	Number	Percent	Number	Percent
1st Juncture: S Pool: Selection				
Experimenter Selection/Rejection	40	62.0	25	38
Mean % loss of *S*s		31.8		
Range % loss of *S*s		11–98.0		
2nd Juncture: Subject attrition: Intervention				
Early (*N* = 12/65)	12	18.5		
Mean % loss		23.5		
Range % loss		7–71.0		
Middle (*N* = 07/65)	07	10.8		
Mean % loss		07.9		
Range % loss		2.5–14.0		
Late (*N* = 13/65)	13	20.0		
Mean % loss		19.0		
Range % loss		2–70.0		
3rd Juncture: Follow-Up				
N/% loss (= 08/65)	08	12.3		
Mean % loss		19.0		
Range % loss		2–74.0		
Overall: 65 Studies	31	47.4	34	52.3
Mean % loss		30.0		
Range % loss		2.5–94.0		
No. Reporting 00% Attrition (04/65)	04	06.0		
(04/31)		13.0		

trition (early, middle, end), the matter of follow-up attrition, (that is, insufficiently reported on or missing data), the percentage of experimenter rejection (or subject loss) at the end point, and finally, the overall attrition loss (at follow-up and cumulatively) as well as it could be determined. These junctures are summarized study by study in Table 3.2.

Examination shows that there are many lapses in the reporting of data. For example, in 35 of the 65 studies the number of subjects the "experimenter contacted" initially for the study are unreported. Experimenter rejection or

TABLE 3.2
Summary of Flow of Cases Based on Landman and Dawes (1982) Report
on 65 Analogue Studies

Subject Type	Study Biblio.	No. Exper. Contacted in (E/C)	Exper. Rejection	Early Attr.	Middle Attr.
Assert. Train.	37	Unreported	0		6/42 (14%)
Anxiety Math	47	Unreported	Unreported		
Anxiety Math	57	Unreported	Unreported		
Anxiety Test	50	500+	Unreported	"25%"	
Anxiety Test	52	930	Unreported	2/30 (7%)	
Anxiety Test	55	Unreported	5/39 (13%)	3/34 (9%)	
Anxiety Test	11	39	None		
Anxiety Test	19	675	640/675 (95%)		
Public Speaking Anxiety	59	Unreported	Unreported		
Public Speaking Anxiety	35	105	None	39/105 (37%)	
Decision-making	61	447	387/447 (87%)		
Depression	53	Unreported	Unreported		
Phobia-Snakes	29	647	64/80 (20%)		
	12	Unreported	Unreported		
	41	2500	2460/2500 (98%)		
	43	Unreported	Unreported	06/31 (19%)	
	46	2500	2420/2500 (97%)		
	48	Unreported	Unreported 04/19 (21%)		
	64	Unreported	Unreported		
	38	1200	1150/1200 (96%)		

End Attr.	Follow-up Attrition	Hidden Attr. (Yes, No Probable)	Exper. Rejec.	Total Attrition N	%
		Probable	None	6/42	14% +
		Probable	Unreported		?
44/143 (31%)		Probable	Unreported	44/143 (31%)	31% +
			Unreported	"25%"	25%
			Unreported	2/30 (7%)	7%
		Probable	13% +	3/34 (9%)	9% +
		Probable	None		?
4/35 (11%)		Probable	95%	4/35 (11%)	11% +
	5/33 (15%)	Probable	Unreported	5/53 (15%)	15% +
18/105 (17%)		No	None	39 + 18/105 (54%)	54%
	6 wks 4/60 (7%) 12 wks 8/60 (13%)	Probable	87%	12/60 (20%)	20% +
		Probable	Unreported		?
		Probable	20%		?
		Yes	Unreported	None	?
		Probable	98%	None	None
		None	Unreported	6/31 (19%)	19%
		Probable	97%		?
3/15 (21%)		Probable	21%	3/15 (21%)	21% +
			Unreported		?
1/50 (2%)	1/50 (2%)	Probable	96%	02/50	4% +

(continued)

63

TABLE 3.2 *(continued)*

Subject Type	Study Biblio.	No. Exper. Contacted in (E/C)	Exper. Rejection	Early Attr.	Middle Attr.
Phobia-Rats	25	Unreported	None		
Personal Growth	02	Unreported	Unreported		
	33	Unreported	Unreported		
	18	72	None		
	17	164	124/164 (76%)		1/40 (2.5%)
	07	731	None	73/731 (10%)	
	08	Unreported	None		
Shyness	60	604	554/604 (92%)	8/50 (16%)	2/50 (4%)
Smoking	30	53	11/53 (21%)		
Under-achievement	40	Unreported	Unreported		
	45	5000	4208/5000 (84%)		
	06	40	0/40 (0%)	5/40 (12.5%)	
	21	181	0/181 (0%)		
	20	683	602/683 (88%)		
	16	Unreported	0/59 (0%)		
	14	109	61/109 (56%)		
	49	Unreported	70/174 (40%)		
	51	Unreported	Unreported		
	58	127	None	90/127 (71%)	5/37 (13%)
	63	Unreported	Unreported		17/135 (13%)
H.S. Age Beh. Diso. Deliq.	44	Unreported	Unreported		
	54	Unreported	None		
Under-achievement	04	Unreported	4/28 (14%)		
Voc. Coun.	31	Unreported	Unreported		
Child. Beh. Problems	01	Unreported	06/42 (14%)		
Anxiety Test	13	64	43/64 (67%)		
Peer Relations	36	265	171/265 (67%)		

End Attr.	Follow-up Attrition	Hidden Attr. (Yes, No Probable)	Exper. Rejec.	Total Attrition N	%
		No	None	None	None
		Yes	16/40 (40%)		?
4/18 (22%)		Probable	None	4/18 (22%)	22% +
		No	None	None	None
		Probable	76%	1/40 (2.5%)	2.5% +
	37/731 (05%)	No	None	73 + 37/731 (15%)	15%
1/10 (10%)		Yes	Unreported		10% +
	37/50 (74%)	Probable	92%	8 + 2 + 37/50 (94%)	94% +
15/142 (36%)		Yes	21%	15/42 (36%)	36% +
04/40 (10%)		Probable	Unreported	04/40 (10%)	10% +
552/792 (70%) 4 sem		Yes	84%	552/792 (70%)	70% +
		Probable	None	05/40 (12.5%)	12.5% +
3/181 (2%)		Yes	None	03/181 (02%)	02% +
		Probable	88%		07% +
		Probable	Unreported		?
		Probable	56%		?
	72/104 (69%)	Probable	40%	72/104 (69%)	69% +
		Yes	Unreported		?
		Yes	None	90/127 + 5/37 (84%)	84% +
		Probable	Unreported	17/135 (13%)	13% +
	12/38 (32%)	Yes	Unreported	12/38 (32%)	32% +
	2/20 (10%)	No	Unreported	02/20 (10%)	10% +
		Probable	4/28 (14%)		?
		Probable	Unreported		?
		Probable	14%		?
		Probable	67%		?
		Probable	67%		?

(continued)

TABLE 3.2 *(continued)*

Subject Type	Study Biblio.	No. Exper. Contacted in (E/C)	Exper. Rejection	Early Attr.	Middle Attr.
Phobia-Mixed	39	Unreported	62/148 (42%)	5/86 (6%)	4/86 (5%)
Self-Esteem	15		None		
Study Habits	23		None		
Alco-holics	26 09	Unreported 62	Unreported 5/62 (08%)	14/57 (26%)	
Heart Attacks	22	Unreported	8/70 (11%)		
Mental Dis. Med.	24	478	388/478 (81%)		
Schitzop.	28 56 65	Unreported 39 Unreported	Unreported 11/39 (28%) Unreported		
Smoking	62	110	37/110 (34%)		
Soldiers In P/S Beh Ds	10	Unreported	Unreported		
Phobia Out-pt	32 05	Unreported Unreported	None Unreported		
Sexual Disorders	42	250	186/250 (74%)		
Asthma	34	Unreported	Unreported		
Phobia Students	03	Unreported	Unreported		
Student Volunteers	27	Unreported	11/74 = 15%		

selection out of cases occurred in 21 studies. Under the Early Attrition rubric, 9 studies report losses from zero to 71%, with only 10 studies reporting at all in this category. We might surmise that there is no early attrition in the remaining 55 studies, but too little data are given to know. Middle and late (within study) attrition is observable in 18 studies, and the loss ranges from 2.5% to 31%. In the estimates of the researchers (Phillips, et al., 1983), the assignment of "Probable" to the likelihood of attritional loss of a "Hidden"

End Attr.	Follow-up Attrition	Hidden Attr. (Yes, No Probable)	Exper. Rejec.	Total Attrition N	%
		Probable	42%	9/86 (11%)	11% +
		Probable	Unreported		?
		Probable	Unreported		?
		Yes	Unreported		?
		Probable	08%	14/57 (26%)	26% +
		Yes	11%		?
69/209		Yes	81%	69/209 (43%)	43% +
		Probable	Unreported		?
		Yes	28%		?
		Yes	Unreported		?
		Yes	34%		?
		Yes	Unreported		?
		Probable	None		?
		Probable	Unreported		?
		Probable	74%		?
7/62 (11%)		Probable	Unreported	7/62 (11%)	11% +
		Yes	Unreported		?
5/74 (07%)		Probable	15%	5/74 (07%)	7% +

nature is applicable in 32 reports and a definite yes answer is relevant additionally 13 times. Thus, in 45 of the 65 cases there is known or suspected attritional loss, ranging from a known 3% (negligible) upward.

The second category, "Experimenter Rejection," allows for the presence of additional known or possible attrition within the study and/or at follow-up. If a study included six sessions and the mean number of subject/session attendance was 3.5, then nearly half of the subject-sessions were not attended.

When and for what reasons did these subjects not attend? We simply do not know. Data are needed, for example, on how many attended one, two, . . . up to six of the proffered six sessions. Maybe three sessions produced as good results as four, five, or six sessions; also, if another researcher were to replicate the reported study, he or she would need to know the internal pattern of attendance/attrition (Rossi & Freeman, 1982). Often the researcher does not break down the attendees' behavior vis-à-vis the study objectives, and data and cases are summarized beyond the limits set by the attrition data. Such reporting is neither complete nor valid; replication of findings is also strictly limited. In 27 instances studies had to be labeled "Unreported" in this category. The final category, "Attrition, N and Percentage," attempts to bring together all known or probable attrition. This category resulted in several findings: 29 studies of the 65 cited percentages of attrition from 2% to 75%; 4 studies had presumably zero attrition; 19 studies are unclear and require the "?" rating; and about 13 studies appear to have very little or no attrition or some person/session data loss (as stated above) and other ambiguities.

Four Examples of Attrition from Landman and Dawes. Four analogue studies are briefly reviewed to show the attrition problem, the first being the Landman and Dawes summary study #21, which reported on 181 underachieving college students. Four training sessions were held regarding improving grades; mode was three sessions attended. Investigators reviewed students' grades 5 years later, losing track of only three: follow-up data on 98%, 2% attrition.

A snake phobia study in Landman and Dawes (#38) began with a pool of 1,200 subjects; 50 were selected; five groups were formed: desensitization, implosion, I/D combined, relaxation and pseudotherapy groups (10 subjects each); five sessions were given experimental groups. Authors report 1 subject lost, each, during treatment and at follow-up, equaling a 4% attrition.

One contrasting study with considerable attrition was from Landman and Dawes (#58), based on a letter from the dean to 127 underachieving students; 52 (40%) failed to respond; 75 (60%) responded; of these, 38 (51%) refused help; leaving 37 from original 127 (71% attrition). Additionally, 5 subjects were lost from experimental and control group; within study loss = 5/37 (13% additional attrition) = 32 subjects; net number, end of study = 32/127 = 74% attrition. Or, 32/75 (52 failed to respond to letter) = 43% attritional loss.

In Landman and Dawes (reference #60), the authors studied shyness; gross $N = 604$ males. Forty-one subjects were contacted by experimenter based on test results; $N = 9$ for non-shy males, netting 50 subjects; of these, 2 dropped out, 6 were eliminated by experimenter and 2 failed to complete three shyness-related sessions; 13 subjects remained at follow-up plus 9 non-shy males = 22/41 at follow-up (19 loss = 46% attrition). Other calculations of data net about same loss.

These four studies illustrate the range of attritional loss in the studies reported by Landman and Dawes (1982); more careful research reporting might make some studies less attrition-ridden, but loss of subjects from study inception, through the experimental or intervention procedures to end-of-study and follow-up, appear sizable and show analogue research along with self-initiated psychotherapy as having sizable attritional problems. The present rating system has some inherent unreliability, but it points up relatively poor data reporting, leaving in doubt analogue research attritional problems. Because many methodological considerations are often given short shrift, some research findings are invalid, ungeneralizable, and unreplicable. With these apparent attritional facts in this sample of analogue studies receiving meta-analysis, it is likely that similar flaws would be found in the total number of citations by Smith, Glass, and Miller. Analogue research and meta-analysis, although a model way to analyze some problems in evaluation and outcome, has failed (in the Landman and Dawes article) to recognize a wide range of attritional problems.

Zeroing in further on the Landman and Dawes review (1982; Landman, personal communication, 1984) it is important to examine the 42 studies (among the 65 reported on) that meet the Landman and Dawes dual design criteria, i.e., the presence in studies of no-treatment controls and random or matched assignment of cases to study conditions. Breaking down the 42 "model studies" from Landman and Dawes (1982) shows that these studies were flawed in a number of ways, following our flow analysis from study inception to termination. These findings are summarized in Table 3.3.

It can be seen from Table 3.3 that there are a number of incidents of attrition from study inception, through early-middle-late features of the intervention itself, and out to a judgment of either clear (yes) or probable hidden attrition resulting from the manner in which the original authors reported on their research. With so many examples of known or likely attrition among these 42 more or less model studies, we are left wanting for better data, for better reporting on research interventions, and for clearer judgments of how random or matched assignments of cases and the presence of controls in studies can mitigate the overall attritional problem. The initial assignment of cases by matching or random methods is a necessary prerequisite for research validity, but this effort in no way guarantees against attrition among either experimental or control groups or both. Attention to attritional matters from study inception to the end is just as important as care in the original design; we would not tolerate flaws in the latter as much as we now appear to tolerate attritional flaws.

The Landman and Dawes study also includes a number of studies — as does the Smith, Glass, and Miller book — that are not the usual cases of psychotherapy. It is not useful to quibble about what is psychotherapy; it is useful to point up that self-selected, walk-in cases may arise for somewhat different reasons than analogue, selected, invited, or conscripted cases. Research on

TABLE 3.3
Showing Attritional Breakdown Per Client Flow Through Intervention Research: 42 Studies Fulfilling "Dual Design" Criteria (from Landman & Dawes, 1982; Landman, 1984). Flow Through the System Identifying Attritional Points

Study #	Percent Exper. Rejection	Early	Middle	Late	F-U	Hidden
1	14					Probable
3	Unreported					Yes
4	14					Probable
6	Zero	12.5				Probable
11	Zero					Probable
12	Unreported					Probable
13	67					Probable
14	56					Probable
18	Zero					Zero
19	95			11		Probable
20	90					Yes
22	11					Yes
25	0					No
26	Unreported					Yes
27	15			7		Probable
28	Unreported					Probable
29	20					Probable
31	—					Probable
35	0	37		14		3%
36	67					Probable
37	0	0	14			Probable
38	96			2	2	Probable
40	Unreported			10		Probable
41	98					
42	72					Probable
44	Unreported				32	Yes
46	97					Probable
48	21					Probable
50	Unreported	26				No

similarities and differences between self-initiated help and analogue population help is sorely needed. The same efforts that lead to greater understanding of attrition in outpatient psychotherapy surely would apply to analogue
research. The loss early on of clients, whether by design or by default in analogue studies, might be as great as it is at intake in self-initiated psychotherapy. The loss of clientele in-process would seem to be more easily identified in
analogue research, but that may still be moot, judging from this review.
Problems with asymptote data appear less likely and to a lesser degree in analogue studies, often owing to the greater ease and neatness in follow-up
evaluations — they know when the study is completed — but there may be
some loss in this respect judging from the Landman and Dawes report.

Methodological Needs. Methodologically, then, the researcher might
well tidy up reporting if this review of attrition in both kinds of therapeutic
intervention is valid. There are a number of choice points at which decisions
about clientele are made and *all* of these should be reported on faithfully. Research emphasis has always been given to the proper matching of experimental and control cases and to random selection and assignment procedures, but
if significant attrition occurs before randomization is put into effect, or if it
subsequently influences different populations differently, the value of the research results can be questioned (Rossi & Freeman, 1982). The research report should, then, contain the number and the description in some salient detail of the large population from which are drawn the cases selected in (or
out) for the treatment/research regimen. Then, cases who self-select-out, together with some of their salient features, should be reported upon. The researcher has the right to select cases for research but also has the responsibility to report fully enough on this process so that replication is possible. Once
a study is under way, there are dropouts; some, as with walk-in therapy, have
decided they either have, or have not, gotten what they wanted; these cases
can often be further studied and important information received, as in the instances of reporting on intake-only cases (see Chapter 4). Within the confines
of an analogue study some clients may attend infrequently even if they do not
wholly drop out, suggesting similarity to those comprising the attrition curve
in outpatient psychotherapy. Follow-up and end-of-treatment assessment
are perplexing problems and often lead to skipping over and not reporting on
important data from which the researcher might learn something. A lot of
analogue research could be shortened — e.g., six sessions may be as good as
eight. The relationship matter — client and therapist liking for one another —
although scarcely mentioned in the analogue research, may turn out to be as
important here as it appears to be in psychotherapy. (Would analogue type of
clients return for help again or refer others to such regimens? We do not
know.) A large number of attritional facts and attitude toward therapy considerations, then, link both self-initiated outpatient psychotherapy and ana-

logue studies of behavior change. There are also some important differences whose further study will probably enhance both types of proffered treatments. The role of attrition is not only of importance in its own right; it may be both the methodological and the procedural consideration that helps organize and conceptualize all manner of intake, process, outcome, and generalization problems. Attrition appears at once to be the heretofore most neglected aspect of psychotherapy and behavior change effort — whether of self-initiated psychotherapy or analogue research — and the most salient in the offering of scientific and practical assessment of behavior change.

REACTIONS TO ANALOGUE/META-ANALYSIS RESEARCH

In addition to the strictures offered concerning the meta-analysis and analogue studies, a number of articles have appeared more recently that reanalyze statistical and other issues raised by the original Smith et al. (1980) book, the Smith and Glass article (1977) and by Landman and Dawes (1982). Further contributions to the several issues raised by meta-analysis in quest of significance in the study of psychotherapy outcome are seen in the Shapiro and Shapiro (1983) article, in Orwin and Cordray (1984), in Kurosawa (1984), in Gallo (1978) and in recent replies by Landman (Oct. 15, 1983 personal communication) and Landman and Dawes (1984) to various criticisms of their work as well as that of the original Smith, Glass, & Miller report (1980).

A more recent review of analogue research in relation to meta-analysis is that of Shapiro and Shapiro. They reviewed 143 studies based on the criteria of two experimental/treatment populations and one control group design, called "a contrast group" design, confining the literature search to the 1975–79 period via *Psychological Abstracts*. Shapiro and Shapiro dealt more explicitly with attrition than did Smith et al. (1980) or Landman and Dawes (1982), providing evidence that attrition among clinical populations in the 143 studies averaged 10.68% ($SD = 13.49\%$) and averaged 9.19% among the control populations ($SD = 13.56\%$) (p. 45). They assert that attrition was "commendably low" in most cases (p. 45). However, the range of attrition with a mean of about 11% and a standard deviation of 13.49% among the clinical cases must have been sizable in many studies. No report was made on how the attrition occurred, the role of experimental selection/rejection, subject self-selection from the studies, and possible problem at follow-up. It becomes even more important from the Shapiro and Shapiro review to note the flow of cases from the inception of the study out to the follow-up period; lacks in reporting on this full range of data leave the evaluator of the research in a quandary and often preclude the opportunity for replication of the studies.

Apropos of the relationship between attrition among walk-in, self-initiated therapy cases and those arising in the analogue settings, the Shapiro and Shapiro review notes that the latter studies were overwhelmingly represented by investigator solicitation (89%), were conducted mostly by graduate students on undergraduate clientele, showed a mean age of 20 years or less, were lacking in the usual anxiety and depression syndrome found among self-initiated clientele, were mostly group therapy studies, and comprised mostly performance and public speaking anxieties (p. 49). Compared to the typical walk-in client in mental health settings, these clients from the 143 reviewed studies were called "sub-clinical," but even aside from the nature of the populations studied by analogue methods, the coverage of attrition problems has left a lot to be desired. The mean number of interviews in the 143 analogue studies was 6.89, closely similar to findings from walk-in clientele, as this report has already indicated. Table 6 (p. 50) in the Shapiro and Shapiro review indicates areas of missing values in relation to treatment, client, context, and design variables. This table reports that 18.9% and 18.7% of the treated and control groups, respectively, had missing data on attrition, a figure nearly twice as large as that reported earlier in the same article (p. 45) and leaves moot the real impact of attritional matters in the Shapiro and Shapiro review.

One reason the Shapiro and Shapiro review of 143 analogue studies advances only slightly our understanding of attrition is that no "flow chart" of subject handling from study conception or inception out to follow-up is suggested. Kazdin (1978) has noted that the clinical-analogue continuum should be broken down into target problems, population, recruitment, therapists, selection, setting, treatment, and assessment. There is no fault with these topics, but the actual "processing" of clientele should, if properly delineated (see our Table 3.3) account for the Kazdin categories. If our Table 3.3 from the Landman and Dawes (1982) review is appropriate to the 65 studies reviewed by them (sampled from the Smith et al., 1980 volume), it would apply as well to the Shapiro and Shapiro review. Not having access to the 143 references, however, precludes rearranging them into the above. Accounting for attrition in analogue studies, although the pattern may be different from walk-in clientele in some important ways, is nonetheless of significance in all ways that influence research outcome: generalizability, replicability, salience of testing of hypotheses concerning behavior change, employment of contrast group or other designs, and of course such practical matters as training therapists, developing service delivery economies and practices, and contributions to behavior change theory. There is, then, no aspect of outcome research not basically influenced by attritional matters; once this is clearly understood, research on attrition can hit a new high in importance and can be shown to ramify into every other aspect of psychotherapy training and practice, including the way clinics and other delivery systems operate vis-à-vis their clientele, regardless of other aspects of the clinic or delivery system such as age of clients, presenting complaints, diagnoses, time-limited (or unlimited) policies, and so on.

WIDER CONSIDERATIONS OF ANALOGUE/META-ANALYSIS RESEARCH

Still other criticisms of meta-analysis findings have been offered (Kurosawa, 1984; Orwin & Cordray, 1984). They may be partially summarized to include the following: sampling problems (e.g., comparing Landman and Dawes results, 1982, with the original meta-analysis samples in Smith and Glass, 1977, and Smith et al., 1980); inclusion of only published studies to compute ES values compared to a wider inclusion of doctoral dissertations; the degree to which studies compare given therapy techniques with controls by use of random assignments of subjects to clinical and control groups; subjects volunteering for a study versus being selected or conscripted; the uneven reporting on research studies found in the literature; the severity of diagnoses among compared populations of patients/clients; and so on (Gallo, 1978; Kurosawa, 1984; Landman & Dawes, 1982; Orwin & Cordray, 1984; Rosenthal, 1979). In addition to these vexing problems is the overwhelming one of attrition, a problem passed over lightly by Smith et al. (1980), and by Landman and Dawes (1982). Orwin and Cordray (1984) note that "clients may select themselves out of treatment, thereby reintroducing the selection bias that random assignment is intended to control" (p. 71). This is a cogent observation as far as it goes, one apparently neglected by Landman and Dawes (1982), but the observation needs further scrutiny. Our data, based on analysis of the 65 studies from the Landman and Dawes article, show attrition by plotting the *flow* of cases from experimenter selection/rejection out to follow-up, this flow including (as cited in Tables 3.2 and 3.3) several junctures, one of which is the client self-selection as one contribution to attrition. Orwin and Cordray report that the Smith et al. data base shows about 68% of the well-controlled studies revealing no pre-to-post attrition (including follow-up?) (pp. 71–72), and that about one fourth of their studies reported client loss (referred to as mortality) in excess of 10% (p. 72). Our figures for the Landman and Dawes 65-sample study from Smith et al. (1980) reveal that attrition is present in 31 (47.7%) of the 65 studies and that attrition may go as high as 60% or more in some studies.

Perhaps more emphasis in looking at meta-analysis results should be placed on the actual flow of cases because this issue comes before various calculations of the final ES. Just as the flow of cases in the walk-in type of therapeutic service has been shown to have very robust characteristics (see Chapters 1 and 2), so might cumulative attrition from the flow of cases in analogue studies be more accurately revealed by flow-analysis. The flow of cases matter comes before any tests of effect size because the latter are based on presumed random assignment of cases to various treatment and control groups. If attrition at any juncture in the flow of cases places in jeopardy the random assignment of cases, then subsequent meta-analysis of effects is vitiated. Not only is effect size hampered in its generality and replicability as and when attrition occurs, the progressive selection of those cases remaining in treatment suggests differences in the experimental (clinical) cases which are presumably augmented (leading people to drop out) as selective attrition operates throughout the flow of cases from study inception to conclusion. If effect size were computed only on data obtained from the remaining cases at the end of a study—based on difference scores—then attritional matters would loom less large; however, if before-after data were based on group means and standard deviations, not accounting for attrition, then effect size would be based erroneously on these statistical operations. Also, because attrition does not appear to occur at any one juncture exclusively, the possible cumulative influence has to be reckoned with throughout the flow of cases from beginning to end.

Further, when there are different effect sizes contributed to by different variables (or tests) and different interventions, there may have been differential attritional effects on these same variables as the study progressed through its course. Some effect sizes are going to be more sensitive to some types of psychotherapy/behavior change intervention than others (e.g., assertiveness training and measures); hence these more "sensitive" measures will contribute in the end more to the effect size than other variables, or be differentially influenced by attrition that will influence ES (Smith et al., 1980, p. 100, Table 5.9). The whole matter of ES, then, based as it is so much on attritional influences, comes out to be more closely related to uncertain results than to convincing evidence that the benefits of psychotherapy are substantial, replicable, and useful. In short, different measures, assessing different intervention procedures and behaviors, will make differential contributions to their final ES; attritional factors, also differentially influencing these various measures will further influence ES; some test-retest measures will be more influenced by attrition.

The Flow Chart Correction.   To correct these many pitfalls, it would appear more useful to first plot the attritional loss of cases by a flow chart for every measure for which effect size is sought before a final effect size is calculated (Shapiro & Shapiro, 1983). Moreover, because this attritional loss is bound to influence different measures of change differentially, separate calculations for each measure being made, taking into account attritional loss, should make the net ES more valid and more reliable. A procedure based on the flow of cases throughout a study, and more particularly noting how attrition at each juncture differentially influences measures, would give a *net* ES more accurate than presently calculated ones.

Factorial studies of client follow-up replies (see Chapter 8), although often suspect as are all self-report measures, may give us a clue of what to expect from a more careful meta-analysis of changes from analogue studies. The factors resulting from the more than 500 questionnaires received from clients rating their therapy experience (in the first three studies reported in Chapter 2) show that about 70% of the outcome variance is explained by "satisfaction" and "problem-solving" (behavior change) factors. It is possible in our present state of knowledge that these two broad measures — "global" as they are — are the best we can do in attempting to assess outcome from psychotherapy short of prodigious efforts to assess behavior directly; and that complicated test batteries and questionnaires will not advance knowledge much beyond the global measures now available (Burisch, 1984). It is possible that behavior change measures will reveal more reliable changes in analogue types of research, because focused intervention is the hallmark of such studies; and that global "satisfaction" will emerge as the most reliable and instructive outcome measures among walk-in, talking psychotherapy cases. If this differentiation were to be obtained in studying the effects from both analogue and self-initiated cases of therapy, it would allow, in time, more concentrated efforts at developing measures that would highlight such changes, thereby permitting, among other benefits, more accurate assessment of ES among both types of therapy. In time, ES would be based not so much on a miscellaneous collection of measures (now so often the case) but on factorially more nearly "pure" measures of change in both types of intervention. In time researchers would be able to identify the most salient effect size measures for each type of intervention and/or each type of presenting problem, assess their net attritional effects, and come out with a final ES more instructive than is now the case. If this kind of attritional-based and improved measurement base were to be implemented, there would remain fewer questions about the benefits of psychotherapy and we would know more clearly whether Gallo's statement (1978) that psychotherapy has a measurable but weak effect on dependent variables is accurate. Feedback from an accumulation of studies differentiating better ES outcomes would allow the flow of cases to either predominantly analogue or self-initiated psychotherapy, perhaps thereby increasing the efficiency and effectiveness of both delivery systems. If further research on therapy and behavior change efforts confirmed the Gallo statement, then we would know better our therapeutic limitations and be able to fashion therapy more explicitly for short-term effects, separating out those cases presumably requiring more or different kinds of therapy.

This state of affairs is doubtless some distance off but its possibilities must be envisioned first, then methods developed for pursuing its implications. Beginning with the attrition problem, then going on to more salient, reliable and replicable measures of ES will enable the development of a more effective and efficient psychotherapy. In the course of these complicated and extended events, however, we will have to back off as therapist/theorists and fashion questions about the conduct of psychotherapy free from the many biases of traditional thinking about psychotherapy, and this freedom-from may include *all* extant psychotherapies because no one of them is based on proper consideration of attritional influences, on the most salient measures, or on the most cogent study of outcome.

ADDITIONAL CONSIDERATIONS

In addition to the problems cited concerning the importance of attritional loss from analogue and meta-analysis research, there are at least two additional issues in the meta-analysis work. The first concerns the use of instruments, questionnaires, ratings, and so on, by which to judge before-after change comparing experimental and control groups in various arrangements. Effect size was calculated in the Smith et al. (1980) volume on the basis of the average net change in each — experimental and control groups divided by the standard deviation of the control group on the particular measure on which ES value was obtained. Because we do not have a very good notion of which questionnaires or measures are valid for given experimental/intervention purposes, we tend to choose those with apparent validity and meaning somewhat close to the objectives of the behavior change/analogue research objective. Thus, if we have a population of individuals relatively low in assertiveness, we will likely use a questionnaire bearing the name "assertiveness" in its title. Or, better yet, we will likely choose some assertiveness measure in which other research has used the questionnaire for similar types of studies (although the populations may differ as well as the study characteristics and objectives). However that may be, the general approach to a behavior change objective involving assertiveness would likely use one or more assertiveness questionnaires. If, then, we obtained some significant difference between the pre- and post-evaluations that are linked to some intervention program that attempts to increase the assertiveness of clients, we would be relatively confident in our results, and perhaps able to generalize them to some extent.

Ordinarily, if the intervention were chosen carefully and if the assertiveness questionnaire also were chosen carefully, the results might be highly exemplary of good research design, measurement, and intervention. But now comes the rub: There are an incredible number of available instruments, many of the same variety (that is, bearing the title "assertiveness" and the like); and there are an incredible number of intervention efforts or programs that have been advanced to improve the assertiveness (or some other characteristic or deficit such as "shyness," "depression," etc.) of a given population of clients. *The large mix of measures and interventions beg for order and for ways to align the measurement instrument on the one hand and the intervention program on the other hand.* This step is needed, along with the fact that the instrument may have been well-based as a result of the coverage, reliability, and validity of the original item pool and the remaining items after cross-validation, plus the application of other possible criteria of relevance and serviceability for particular evaluative purposes (Burisch, 1984).

The large number of ES figures in the Smith et al. (1980) book — 1766 among 475 research reports — covered a number of topics such as assertiveness, underachievement, depression, anxiety, shyness, self-management, and so on (p. 109). It would be useful and heuristic to arrange the hundreds of tests used in the Smith et al. review of meta-analysis value in a table such as the hypothetical one proposed (see Table 3.4).

This hypothetical table begins with a column of tests according to the name and/or type in the left-hand column; in turn, the next column shows an intervention of an analogue type. The final column suggests that different examples of the "same" test are used quite variably, or inconsistently, in widely dif-

TABLE 3.4
Hypothetical Model for Improving Analogue Studies: Applications to
Tests/Measurements, Interventions and Effect Size (ES)

Tests/Measurements (Pre-Post Assessm't.)		Analogue Intervention Programs	Effect Size
Assertiveness	1	Social Skills: Male Dating	0.59
"	2	" " : Job Interview	0.77
"	3	" " : Overcoming Shyness	0.51
Shyness	1	Social Skills: Introducing/Conversation	0.81
"	2	" " : Dancing	0.30
"	3	" " : Handling Anger/Disappointment	0.90
Depression	1	Handling Moods, Mood Swings	0.66
"	2	Complaining About Others	1.05
"	3	Self-Abnegation	0.92
Achievement	1	Study Skills	0.66
"	2	Exam Taking	0.49
"	3	Test Anxiety/Oral Presentations	0.71

(The Tests/Measurements are simply illustrations of named tests; the interventions are likewise illustrations; the ESs are arbitrary; the dashed lines suggest how tests with one name may relate to interventions with different names, and vice versa; all leading to the point that from left to right, there must be a tighter alignment between these activities, so that at the right the ES is optimized, feeding back successful effort.)

ferent intervention efforts, sometimes based on purportedly similar intervention programs; and that the test findings (pre-post) accumulate widely different ES values, plus or minus, without much rhyme or reason.

This kind of table could be made up of data from an extensive collection of measures as applied to a variety of intervention efforts with wide-ranging effect sizes. A table of this type would show how well particular tests or measures and/or classes of tests or measures (e.g., tests of "anxiety") stand up against various analogue studies in terms of the final ES values (doubtless being shown to vary considerably). For example, if "assertiveness" as a construct really draws under its label, in terms of its item pool, those aspects of behavior that respond most favorably to an easily identifiable intervention process, then we may hypothesize that this combination of specific test/ questionnaire items and interventions would combine to produce more significant ESs. Such a coupling of items and intervention procedures might also prove to be more generalizable and replicable over a range of problem areas; this would provide, if true, important information on the efficacy of given analogue interventions. Also, statistically testing item validity against total test score on several questionnaires of the "assertiveness" type, one could identify in time critical items for pre- and post-assessment and their relationship to later *overt* changes in the client's behavior, as well as better identify topics for use in the actual intervention process itself. This procedure would enable the researcher to identify packages containing intervention modules linking earlier assessment efforts with intervention efforts, hence with later outcome results, making for a more reliable ES. Field tests would then follow.

Following this hypothetical analysis, other problem areas (e.g., "depression") might not yield as appreciable results as the study of assertiveness; at least it would be an empirical problem of how well any other assessment area would stand up under scrutiny. We could, then, trace the flow of results from each kind of named test, through the intervention packages or modules out to ES outcomes, a kind of bootstrap operation. Arranging the data this way would expose the weakness and strengths, the similarities and differences, between the test/measure used, the intervention and the outcome results in terms of ES. Some tests would fall by the wayside quickly and only a few could be expected to survive such a flow analysis when ES became the criterion of worth in the comparison of experimental/clinic groups with controls. We would soon learn where to put our efforts most economically. A further step could be taken by factoring tests of a given classification (e.g., "anxiety"), in order to extract the substantial features of the combined item pools. This type of analysis would simultaneously improve the test/measurement and the intervention program as they combined to produce more respectable ESs. Still further steps could be taken in that factored tests of different names ("depression," "anxiety," etc.) would be used in combinations with various intervention programs and thereby make up the best combinations that would arrive at the most respectable ES values.

The same procedures could apply to walk-in, self-initiated clients. Running two sets of research programs, side by side, so to say, in a variety of outpatient settings, would tell us how similar analogue studies and the self-initiated interventions were in pre-post characteristics and how well they yielded appreciable ESs. We would then have in one extensive programmatic research package a leg up on the two general types of intervention (analogue and self-initiated clientele), the most heuristic tests/measures, and the most economical intervention programs yielding the most robust effect sizes.

A substantial but derived benefit with such a programmatic research posture would be to highlight further the total *flow of cases* through both intervention systems, thereby describing more accurately the strengths and weaknesses of both and the pitfalls of research on behavior/personality/psychotherapy change. This would enhance the notion of how delivery systems operate and enable us to look to ways to change the system. The additional development of item pools, assessment instruments, outcome research, and the like, would all combine strengths in the same systematic framework and we would not be obliged to change one aspect of the system without regard to other aspects, as we now are. Lacking a comprehensive appreciation of the flow of cases, we now enter into this flow at different points without realizing it and thereby vitiate the value of probes into changing behavior from either an analogue or a self-initiated walk-in perspective. Every feature of this flow-of-cases system is amenable to ready retest and replication; every feature is, so to say, exposed to research scrutiny, thereby identifying early on untestable or unproductive hypotheses.

What can we then say about ES? It is a Phoenix arising out of the ashes of scattered research methodologies, unreliable measures, not clearly specified intervention procedures, and other faulted research efforts. It is potentially a very heuristic way of looking at change phenomena that are in need of improved methodological bolstering at the intervention and measurement levels, all possibly leading to improved ES. When ES arises from an "in tandem" alignment of assessment/measurement and intervention, with improvement based on repeated feedback of results, ES will be increased and lead to a coalescing and simplification of intervention packages. In time, this procedure — which is, in effect, a more precise study of the flow of cases through the change or intervention system — will lead to a real science of behavior change; and, of equal importance, to a simplification of diagnosis in ways bolstered by observed and measured behavior, not based alone on administrative or theoretical niceties.

One demur must be offered. The demur is based not on the flow of cases but on the fact that all assessments may ultimately reduce down to two factors — client satisfaction and appropriate behavior change (problem solving, or whatever one wishes to call it). This prospect would probably mean that all of our hard-earned research measures — assertiveness, shyness, anxiety, depression, and so forth — might reduce down to specific behavior change and to client-reported satisfaction with the intervention process. It still may remain important in a programmatic sense to begin by searching out available measurements of the presently respectable and conventional sort before expecting a factor distillation to yield valid general factors, although there is some present indication that this will come about (Berzins, Bednar, & Severy, 1975). Whichever way research leads us — to fewer and better assessment instruments requiring considerable effort and detail or a synthesis of all these varieties reducible to behavior change and client satisfaction — it will be very interesting, will yield more practicable results at the clinical level, and will also be of immense theoretical and conceptual importance. We will presumably hit research gold either way; and the mining of the gold will be continuously rewarding and heuristic.

These notions will also test in a variety of ways the hypothesized importance in this book of the general systemic, flow-of-cases point of view; it will give confidence to these notions as they might also apply to other than psychotherapy/behavior change systems, such as medical compliance as an obvious example.

$$4$$ The Intake Interview and Its Implications

The three previous chapters have shown that the course of therapy in a variety of settings and from almost any vantage point (age, sex, diagnosis, short- or long-term) results in the same type of Poisson curve that describes the flow of cases from the inception of therapy to the end. We have seen, moreover, that most of the loss from therapy occurs at the beginning point, the intake. What is it that characterizes the intake so unmistakably as the crucial juncture it is, even when therapy has hardly started and what the intake actually accomplishes, or what it is presumed to do, has not been clearly defined. Several ways of studying the intake are examined here. (Chapter 6 by Peter J. Fagan goes further into the intake issue.)

First, therapy may be different from what we have all been taught to believe. Therapy is not the long-range, allegedly penetrating process that uncovers the unconscious, analyzes resistance, melts defenses, reconstructs personality, divines motivation, or creates remarkable behavior change. It is rather a most modest, sometimes uneventful, sometimes unsuccessful process. Some unusual changes may occur with therapy, but not often. Relatively large changes may occur occasionally not only with therapy but with weekend marathons, with religious conversions, with falling in love, and with harrowing exchanges with reality. Most change is slow or faltering, almost imperceptible, and woven into the fabric of life so deftly that at the end of an experience one can hardly tell exactly what has happened or how change has been wrought. How any of the changes from any source will hold up is still another formidable problem.

Second, if therapy is so modest an undertaking, then, it should be more respected for this role, not for some prime moving role. Therapy should be considered by this reasoning to occur under a number of equally modest circumstances, from the minute one "decides" to engage in therapy, from the day one walks into the therapist's door, from the hour one finishes the intake interview, or a few interviews, and "decides" at any of these junctures that no more help is needed. Bloom (1981) reports that about 70% of the cases having only one (intake) interview reported satisfaction with this experience, evidently enough so that more sessions were not indicated — at least at that time. One can always come back later if the need arises, just as one would do with a dentist, a lawyer, a physician, a tailor, or anyone serving a limited but useful purpose. The patient is a kind of consumer of services (Lazare et al., 1972; Lazare, Sherman, & Wasserman, 1975) and as such, therapeutic behavior relates clearly to other consumer behavior.

INTAKE INTERVIEW STUDIES, 1981–1982

The first intake study consists of an examination of intake therapist ratings of clients they interviewed ($N = 45$) and the corresponding ratings of clients ($N = 35$ available ratings from the same 45 rated by the therapists; 10 clients failed to respond to the query) on several questions pertaining to their ratings of their experience at intake (1981–1982). This research arose from observations that therapists appeared less optimistic about client prospects in therapy than did the clients themselves.

To the question put to the clients immediately following intake, "Would you recommend the Counseling Center to others?" clients rated this item 4.5 on a 5-point scale; and to the question, "Would you return (yourself) to the clinic if the occasion arose?" the mean ratings for 35 clients, same scale, was 4.10. These relatively high global ratings are supported in the literature (Gelso & Johnson, 1983; Silverman & Beech, 1979; Ursano & Dressler, 1974). Comparable ratings by the therapists on their 45 clients netted the following results: "client appeared to me to be one who would improve with therapy," a mean of 4.73 on a 7-point scale; and "would like to work with this client" produced a mean of 3.67, same scale. Clearly, then, the ratings by therapists at the client's intake point are lower than those by clients. Following up on these findings produced some even more interesting ones. Updating the 45 clients to the end of the semester indicated that some were "rejectors" of therapy (that is, did not return after the intake); some were "dropouts" (that is, had one to three interviews); and some were "remainders" (had an average number of sessions — four or more). The therapists at intake rated the 15 potential "rejectors" 4.33 on the item, "client appeared as one who would improve with therapy"; the potential 15 "dropouts" at 4.44; and the 15 potential "remainders" at 5.29, on the same item. Further, the therapists at intake rated the item, "would like to work with client" as follows (7-point scale): means of 3.23 for "rejectors"; 3.69 for "dropouts"; and 3.88 for "remainers." As one can readily observe with these findings (although not statistically significantly different, they are congruent), either something is going on at intake that is remarkably prescient or the ratings represent the beginning point of a self-fulfilling prophecy, namely, that therapists exert a remarkably subtle but somewhat far-reaching influence on clients at intake. Although the clients were not wholly persuaded by the therapist at intake, the difference and congruencies in these ratings suggest appreciable therapist influence (or unusual clinical judgment).

ANOTHER APPROACH TO INTAKE RESEARCH

Curious about this intake phenomena, we conducted more studies at The George Washington University Counseling Center in an effort to probe more fully into the process (Phillips & DePalma, 1983). We telephoned 46 people who had had only one (intake) interview to determine why they felt they did not need to return for therapy. These 46 people constituted about 11.5% sample of the whole year's population (1982–83) of 416 cases, about 50% of whom came for intake only. Table 4.1 lists the questions these clients were asked and their answers.

Thus it is apparent that the overall client ratings of therapist and the dozen or so items regarding general matters concerning the clinic, the intake experience, and so on, were high. Perhaps any clinic that considered its job seriously would turn in comparable ratings. However, these were all college students (undergraduate and graduate students) who are somewhat prone to criticize the university; thus, comparatively, the Counseling Center stood up well in their eyes. These results compare well with those reported in the literature (Bloom, 1981; Budman, 1981) on client ratings of a single therapy (or intake) session. (Some clinics begin therapy without an explicit intake; hence one-session-only contacts might be either intake or the first therapy session.)

In this study over 85% reported positively to general questions about the intake interviewer, clinic policy, and the like. It is important to note, too, that half or more said they knew what to expect at intake or during therapy, some 40% having had a therapeutic experience previously, a fairly high proportion in such a young population (age range: 16 to 35, with a mean age of 23 years). Other than personal experiences with psychotherapy, these fairly economically advantaged youth and young adults had heard and read about psychotherapy and some had participated in family therapy when they were as young as 6 to 12 years of age.

It is quite possible, from the answers to the questions posed the intake-only population, that they were just "checking in" about therapy, getting something from the process, and seeing whether or not they then felt the need to

TABLE 4.1
Questionnaire Responses from a Sample Intake-Only Population, 1982–1983 ($N = 46$)

Item Content	Response			
	Yes or Positive	*No or Negative*	*Neutral*	*No Answer*
1. General reactions to the intake interview	34 (74%)	06 (13%)	04 (09%)	02 (04%)
2. Knew what to expect at intake	22 (48%)	24 (52%)		
3. Knew what to expect in therapy	27 (60%)	19 (40%)		
4. Prior therapy experience	19 (40%)	27 (60%)		
5. Liked the intake therapist	43 (93%)	03 (07%)		
6. Reaction to having a different therapist	03 (07%)	01 (02%)	42 (91%)	
7. Therapist ratings — see below				
8. Other feelings about therapist	16 (35%)	05 (11%)	25 (54%)	
9. Discomfort with clinic procedures	07 (15%)	39 (85%)		
10. Aware of ability to change therapists	33 (72%)	08 (17%)		05 (11%)
11. Able to solve problem on own	39 (85%)	03 (07%)		04 (08%)
12. Plans to continue therapy elsewhere	09 (20%)	37 (80%)		
13. Would return to CC if necessary	42 (91%)	04 (09%)		
14. If returned, any changes needed	09 (20%)	01 (02%)	36 (78%)	
15. Would recommend CC to others	46 (100%)			
16. Overall Center rating: Mean = 4.14 S.D. = .83				

Ratings (5-point scale)	Mean	SD.
7. Therapist ratings		
a. Interested in me	4.01	
b. Helpful suggestions	3.86	
c. Sensitive, understanding	4.02	
d. Warm and supportive	3.91	= 0.95, Series
e. Helped solve problems	3.78	
f. Worked well together	3.78	
g. Turned my concerns into major psychological problems	1.39	

85

continue. It is also understandable that, given the highly positive responses to intake-only, these clients would need only a few interviews if they were to continue with therapy (keeping in mind that this counseling center ranged between a mean of four to six therapy interviews over an 8-year period, a highly stable figure, with standard deviations in the same range as the means).

TWO SPOT-CHECK STUDIES OF THE INTAKE

It is clear that we do not know much about the intake interview save for the number of clients not returning and a few demographics associated therewith. Two spot-check studies are of interest in this connection; they followed from the aforementioned studies.

The first spot-check study was based on brief interviews with clients as they finished the intake session and before they left the Counseling Center. This check was to ascertain client reactions to the intake interviewer and to assess the likelihood that the client would return for therapy. This spot-check was carried out during three semesters: spring, 1982, fall, 1982, and spring, 1983, netting a total of 210 interviews, about 35% of the total number of intake interviews (personal/social problem cases) conducted during that three-semester period. The study missed clients who finished their intake session when the spot-check interviewer was unavailable; others were unable to take the time for the brief spot-check, or declined the interview (some offering to answer questions another time).

The second spot-check following intake was conducted during the 1981–1982 school year and included both clients and therapists, where each answered a matching six-item questionnaire concerning the just-held intake. These two studies are reported on in turn.

The First Spot-Check Study.   The first "spot-check" study covering three semesters, 210 cases, was based on a six- and nine-item questionnaire obtained with clients before they left the Counseling Center following intake.

This study took place following a number of staff discussions concerning the intake juncture and what clients might know, feel, expect, and so on, at this point in their help-seeking behavior. Students were asked to complete the intake interview before it was known whether they would be returning for therapy or whether other dispositions would be made (if they had not already been referred out during the intake interview). Every client was interviewed for 5–6 minutes using the six-item questionnaire (spring 1982) and the nine-item questionnaire (the following two semesters). Constraints on who was interviewed were previously cited. Very few refused the interview invitation (5 out of 215 solicited), and all responded well to the brief spot-check interview. Data on the first spot-check interview are shown in Table 4.2.

TABLE 4.2
First Post-intake "Spot Check" Data Summary, Client Replies; 3 Semesters, N = 210 (% Data)

	M	F	#1 Meet Exp. +	−	?	#2 Help/Like +	?	#3 CC Confid. +	−	#4 Recomm. CC +	−	?	#5 Return CC +	−	?	#6 Help Before Y	N
Spring '82 (N = 60)	20/33	40/67	90	08	02	93	97	93	07	97	01	01	92	06	02	47	53

	M	F	#1 Gen.	Int.	Dis.	#2 Expec. Y	N	#3 Help Before Y	N	#4 Improve Y	N	#5 Int. Bother Y	N	#6 Recomm. Y	N
Fall '82 (N = 74)	31/42	42/58	99	90	08	54	46	57	43	42	58	10	90	96	04
Spring '83 (N = 76)	30/40	40/60	95	84	18	51	49	54	56	26	74	17	83	97	03

	#7 Contin. Therapy CC	Other	Unsure	No Need	#8 Reasons Not Return/Therapy None	Better	Ther. Rel.	Money	Time	Misc.	Total	#9 General Comments Pos.	Neg.	None
Fall '82 (cont.)	84	16			19	23	24	11	08	15	100	40.5	12	37.5
Spring '83 (cont.)	76	04	17	03	13	22	14.5	11	14.5	25	100	32	30	38

It will be noted that the spring 1982 population of 60 cases were asked only six items; added to these six were three more items for the fall 1982 population ($N = 74$) and the spring 1983 population ($N = 76$). As expected from the literature and from our own experiences, ratings of the intake experience were "high" for all items. Item 1 asked if the intake interview met the client's expectations; 2, if the client liked the intake interviewer; 3, whether the Counseling Center gave the client confidence in getting help; 4, if the client was willing to refer friends in need; 5, if the client would return again if occasion arose; and 6, whether the client had sought similar help before. Items 7, 8, and 9 for the two following semesters included: 7, whether client planned to continue therapy here or elsewhere; 8, why clients might elect not to come back; and 9, general comments. Some researchers have said that the baseline range for satisfaction of client contact with counseling centers and mental health facilities ranges between 75% or 80%, up to 90% to 95%, and that a suitable "baseline" for this phenomenon is about 80%–85% "satisfaction" or approval, similar to some industrial/organizational psychology data on job satisfaction.

Approximately 95% of the clients in the spring 1982 population averred they would return to the Counseling Center for therapy, whereas our records show that only about 50%–55% actually returned for the first therapy interview; possibly the positive responding to this item was a client tendency to state what he or she felt was a socially expected response, or it represented the aftereffects of some immediate satisfaction with the encounter. However the shrinkage between avowed intentions to return for therapy and the actual return rates came about, apparent failures to return seem not to be based on any substantial negative reactions to the center or its personnel or policies. This set of facts means, also, that if the clinic developed the policy of capitalizing further on positive client attitudes at intake, there would be a number of policy matters a clinic could invoke with apparent client approval, such as lengthening the intake interview and then suggesting that, variously, clients return for a follow-up in 1 month, 2 months, or more to report on progress (allowing, however, client choice for an earlier return or more interviews if need were sufficient).

Data for the two ensuing semesters (fall 1982 and spring 1983) net similar results. Item 8, however, concerning reasons for possibly not returning for therapy, even though the offer was made, shows the number of considerations clients offer as possible reasons for their demur: From about 15% saying "no reason," the other possible deterrents were "getting better" (about 23%), "therapy no longer relevant" (15%–24%); "money" (11%); "time" (8%–15%) and miscellaneous items (about 20% on average the last two semesters); occasionally clients offered more than one reason for not returning for therapy. Therapy appears to be similar to a possibly large number of activities they may or may not engage in, there being no great formality, necessity or certainty associated therewith, even though about 15%-25% said after intake they saw "no reason" for not coming back for therapy. This opinion does not mean, however, that return for therapy is a certainty or that it is strongly needed. There appears to be nothing in the data for the vast majority of clients attending a university counseling center to allow us to say therapy is the serious, formidable process that it is characterized as being in much of the literature. Although attitudes toward therapy, toward the clinic and its processes and policies are positive, there is a "be or let be" attitude running throughout the present surveys of client attitude; and because about 35%-40% have had some contact with therapy before, either individually or in the parental/family setting, there is still the same attitude of conditional acceptance, not necessity (Emrick & Lasser, 1977; Emrick, Lasser, & Edwards, 1978).

The Second Spot-Check, Post-Intake Study.   This study of the intake process came immediately following the intake and before the clients left the Counseling Center building. Clients and therapists filled out a six-item questionnaire assessing their *immediate* reactions to the intake and their attitudes toward continuing therapy. These were independently turned in to the receptionist who collated returns for the computer analysis. The major hypothesis examined here was that clients would rate their intake experience, item for item, higher than therapists would (at intake) rate the same items (but stated from the therapist's vantage point). Table 4.3 shows the results of the six-item questionnaire, which included questions concerning whether the interview was *helpful* (from the client's viewpoint and, correspondingly, if the therapist felt this way also); item 2 covered their respective ratings as to whether *understanding* occurred; item 3 was based on each feeling *encouraged* by the intake process; item 4 referred to each *liking* the other; item 5 assessed each, client and therapist, being willing to work together in therapy; and item 6 referred to *expected progress* were the therapy to go on, as assessed by each participant.

Table 4.3 presents the correlations between client and therapist for each of the six items; the *F* values, respectively, for client and therapist, with significance levels. Only item 6, therapist ratings (*F* value 3.74), reached the .05 level of significance. The forward-looking nature of this rating (item 6) suggests that early on assessment of client/therapist attitudes should attempt to assess not only present status but also *future workability* for therapy, for the therapist and client in question, and for help-seeking in general (see Fagan, Chapter 6, in this connection). As we know from the literature, clients tend to rate their therapeutic experience higher than do therapists — especially in short-term therapy (therapists traditionally expect therapy to last longer for a good job to be done) — but also often in longer term therapy. It is evident that therapists and clients have different "sets" or "expectancies" concerning ther-

TABLE 4.3
Client and Therapist Results on the Post-intake Questionnaire, 1982–1983 (Type IV Sum of Squares)[a] N = 353 Matched Pairs

| | Client | | Therapist | | | | Client | | Therapist |
	Means	SDs	Means	SDs	r[b]	"F"	Significance	"F"	Significance
1. Helpful	6.07	1.16	5.34	1.06	0.29	0.15	0.70	0.45	0.50
2. Understanding occurred	6.28	1.05	5.82	1.06	0.16	3.79	0.05	4.32	0.04
3. Encouragement occurred	5.90	1.33	5.64	1.33	0.40	0.03	0.86	4.41	0.04
4. Liked the other	6.39	1.03	5.47	1.33	0.21	1.66	0.20	1.21	0.27
5. Wanted to work with each other	5.69	1.56	4.86	1.70	0.25	0.34	0.56	0.16	0.69
6. Expected progress	5.43	1.48	5.07	1.41	0.25	3.01	0.08	3.74	0.05

[a]The 6-Item Questionnaire used by clients had a split-half correlation of 0.96; that of therapists 0.94.
[b]All r's significant at the .0001 level.

apy, as these results indicate. Perhaps therapists would be helped in their short-term therapy posture if they saw more clearly that clients are usually ready for immediate help, that they are somewhat optimistic, and that they are often looking *forward* to a successful therapy interaction. The therapist's more formidable view of therapy may act to discourage client optimism, workability, and perhaps later assessment of results. The process of early, post-intake assessment of client and therapist attitudes is reviewed again with a somewhat different research posture in Chapter 6 by Fagan.

PRE-INTAKE DATA

Once the intake process has been characterized as a definite juncture in the flow of cases through a mental health facility, it is soon apparent that the pre-intake phenomenon might, itself, contain some interesting information (Albers & Scrivner, 1977). If intake data of the type studied in most of the predictive literature concerning psychotherapy lacks power, and if the intake process itself seems to present a "new ball game," then the pre-intake process would appear to be interesting in its own right and possibly related to the later intake process.

A study of the daily intake log at a Counseling Center showed that a number of people called and made appointments, but they cancelled or did not appear for the intake interview. This phenomenon was studied over the entire academic year, 1982–1983 (and was repeated for 1983–1984 ending April 27, 1984) and netted a number of interesting findings, which were then pared down for more detailed investigation (Phillips & DePalma, 1983).

Some research shows that waiting lists and the transferring of clients from one therapist (or intake interviewer) to another may increase clients' dropping out from therapy (Caggiano, 1981; Levy, 1963; Shuelman, Gelso, Mindus, Hunt, & Stevenson, 1980; Sinnett & Danskin, 1967; Tantem & Klerman, 1979). Attempts at pre-therapy structuring or preparation for the ensuing therapy has had, at best, mixed results and may have influenced client in-session behavior but not attrition rate (Barnett, 1981; Brosch, 1980; Holliday, 1979; Levitt & Fisher, 1981). Pre-therapy information might even increase attrition inasmuch as it may "disconfirm clients' expectations." It is hard to predict what pre-therapy behavior is related to what in-therapy or post-therapy behavior. This is all the more salient in that client-expressed satisfaction with clinic procedures and initial interviews appears to bear little or not at all on subsequent client attrition (Heilbrun, 1972; Zamostny, Corrigan, & Eggert, 1982). The attrition phenomenon as described in previous chapters may lead us to expect pre-intake attrition to show some of the same characteristics. The problem is how to investigate the pre-intake attrition, or loss of potential clientele, a matter not previously studied but one we have attempted here.

Perusing the 1982–83 flow of cases, we discovered that of the 416 applicants (ostensible therapy cases) a *prior* or pre-intake population of 32 clients also existed. They comprised about 7% or 8% of the 416 applicants. Of these 32 pre-intake potential clients, 15 made appointments but did not show ("no show") at the agreed-upon time. Another 17 clients made the initial appointment and cancelled but did not reschedule. Additionally 22 clients who had also cancelled before the intake subsequently rescheduled. Thus, there were three pre-therapy intake populations for study. These three populations ($N = 54$) are to be seen in the light of the population that did not return after the intake ($N = 228$). Thus the total intake picture for 1982–1983 appears as follows: Total number of applicants = 416; number having intake only = 228 (55%); number having one or more therapy interviews = 188 (45%). Prior to this attritional résumé, then, the pre-intake clients have their place, so to speak.

The research notion guiding the study of the pre-intake population was that they would appear in attitude similar to the therapy cases in regard to therapy, the clinic, readiness to avail themselves of therapy, and the like. On the basis of a seven-item questionnaire, the pre-therapy, "no show" and "cancelled" cases were phoned for an interview (Gates & Colborn, 1976; Shepard & Moseley, 1976). The no show and cancelled cases were 65% female, compared to 60% female at intake over several years; the total group had a mean age of 23.1 years. Table 4.4 summarizes the questionnaire findings for these two pre-intake populations.

Table 4.4 shows that the "no show" and "cancel-no rescheduling" cases are largely positive in their responses to questions about the Counseling Center and their aborted intake appointments, the "no show" cases being more reluctant to follow through and harboring somewhat less positive attitudes toward the whole enterprise of applying for help at the center. Some may think there is inconsistency in the replies of the two groups of students who failed to follow through on appointments inasmuch as about 50% of each group had sought help before in some setting, including the present Counseling Center; and more then 80% said they would reapply should the occasion occur prompting them to do so. However, the demur was apparently not based overwhelmingly on "anxiousness about coming to the Counseling Center" as evidenced by 35%–40% saying there was no felt anxiousness. If we regard the "no show" cases as the most distant from accepting help at the Counseling Center, and the "cancel-no reschedule" cases as next in line in this respect, we see evidence that the "no show" cases were more problematic in their acceptance of help: 54% report schedule conflict or having changed their minds, compared to 35% in these two categories among the cancel cases; and fewer of the "no show" cases reported that they knew what to expect at intake (20%) compared to the cancel group's 30% frequency in this category.

Add to these two populations of demurring cases at intake 22 "cancel-reschedule" cases who became part of the 416 intake cases for the 1982–1983

TABLE 4.4
Summary of 7-Item Questionnaire: Pre-Intake 15 "No Show" and 17 "Cancel" Cases

Item Number	Questions and Answers	No Show N	No Show %	Cancel N	Cancel %
1	Reasons for no show?				
	Schedule conflicts	3	33	3	17.5
	Changed mind	3	20	3	17.5
	Forgot	3	20	–	–
	Problem left	3	20	7	41
	Illness	1	07	–	–
	Got help elsewhere	–	–	4	24
2	Sought help before?				
	This CC	3	20	3	18
	Health Service/CMHC	2	13	3	18
	Private Practice	3	20	2	12
	Never	7	47	9	52
3	Would reapply to CC?				
	Yes	12	80	14	82
	No	1	07	2	12
	Uncertain	2	13	1	06
4	Know what to expect at intake?				
	Yes	3	20	5	30
	No	12	80	12	70
5	Anxious about coming to CC?				
	None	6	40	6	35
	Some	7	47	10	60
	Much	2	13	1	06
6	Recommend others to CC?				
	Yes	14	93	16	94
	No	1	07		06
	Uncertain	–	–	–	–
7	How well you think CC serves students? (Scale 1–5, 5 high)				
	Means		3.33		3.80

academic year. This pre-intake, step-wise progression in terms of distance from or movement toward intake appears to make sense and further appears as an approximation toward keeping the intake appointment. Figure 4.1 shows how the pre-intake progression takes place in the successive approximation sense. Data for 1983–1984, on the same subject, are covered in Fig. 4.2. These are the only 2 years on which we have reliable pre-intake data; this topic will be expanded in future years. It adds credence to the notion that the "real world outside the clinic" — even in the university community — embraces a potential number of users of mental health services and that the intake — even though sometimes approached reluctantly by a percentage of potential

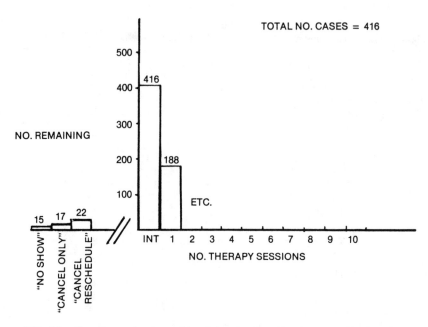

FIG. 4.1   Showing pre-intake attritional data for "No Show" ($N = 15$), "Cancel-No Reschedule" ($N = 17$), and "Cancel & Reschedule" ($N = 22$); Total Pre-Intake, 1982–83 $N = 54$.

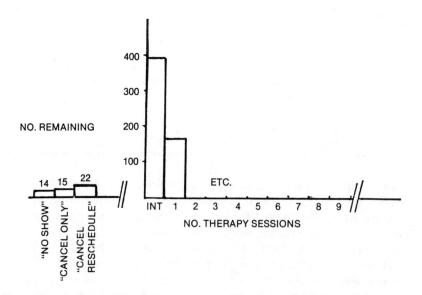

FIG. 4.2   Showing pre-intake attritional data for "No Show" ($N = 14$), "Cancel-No Reschedule" ($N = 15$), and "Cancel And Reschedule" ($N = 22$). Total N, 1983–1984 = 51.

94

clients — serves as a tryout, or bridge, between the formal services of the clinic and the somewhat vague and ambivalently felt "need" in the larger community, or the relevance of the support system for the client in the larger community.

In further comparisons of the pre-intake clients with those having an intake-only session, we note in the latter cases that 11% offered negative replies concerning "other feelings about the therapist" (Table 4.1): feeling that the intake therapist did not structure the process enough, apparently did not answer client questions sufficiently, and seemed to give no overall direction to the potential offer of therapy. On balance, this criticism seemed to be the most cogent of therapist activity at intake, and may be related, in turn, to the 17% (among intake-only clients) who reported they did not know they could ask for a change of therapist.

In comparison to the reasons given (Table 4.4) among the "no show" and "cancel-no reschedule" cases, these intake-only clients said they did not return to the clinic because they were able to solve their own problems (85% so reported); and, somewhat overlapping, only 20% planned, they said, to pursue therapy elsewhere; perhaps all to the point that this intake experience was a fact-finding, direction-seeking, even transitory experience for the intake-only group of 46 cases. No great matter, then, ensues from the intake experience; 91% said they would return if the occasion arose, apparently without any strong bias against the center or its processes/policies, and all would recommend the Counseling Center to others (some volunteered the statement that they "felt it was a 'good idea' to seek psychological help" if one felt the need.)

The overall center rating was understandably a bit higher (4.14 mean; $SD = 0.83$; Table 4.1) for these intake-only clients, compared to the pre-intake clients, perhaps based on the more concrete nature of their experiences with the clinic. Additionally, the client ratings in Item 7 concerning the intake interviewer netted an overall mean for seven sub-items of 3.9 ($SD = +0.95$), and a mean of 1.39 (5-point scale, 5 highest), indicating the intake therapist/interviewer did not "pathologize" the clients (their version of the intake process as an evaluation of client status and future use of the clinic).

In summary, then, of the pre-intake and intake-only population attitudes, a potential population of help-seekers show varying degrees of ambivalence concerning mental health help — at least in the university community and, we aver, in communities at large, as well — and the stronger the positive inclinations, the more likely the person will get to the intake process itself, although with some demur at different points along the way.[1]

---

[1] Data are presented on some exploratory attempts to ferret out more aspects of "help-seeking" behavior between or among clinics in a relatively compact geographic community, wherein the behavior of clients/patients is described in terms of their previous therapy contacts; this curve, also, is expected to show a negatively accelerating declining ("decay") curve of the Poisson distribution type.

THE ROLE OF PRE-INTAKE INSTRUCTIONS

Attempts to understand the intake process can take a number of directions. One obvious method is to try to structure the intake interview and the subsequent therapy by introducing to the prospective client more instructions concerning intake and therapy. This has been tried by several researchers but positive results have been lacking insofar as convincingly cutting down on loss at intake (Strupp & Bloxom, 1973).

The present study was carried out during 1982–1983 and included between 375 and 407 clients, the *N*s for different comparisons. The procedure was to invite the prospective client, upon filling out the pre-intake demographic data, to listen with earphones to a 5 to 6-minute tape stating the clinic services, conduct of the intake interview, and how therapy *if it eventuated* would be handled. On alternate days clients were given the tape to hear: Monday/Wednesday/Friday one week and Tuesday/Thursday the next. Approximately 36% heard the tape, 64% did not; the difference (from 50/50% ratio) arose presumably out of some carelessness by the administrative staff in providing the tape for waiting clients, because of time pressures that disallowed some people listening before the intake interview, and on occasion when several prospective clients were awaiting interviews and not enough cassettes were available.

The first hypothesis examined was related to the expectation that the tape-listening would — through realistic instructions — encourage more sessions. This hypothesis arose from some staff discussion about the importance of instructing prospective clients more fully about therapy, and assuming that more knowledge would lead to more participation. The literature on this subject is not extensive and the findings are somewhat moot. However, the short-term context allows for a more exact test of the hypothesis that more knowledge = more therapy.

Results did not conform to the hypothesis. Clients who heard the tape (N = 145 or 36% of total intake) had a mean number of therapy sessions of 3.59 (SD = 4.77); those not hearing the tape (N = 230, or 64%) had a mean number of sessions of 3.74 (SD = 5.48); an insignificant t-test difference between the two groups (p = .77). One can always say that a better tape would have made more of an impact, or that a tape and a printed sheet of explanation would be expected to yield more definitive results. Perhaps a special verbal message by the intake therapist before the interview got under way, together with a handout sheet highlighting the major points about therapy and clinic procedure, would be productive of differences. Clinics can be encouraged to give other methods a try. If an introductory explanation were to be productive, it would seem that the number of therapy sessions would be the variable most sensitive to change. This reasoning may be challenged somewhat by an alternative hypothesis relating to the quality of therapy; i.e., the subsequent ratings of those hearing the ·tape and conntinuing therapy would be higher than those not hearing the tape but also continuing with therapy.

A second comparison utilizing the tape-no-tape populations was with the proportion of senior staff ($N = 7$) versus externs ($N = 7$) who served as the *assigned* counselor for the incoming client. The senior staff received by assignment 66% ($N = 269$) of these intake interviews ($N = 407$) compared to 34% ($N = 138$) for the externs (the latter group served half-time or less whereas most senior staff members were full-time or nearly so). This comparison showed that each group — senior staff and externs — was assigned the same proportion of tape and no-tape clients as they had intakes in the whole population of clients; hence there was no bias by chi-square test introduced due to experience level ($p = .34$).

Considering the notion that there might have been a sex difference in regard to the number hearing the tape, M/F comparisons were made using the 8-year 60% female population as the baseline. In this population of 405 clients, 245 females (60%) were in the intake population (160 males = 40%), and their proportion listening or not to the tape (females/males = 62/38% listening and 60/40% not listening to the tape) shows no significant difference by chi-square test ($p = .75$). Thus no bias in the M/F proportion listening to the pre-intake tape was present.

The final comparison of the tape-listening conditions possibly causing a bias was a comparison of senior staff versus externs in relation to the percentage of clients listening or not to the tape compared to the total listening/not listening population, at intake. Externs saw at intake 65% of the clients who listened to the intake tape ($N = 116$), whereas the senior staff saw at intake only 35% of the intake clients who had heard the tape. The p value here is .0007, indicating that subsequent to the incoming client hearing the tape the externs were disproportionately represented in the intake process. One could argue that the externs being on hand more for intake (which is normally the case as the senior staff conducts, in proportion, two thirds of the therapy and the externs conduct about two thirds of the intakes) would bias the subsequent behavior of the incoming clients as to the number of their therapy sessions. Among the senior staff, 27% ($N = 39$) of their clients heard the tape and 73% ($N = 105$) did not; comparable figures among the externs was 44% ($N = 116$) of their clients heard the tape and 56% ($N = 147$) did not. We are not able to explain this disproportionate set of figures comparing externs with senior staff.

SUMMARY

The intake juncture appears to be the most crucial one in the delivery of psychotherapy services insofar as the literature states and insofar as the current array of data indicates. Before intake there is an attritional phenomenon; at intake, attrition asserts itself most boldly; and, of course, following intake there is a progressive lessening of the number of cases appearing for therapy, which is described as the negatively accelerating ("decay") curve of the Poisson distribution type. Thus, if one wanted to do meaningful research on the whole of psychotherapy delivery, one would do no better than to concentrate on the intake process itself.

It is also fairly clear that pre-intake efforts to predict who will continue in therapy, who will get the greater benefit from therapy, and whether longer attendance is actually associated with improved outcome are all more or less moot in the research literature. Although there is some support for the expectation that more therapy equals better results, the constrictive number of sessions involved in short-term therapy militates against this generalization having much value; and, too, even in the short-term context, the relatively longer number of sessions does not produce the better outcome results, however they are measured.

We have said over the course of the studies reported on here, that the intake is the start of a new ball game. The intake is a social phenomenon in its own right, only scantily related to any so far determined pre-intake characteristics of the client, the therapist, therapeutic persuasion, and so forth. Concentrating research on the intake will probably bode best for increasing our knowledge of psychotherapy and behavior change. The intake, combining as it apparently does the features of the client, the therapist and the delivery system, qua system, emerges as the substantive unit of study of psychotherapy and appears to convincingly override any set of variables heretofore examined as to client, therapist characteristics or type of diagnosis/therapy, and the like. Insofar as the intake is the crucial juncture in the whole attritional matter—described as it has been herein via a large number of studies—it now behooves researchers and practitioners of all persuasions to examine as fully as possible the intake process.

There are a number of ways in which the intake may be further studied. Some of them may be the following: Arrange the intake only partly as a fact-finding process, a process preliminary to therapy, but consider it the actual beginning of therapy. Some people and some clinics do this explicitly, and minimize the preliminary feel of the intake by launching directly into therapy. What would this mean? It would mean that problem statements by the client—or those ferreted out by the therapist—would constitute points that were "up-for-change" and would be viewed in this explicit manner. Several points of departure would be identified and plans made for a change process, involving, of course, as totally as possible the client's understanding, participation, and so on. If the intake interview took more than an hour, by plan, the ways in which the problems-cited-for-change could be pursued would be further adumbrated and an "action plan" would result. This sometimes happens anyhow, and it is possible that the most adroit therapy—that therapy taking the lesser amounts of time that produces equally good results, measure by measure—would be supposed to operate in this explicit manner.

A second way to pivot new procedures on and following the intake would be to extend the time when the client would return for another session. An hour or 2 might provide the needed structure available in an intake. The amount of time—1, 2, or more hours—could be systematically varied over populations in order to have the client try out the value of assignments, tasks, data keeping, and so forth, under varying intake conditions. The client could then have the option of calling in for another appointment, on demand; or the client could be scheduled out for follow-up contacts 2, 4, 6 weeks later, a time when evaluation of the intake matters would be held and new plans made (if needed) or extended if that were indicated. It would be expected on the basis of present knowledge that about one half of the clients would not return after intake; using this figure as a baseline, the number returning in 2 to 6 weeks would constitute a kind of test of this attritional matter and perhaps give a leg up on the study of the amount of change expected, client or other ratings of change, and so forth, as a function of the time between intake and some follow-up; thus the length of the intake (1 or 2 hours or some other plan) versus the follow-up period of time (say 2–6 weeks) versus some indication of change, would constitute the research matrix. In this framework would occur, also, the number of subsequent sessions following intake needed to produce various incremental results, together with client satisfaction, behavior change reported/observed, and so forth.

A third way to assess intake more fully would be to offer intake as a one-time-only contact. Offhand, this procedure would be expected to yield some favorable results about 70% of the time, but one would not know, in a research sense, if that were true unless some follow-up were conducted. The differences, then, between the second intake study plan previously cited and this one would be in the pre-arrangement at intake that there would be a follow-up in exactly 2 to 6 or so weeks; in this third case of studying intake, the follow-up might be unannounced at intake and conducted after some longer period of time, say 3 to 6 months later, with similar variables in tow as with the second plan mentioned. Holding to a fairly constant set of variables for study, this procedure might yield some pretty interesting results for most outpatient settings (counseling centers, community mental health clinics, etc.).

A fourth way in which intake could be conducted in more experimental ways would be somewhat of a simulation of analogue type of studies, where people who contacted a clinic would be asked to identify as clearly as possible their presenting (or main) problem. Then a small group of such persons would constitute a discussion group as an intake process, wherein a number of efforts would be made to set up change plans, plans for a "buddy system" of help among group members (similar to many such plans extant in group therapy now), and an agreement that the group members would confab and confer with each other and return as a group in a given period of time. This procedure would activate a process of active support or interpersonal help ("buddies"), would present a change plan together with specifics about implementing the plan, and would designate a follow-up point when group members would return with reports on their successes, suggestions for further work (or not) and so on.

These four plans are certainly not exhaustive; others may already exist in the literature or possibly in the non-reported efforts of clinics and counseling centers. Combinations of the proffered plans also could be tried.

Lest the reader gain the impression that altering the intake would address only how fast one could get clients in and out of treatment, the point should never be forgotten that as things now stand, somewhere between 40% and 55% of the clients/patients who approach a service delivery system do not return after the first visit (whether it is intake or a bonafide therapy contact); that most people report favorably on a single contact with therapy; and that any system for experimentation would have a "fail safe" arrangement whereby people who could not profit from the proposed structure would switch to a preferred plan. In fact, any clinic that attempted to do the kinds of research on the intake as proposed here should tell the prospective client at intake that the proffered plan was one in which the clinic had confidence (and, possibly, experience) but that exceptions were anticipated and would be respected, thereby avoiding any impression of coercion.

A possibly equally valid reason for experimenting with intake is that a staff willing to do so would doubtless serendipitously hit on still other ways to offer more effective and efficient services, all to the client's advantage. The research posture implied in a willingness to experiment with the intake process (as well as other portions of the delivery system, to be addressed later) would reveal an "open" system of service delivery more compatible with humanitarian and research objectives than is now the case among most clinics and counseling centers. Orthodoxy in adherence to clinic policy, therapist "style," the length of therapy, notions about what has to change in order for the patient to benefit, notions about client preparation for therapy, not to mention the ubiquitous diagnosis, and so on, would all give way to a more open and experimental/research posture which, in time, would more clearly address all the mental health issues inherent in any delivery system, from funding out to final evaluation of results.

NEW PRE-INTAKE MEASURES AND THE COMMUNITY

Addressing the importance of pre-intake events is in some ways a preventive measure. In the previous references to the no show and cancel conditions, we saw an approximation toward making and keeping the intake appointment. In the vast area of the university population (or in a community) there are many potential users of the mental health services offered. Some are in great need and do not utilize the services, some are in need and do use the services, and many lie in between — those perhaps who are about to use the service but are ambivalent about it — and possibly other subpopulations of users or potential users. If these could be defined more accurately, we would be able to direct mental health education to the vast population of persons who are yet to use the various clinics available (Veroff, Kulka, & Douvan, 1981). Veroff et al. did household surveys of potential mental health service users in 1957 and 1976. They found that the conventional psychiatric/psychological service delivery systems, private practice and community-based clinics alike, tend to operate by severing the individual needing help from his or her social context (pp. 6-7), whereas so-called nonprofessional forms of healing (faith healing, shamanism, prayer, etc.) bring the community into the healing effort. Research that is done in, say, a university community covering potential users of mental health facilities should take into consideration as many aspects of the social/community setting as possible, and try to juxtapose the potential client alongside the actual delivery system. As we gain more confidence in replicating the kinds of pre-intake research undertaken here, researchers can identify more aspects of the community that will affect the client's availability to the delivery system and the delivery system's responsiveness to the potential client. It will be necessary, however, for the clinic to see its delivery system obligations somewhat differently from the customary ways now practiced.

Social/Community Intervention (SCI) efforts (Bloom, 1981; Cowen, 1973; Iscoe & Harris, 1984; Veroff et al., 1981) are making it increasingly clear that mental health is not just an individual matter, pivoting on the proper diagnosis, treated by the therapy of choice (Andrews, Hewson, & Vaillant, 1978; Collins & Pancost, 1976; Durlak, 1979; Gottlieb, 1981; Lenrow & Cowden, 1980). Health and psychotherapy measures are to be seen in a much more complex amalgam of factors that arise from the social matrix which, in turn, may "cause" or foster the expressed problem. This treatment matrix may indicate the most likely forms of therapeutic intervention (social or religious groups expressing already given and extant social pressures and the like); and may point to treatment efforts that will look somewhat different from a manual on how to treat this or that set of complaints. The work of Glasscote (1980) suggests that although preventive mental health efforts have a positive and familiar ring, when actual practices among six selected CMHCs were investigated, only about 3% of the clinic's time was spent in preventive work and there was no preventive policy in effect. That condition arises, in part, due to the absence of relevant information about the community, the incidence of various mental health needs, and salient features of mental health service delivery systems that might be employed in some way to effect preventive efforts and measure them. A university (contained) community might serve as a wellspring for some types of preventive mental health work — in the residence halls, in classes, in expressed university policy and the like.

Following up on the small effort begun here in the pre-intake study, we might better define community needs in college or university residence halls (as one example of an entry point) and ascertain in such settings how attitudes toward psychotherapy (as one example of a mental health service delivery effort) might be obtained. It would be important to know how information dispensed to the students would reduce the need for formal therapy services, how groups could be formed to interact with each other as a kind of "mental health network". These efforts could be followed forward to see what, if any, impact they had on students seeking psychotherapy, inside or outside the university setting. Although social support systems or networks are often touted as panaceas, there likely is a more modest substantive core in them that can be studied to see how they function. The dispersal of informal and formal information about mental health and mental health facilities on campus, and other related issues (Veroff et al., 1981, p. 11) would be vital information for all community members. Although research methodology would call for more stringency than is now likely, some examples of preventive work could be examined in the residence halls wherein baselines would be ascertained on mental health usage and attitudes, followed by planned network intervention programs, to see, in the end (of a semester or a year) what effect was noticed in the admissions to a mental health service on campus. For continuing data collection, a clinic (such as the one affording the pre-intake study previously cited) could be used as a baseline system for clients calling in for help, then failing to show, cancelling (and rescheduling or not), coming for one or more interviews, and so on, in the utilization of the proffered services. Moving backward in time, so to say, these no show, cancelling cases could then be studied more fully to see if there were aspects of the network of support and information of value to them in preventive ways, and/or where improvements could be made. Most clients get some help forthwith in consulting with a counseling center or mental health facility; if this kind of service could be backed up by social/community network intervention and preventive efforts, it would be supposed that a fairly high degree of effective preventive work could be accomplished. Thus what is needed is not so much surveys in the community at large — although such work may have some bearing on understanding the community (Veroff et al., 1981) — but *focal points in the delivery of services* that could be used to register changes in utilization, cost, prevention, and so on, over time. A university community, or possibly a high school or an apartment complex, could be used to study and assess changes in utilization, cost, preventive efficiency of mental health services. Guides for this kind of study are found in the Veroff et al. volume (1981, p. 79), wherein are assessed replies to questions concerning the citizen's potential "readiness for self-referral" (Table 5.1), including past use of mental health referrals, reflective answers on whether one could or might have utilized such services, how self-help is developed in lieu of formal referrals, and so on. Baselines of several types of questions conducted on a number of populations could service as guidelines for service delivery system plans. Because a residence hall exists in a potentially research-skilled setting — the university — what information obtained there about formal and informal help utilization could be generalized to other settings? Presumably such information would enable community members to better see mental health help as community-centered in final analysis and not as a service that separates the user from the community at large (Veroff et al., 1981, p. 11). The Veroff et al. report (p. 131, Table 5.11) might serve, as well, as an informational base on types of problems people would consider as ample reasons for help-seeking, including problems relating to marriage (and spouse), children, other family questions, and so forth. Other content areas relating to jobs, to education, to health, would doubtless suggest a different set of salient questions. This model could suffice well in a university setting in which a survey would include study problems, depression, relationship conflicts, substance abuse, roommate problems, and so on, thus instructing a clinic, broadly speaking, on what kinds of service delivery problems they might "tune into" to be of better service in both preventive and immediate service delivery ways. Here, again, the preventive focus has to be on some demonstrably present and often utilized resource — such as a university counseling center or mental health clinic — in order for the SCI preventive efforts to have ample test of efficiency and efficacy.

In final analysis, then, once the intake interview has begun, the emergence of a new set of interrelationships seems to be under way. The client appears to be reassessing his or her need for help, the salience of the present interview situation for delivering that help, the effect of the clinic and its policies on the potential therapy client, and whether therapy as a continuing process is indicated. These questions occur most in relationship to the client being separated from his or her community, which need not be the case, as we are learning in studying community attitudes toward mental health. The clinic not only operates as a delivery system the moment the client contacts it, but the springboard from which the client moves toward the clinic is, itself, a mental health network — more or less defined — and may serve not only as a backdrop for the client's immediate moves, but may be a resource the client can fall back on or even utilize in lieu of the formal mental health delivery system. The more, then, the clinic as a delivery system places itself in the larger community context, and the more it entertains questions about how the whole delivery system operates, the more it will grow into a mature point of focus for the utilizer of mental health services. The upshot of the clinic as a delivery system, qua system, beginning with the client's first contact (even pre-intake, as we have seen), is that the clinic should not see itself, or its function, as a facility that separates itself from the community (in order to treat the individual or the family) but that works in tandem with the community. The study of the intake process is the first and most vital way of assessing the delivery system, qua system, in whatever ways we wish, from pre-therapy attrition, through intake and subsequent therapy attrition, out to the length of the asymptote and to the evaluation of the services delivered.

5 Client and Delivery System Characteristics: The Flow of Cases Over Time

One of this book's main messages is that the study of psychotherapy has to submit to the characteristics of the delivery system, as a system. Studies of individual cases, small group research (even though well-conceived and executed), and the vast panorama of outcome research (seldom recognized to be beholden to attrition as it is) are all interesting and useful to a point, but they do not address the most salient issues regarding psychotherapy theory, research, or practice. What is needed, it is held, is research that deals in a variety of ways with how the system as a whole operates, how systems compare with each other, how they are similar or different across age, sex, demographics, diagnostic categories, and so on. This chapter, along with the rest of this book, pinpoints a few questions about systems as a whole as they deliver psychotherapy services (the same matters apply, of course, to medical service delivery and perhaps to other delivery systems as well, all vastly open terrains for new research and practices beyond the limits of this volume). Because the study of how mental health delivery systems operate has been miniscule, our own present efforts only suggest a few leads and contribute a beginning to a data base on an important and ranging topic.

THE UNIVERSITY COUNSELING CENTER AS A SYSTEM

A university counseling center setting is an appropriate one in which to begin some kind of research on how delivery systems operate. The counseling center is in operation chiefly during the regular academic year, from September to June, and can be expected to show definite characteristics associated with the availability of actual or potential clientele. Community mental health centers would be expected to have a different in-flow of clientele, less seasonally controlled and certainly not with the vast fluctuations in potential clientele in the community that the university setting shows. All delivery systems might be expected to show some seasonal or other changes and just what such changes are on a month-to-month or trimester or semester basis remains to be researched and described. There is one very interesting research area for people influenced by the notion that delivery systems, qua systems, make up the information base needed in most if not all mental health areas, because the delivery system itself influences how the theory and practice of mental health intervention is carried out (how delivery systems in medical areas operate may also be influenced by the theory and practice related to the particular disease or illness). If it can be shown that mental health delivery systems of any type (counseling centers, mental health centers, etc.) are influenced by cyclic patterns, then this information is of importance in its own right for matters of efficiency and economy, but may also range into other areas of importance relating to the theory that purports to guide mental health practice. The rest of this chapter is devoted to a very preliminary exploration of some cyclic or patterned aspects of the delivery system in a university counseling center.

EXAMINING FOUR HYPOTHESES

Even though the university counseling center is in operation throughout the calendar year, the bulk of applications for mental health services occur during the academic year, from August or September to May or June. Within this 8–10 month period of time, the flow of intake cases varies; this variation must first be described, then possible implications of the variability further examined.

Covering the 1981–1982 period as the data base, the following hypotheses were studied:

1. The flow of cases will not be the same, month by month, throughout the academic year. Although this is an obvious hypothesis, its descriptive content has been lacking in the literature and is further needed for explication of the other hypotheses, to follow.
2. The male/female breakdown, although known for the whole year— over an 8-year data base span (60/40, F/M percent)—is not expected to be the same month by month throughout the academic year. Considerable variation is hypothesized.
3. The mean number of therapy sessions will vary with the month of the year, being larger at time of low intake (early fall), descending as intake and

academic year moves to the end (late spring), then rising again as intake diminishes.

4. Some personality characteristics will be associated with earlier admission to the counseling center on the basis of assertive, self-examining interests; this will be shown by higher Bem "masculinity" scale scores for both sexes earlier in each semester and such scores will diminish by the end of each semester.

Figures 5.1 through 5.4, respectively, display the results associated with these hypotheses.

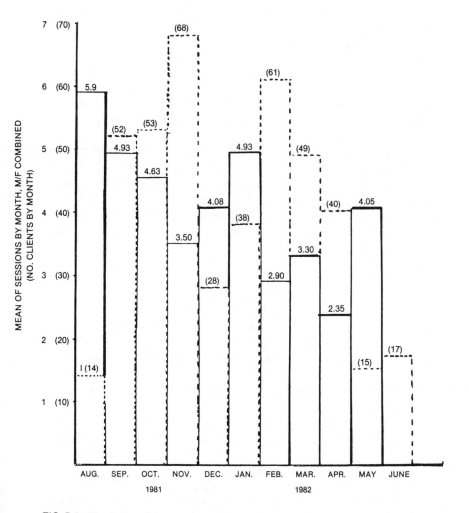

FIG. 5.1 Total clientele by month, 1981–1982. Comparing length of therapy with number clients at intake.

HYPOTHESIS 1

Figure 5.1, total number of client intakes, month by month, 1981–1982, shows considerable variation, from 14 intakes at the lower time (August, 1981) to a high level of 68 (November, 1981), an intake ratio of more than 5-to-1. Comparing August, 1981, with February, 1982, a ratio of 13 to 61, respectively, nearly 5 to 1 again, displays considerable variation in clinic activity at different points in time. The fall, 1981, semester (September through December) showed 201 intakes; the spring semester (January through May, 1982) showed 203 intakes. If we leave out May, 1982, a short month as far as students attending classes is concerned, the January through April N becomes 188. Each semester averages 45 to 50 client intakes per month, the fall for 4 months, the spring for about 4–4 1/2 months. Relatively low intake months, then, such as August (before the semester formally begins) and May and June (toward or after the close of the spring semester) are distinctly different from the regular school months insofar as intakes are concerned, *and insofar as length of therapy is concerned.* The correlation between number of intakes for personal/social therapy and the subsequent length of therapy was − .44, with $p = .20$, showing a small but unreliable trend. Drawing clientele from one or another month for research or other purposes may have some impact on a number of variables such as length of therapy, male/female intake per month, and perhaps personality characteristics of the incoming clientele. The lack of homogeneity from month to month in at least the number of intakes likely influences — and is influenced by — the system, qua system, and may ramify into other areas. Some of the other areas of impact are related to hypotheses 2, 3, and 4.

HYPOTHESIS 2

Hypothesis 2 states that the female/male breakdown will vary also by month, even though the overall average for the year was 65/35% (1981–1982 only); the overall F/M ratio for an 8-year period was 60/40. Leaving out July and August in the present tabulation may have had some influence on the 65/35 ratio, pushing it away from the 60/40% level, but this is a relatively minor variation.

Month by month breakdown (see Fig. 5.2) shows females even with males in August, 1981, but with the advent of the academic year, the female population looms much larger and exceeds the 60/40 ratio for the overall figures as well as the 65/35 ratio for the 1981–82 academic year. In September, October, and November the total number of F/Ms is 118/53, well over 2 to 1. Observing further the 1982 portion of the 1981–82 academic year, we see again a near-equal January intake, then return to the predominant female ratio in-

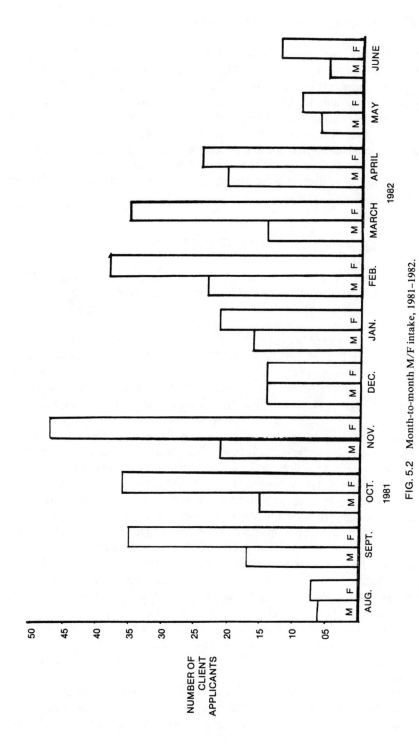

FIG. 5.2   Month-to-month M/F intake, 1981–1982.

NUMBER OF
CLIENT
APPLICANTS

109

take for February to April (the latter F/M Ss = 117/53, a 2.2 ratio compared to a 1.5 to 1 for the 8-year period). May, 1982, returns to the standard 1.5 to 1 ratio, but June, probably with more female summer school enrollment in proportion to males, rises again to over the 2-to-1 ratio. The point here is that the variation from month to month ranges widely and barely approximates the yearly overall figures, and that this wide gender variation can influence client responsiveness to a number of service delivery and research considerations. There is, then, a far from homogeneous flow of cases from the beginning to the end of the academic year as to total clientele intakes as well as to F/M ratios.

HYPOTHESIS 3

Hypothesis 3 concerning the number of therapy sessions as a function of the month of intake begins to put more flesh on the skeleton of impact from time-of-year data (see Fig. 5.3). The mean number of therapy sessions for August, the sparsest intake time, is 4.80 for males (N = 6, from Fig. 5.2 data) and 7.0 for females (N = 7 from Fig. 5.2 data). These mean figures are higher than the overall mean for the year, 1981–82 (4.11). September and October intake data for number of sessions fall back closer to the overall mean for the year; but December breaks the pattern and on the face of the data (as means) we would have trouble explaining this variation save for the possibility that the near-equal F/M intakes for December (14 cases, each) may show some other kind of slight atypicality in who comes for intake at this time, perhaps based on variables we have not yet identified. January, 1982, average number of therapy sessions for both males and females rises somewhat along with the lesser number of intakes; both variables subsequently change — according to the hypothesis — for February to May, in that as the intake number goes up during this 4-month period the mean number of therapy sessions goes down. The end-of-the-year phenomenon of female change in number of therapy sessions (for April admissions) is interesting, suggesting further that females and males behave quite differently in the number of sessions and that the April intake of females may mean they are somewhat different from what they have been during the year and different from males as well. It should be remembered that these are all personal/social/emotional problem cases, not problems such as study skills or career choice; hence the impact of the semester's end or the year's end would not seem to relate to the more strictly academic matters. In general, then, the slope of the mean number of therapy sessions per month against the number of intakes per month, combined M/F figures (despite some gender differences), shows a negative relationship. This now becomes a system variable in that as the system is low on intake clientele it tends on the average to give more time to incoming patients, but as the sys-

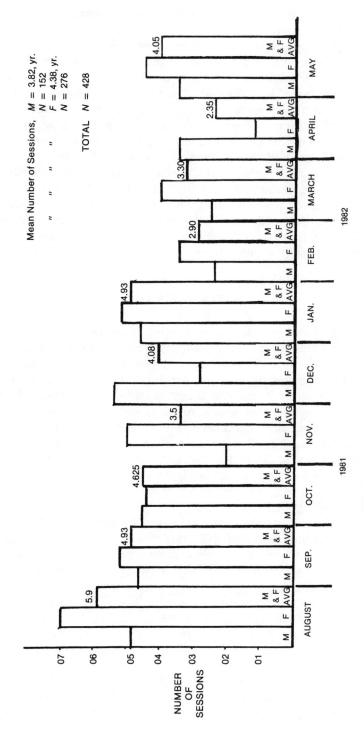

FIG. 5.3 Mean number therapy sessions by month of intake.

111

tem gets loaded (or overloaded?), the average number of sessions works out to be less. It is a way, perhaps, that the system accommodates itself to the intake phenomenon, despite need or degree of disturbance (we have no direct information on "need" or "disturbance" but it will become a matter for research in the future). If the presumed need in the form of the number applying for help each month were to stay constant — say an average of 35–40 clients per month instead of the observed variation — what would the system do to accommodate itself? Would the average number of sessions per month be more nearly equal? Would there still be an imposed variation owing to the end of the semester (or the academic year) that would impose time limits similar to those observed now? Or would some other pattern emerge? These are interesting research questions and will have to be answered over time among clinics offering different patterns of time-related services, i.e., less variation from month to month or with different patterns during the year.

HYPOTHESIS 4

Pursuing the fouth hypothesis calls attention to the possibility that some personality variable might be related to the time of the year when clients apply for help. Upon inspecting data early on from the Bem scale, it appeared that the clients coming early in the year were more assertive, clear, and definitive about their need for help — not implying greater need but more likely a better definition of presumed need — compared with those coming later, perhaps procrastinating more, being less certain about help-seeking or more ambivalent about what it might offer them. Whatever the accompanying attitude basis, it appeared that higher masculine scores for both sexes might accrue as a function of time of intake. Figure 5.4 summarizes the month-by-month data, each sex, Bem "masculine-feminine" scores, throughout the 1981–1982 academic year.

Although Fig. 5.4 suggests that male scores are higher on the Bem scale from August through December, 1981, this variation does not hold up for females. In fact, female Bem-masculine scores tend to be lower than Bem-female scores and tended, moreover, to go down somewhat between August and December. During the second semester, January to May, 1982, the scores for male clients appear to diminish from January through March, but then appear to rise for April and May, indicating that there may be some other factor than time of year, perhaps variables other than assertiveness, that would account for this Bem masculine scale phenomenon. At the same time the females, January to May, 1982, show a "masculine" shift downward only between January and February, then an upward trend from March through May, a pattern inconsistent with the fourth hypothesis. These variations are not statistically reliable, as stated, but they may be noted for later study.

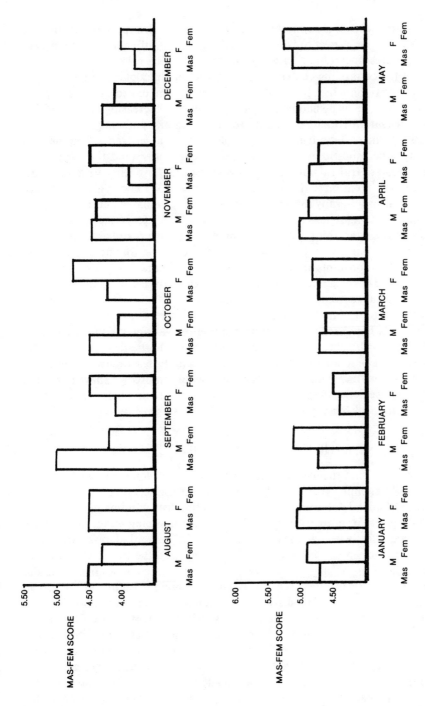

FIG. 5.4 Bem scores, by month, sex, and masculine (mas) & feminine (fem) score values. Total = 428.

Despite the meager support in relation to the fourth hypothesis, it could be that some other aspect of "decision making" might influence how long a client tolerates uncertainty, frustration, or ambivalence before applying for help at the counseling center. Fortuitous matters may play a role here—the casual mentioning by a friend of going for help, someone jokingly saying to a person that she or he had better get some help, or increasing conflict with a lover, friend, or roommate might prompt the intake-pursuing decision. It is doubtful, then, that any nuclear variable such as "assertiveness" on the Bem or any other questionnaire would now, as we understand these questionnaires, lead to fruitful notions of just when a potential client carries out some felt need or intention to the point of intake action. We know, also (see Chapter 4) that pre-therapy intake ambivalence and graduated action taking are common to a small percentage of the potential (and later actual) clients of the counseling center; this phenomenon might erase any possibly assertive effort on the potential client's part and render the likelihood that no consistent set of conditions prompts applying for help, anymore than the passage of time, the smelling of certain foods, or the like, prompts for certainty the subjective feeling of hunger and/or leads to eating.

The relative failure of this hypothesis about "assertive masculinity" might show again how hard it is to obtain pre-therapy variables with validity concerning going to, staying in, or profiting from psychotherapy. Whatever variables might be so identified would have to stand the test of attritional loss of clients—as we have abundantly seen—and would, moreover, have to remain valid and predictive despite flow of time (or month to month) changes, a sizable requirement for any variable at our present stage of knowledge.

THE ISSUE OF TREATMENT DELAY

Many clinics find themselves caught in the throes of long delays between intake and beginning therapy. The university setting seems to vary in this respect. Gelso and Johnson (1983) report waiting lists building up for periods of 6–10 weeks or more (p. xxi). In the present counseling center, delays have characteristically been in the order of 2–3 weeks, somewhat longer over holiday periods such as Thanksgiving, Christmas, and the Easter spring break period. Part of the cause of delays getting into therapy arises from inability to contact students to tell them an opening is available. Phone calls often fail to produce good communication with students; usually after two or three calls and messages, the potential client is written to with a specific appointment time indicated. This procedure appears to net better results, but no hard data are available on oral or written communications. Students have often remarked that calls concerning their impressions of the counseling center, their therapist, and their therapy experience allow them to feel warmly regarded with a personal interest taken in their impressions; however, phone calls for appointments for therapy are apparently fraught with more ambivalence by students; hence there is some slippage in this matter.

Data were accumulated over an entire academic year, 1982–1983, to determine first how long the delays were on the average and the range; the shortest delay was, of course, that of taking the client in for therapy the same or the next day following intake; the longest single delay for the specified period was 49 days, occasioned by failure to reach an ill and hospitalized client; other delays related to a client on an extended trip or ambivalent about continuing in school.

It is generally thought that long delays produce attrition from therapy. Although that notion has seldom been systematically investigated, it seems intuitively valid. Surely if delays getting into therapy are more than a few weeks, the propitiousness of the matter would seem to have passed, and more likely than not the problem requiring attention will have passed or help will have been received in alternative ways.

Research on delay getting into therapy was accomplished by taking a random sample of 58 cases from the year's clientele, 1982–1983. The mean number of days delay was 16.88 calendar days (subtract 4 week-end days, leaving a school days accumulation of 12.88 days, about 2½ weeks), with a standard deviation of 12.33 calendar days, yielding an r of $-.146$ ($p = .274$) with number of subsequent therapy sessions. Extracting the very longest delay cases from this flow — $N = 13$ cases — yielded a mean delay of 23 calendar days ($SD = 11.33$), and a mean number of subsequent therapy sessions of 6.00 ($SD = 8.19$). It is unlikely from these data in this particular counseling center setting that the length of delay is intolerable; and that only very extensive delays of 2 months or more will have a depressing effect on client readiness to enter therapy (in the immediate clinic where the long delay is encountered). Perhaps, too, the compactness of the university setting diminishes the meaning of delay getting into therapy inasmuch as the counseling center is always there physically and people are known to utilize its resources, possibly leading to a philosophical attitude that the prospective client will "sooner or later get in." This is not an attitude to be encouraged however; perhaps with more alert methods of handling intake generally there would be even less of a waiting period throughout the year. We have seen in the aforementioned how intake varies from month to month and how length of therapy appears to vary inversely with the fluctuating number of intakes per month; some of the longest delays getting into therapy may be occasioned by some of the longest-delay-clients coming in at peak intake times, becoming discouraged at any waiting more than a few days, hence, backing off from accepting therapy when it does become available. We do not have any data on this possible factor, however.

The procedure in the clinic reported on here is based on telling the client that he or she is placed temporarily on a waiting list but will be called soon by a therapist for an appointment. The client also is given the choice of a male or female therapist; if the client has further desires, such as a regular staff member (in contrast to a student/extern), or if there are any particular time arrangements that are narrowly necessary, those requests are honored if possible. Seldom, however, are extraordinary demands made on clinic time or personnel; the client being given options, however, leaves an impression that the staff is working hard to accommodate the student. This support appears to help tide the client over to the next regular appointment.

CLIENT RATINGS RELATED TO NUMBER OF SESSIONS

People who have one visit to a mental health setting may refuse to give a rating on their experience, saying, as expected, that they did not know enough about the whole matter to consider it validly. In spite of this demur, however, many clients with an intake-only or an intake and one therapy session do come up with ratings of their experience as we have seen in the early chapters of this book.

Keeping in mind that not all clients reply to questionnaires, data on the number of visits and client ratings of those visits are nonetheless somewhat informative. The baseline data for therapy clients responding to follow-up questionnaires are somewhere in the 35% to 40% range (see Chapter 2 data). Also, selectivity among clients who have had more sessions leads them to conform more to clinic requests, and to be willing to rate their experience in therapy more readily. Research on 56 randomly selected cases, 1982–1983, showed that the correlation between "global" ratings and therapy sessions attended netted an r of $+.015$, with a p of .28, an insignificant relationship.

THE ASYMPTOTE AND THE EXTENDED CASES

Filling out the picture of the flow of cases over time, the final consideration concerns the asymptote. The first two chapters have illustrated the importance of the asymptote and the extensive variations in the delivery of services it addresses. In the traditional literature on the length of psychotherapy, usually the range and the mean are the only data provided. Analysis of the flow of cases from study inception (or therapy intake) to termination and follow-up has been made explicit in this book by the attrition curve. In the Poisson distribution the mean and standard deviations are approximately equal. This distribution seems to characterize the flow of cases among all clinics we have been able to identify.

It is readily possible to compare clinic activities in the overal handling of cases via the Poisson distribution; in this section the extended cases, those going approximately three standard deviations beyond the mean, have been examined.

Research on short-term psychotherapy often omits reporting on relatively longer term cases (Baldwin, 1978; Cummings & VandenBos, 1979; Gelso & Johnson, 1983). At The George Washington University Counseling Center the staff has noted that about 8% (33 out of about 400 clients) extended beyond the 10-session limit 1982–1983; such extensions occurred among all but 2 of 14 therapists. No research on extended therapy cases has appeared in the literature; hence this study is of particular research and practical interest.

Subjects

For the academic year, 1982–1983, the total population of ostensible therapy cases was 399; their mean age was 23.19 years (SD = 6.48 years), and their F/M ratio was 60/40. The present study sample of 33 extended cases fell within this population; their mean age was 21.1 years (SD = 3.19 years), and the F/M ratio was 74/26; these cases were matched on the basis of age and sex with 27 client controls from the same therapists. These control cases had 10 or fewer sessions, an age mean of 21.3 years (SD = 3.10 years), and the same F/M ratio (74/26).

Procedure

Extended therapy cases were identified at the end of the 1982–83 year; their mean number of therapy sessions was 14.12 (SD = 2.95), compared to the control cases' mean of 5.58 sessions (SD = 4.99). Extended and control case files were reviewed to obtain demographic data and to confirm the accuracy of therapist interview information. All files were in the hands of the investigator during the therapist interviewing period.

The therapists (N = 12) were composed of five staff (Ph.D. plus 5 or more years therapy experience) and seven psychology graduate students with a minimum of 2 years therapy experience. Therapists were interviewed via a 16-item questionnaire covering client demographics and other intake and termination data. The interviews occurred over a 6-day span. All cases were covered in a single interview — except in two instances where time constraints necessitated a second interview — and cases were covered in a random order for each therapist's clientele.

Hypotheses

Six hypotheses were examined: (1) There would be a significant difference in the mean number of therapy sessions between extended cases and controls; (2) extended therapy cases would be rated by therapists as more disturbed both at the start and end of therapy; (3) extended cases would have experienced more extenuating life circumstances (serious illness, death in family, job/school failure, etc.) than controls; (4) extended cases would more often be from the same sex therapist/client pairs; (5) extended cases would be more "therapeutically responsive" in sessions, i.e., more self-disclosing, better liked by therapists, and more willingly seen again by therapists should the occasion arise; and (6) extended cases would more likely be referred out for additional therapy, despite their already higher mean number of sessions, due to the still remaining seriousness of their problems or life circumstances. Hypotheses were considered confirmed if they reached the .05 probability level.

Results

Findings were organized around replies to the 16-item questionnaire and client demographic information. The first hypothesis was confirmed; extended therapy cases showed by t-test a mean number of sessions significantly larger than the controls ($p < .01$). The significance of this hypothesis was pivotal to the testing of the remaining hypotheses, which netted the following results. The second hypothesis was rejected, showing that the extended therapy cases were not rated by therapists as more disturbed than control cases. The third hypothesis — that of extenuating circumstances of a serious nature in their own or family's lives — was not supported. Quantitatively, the extended cases did not have significantly more debilitating events in their own or family's lives, compared to controls. However, they did have qualitatively more serious incidents, including one suicide of a boyfriend, two stroke/heart attacks among parents, two abortions, and one probationary status for a legal offense. Extenuating life circumstances among the control cases were not as serious and included none of the previously mentioned.

The fourth hypothesis anticipating the extended cases to be generally more responsive to therapy was disconfirmed. The occurrence of like-sex F/M pairs more frequently than opposite sex pairs among the extended cases compared to controls (the fifth hypothesis) was disconfirmed. The sixth and final hypothesis that the extended cases would more often be referred out for more therapy was also disconfirmed. It could be that reasons for referral out were qualitatively different among the extended versus control cases, but this matter was not examined.

Implications

Although several factors may contribute to the occurrence of extended cases of therapy in a time-limited (10 session) context, no one reason or set of reasons, as herein examined, proved significant statistically. It was fully expected that the therapist-rated seriousness of the client's disturbance, the presence of formidable life problems, and therapist tendency to refer out the longer term cases would all occur, but not one was statistically significant. Qualitatively, the extenuating life circumstances were present in more serious degrees among the extended cases, but the overall incidence of such events — item for item across extended and control cases — was less than the amount needed to show statistical significance. However, this possibility among extended (or potentially extended) cases must always be held open.

Perhaps all clinics that utilize a time-limited framework will nonetheless have extended cases. Their occurrence, although less than 10% of the cases, inevitably takes considerably more staff time and should be planned for in clinic policy. Other factors that might contribute to the presence of extended therapy cases should be examined: time of year when clients enter therapy, the acute or chronic nature of their reasons for pursuing help, whether they have had prior therapy, and whether they later seek more therapy. (The last factor, seeking further therapy, is now under further investigation.)

An interesting finding from the mean number of sessions for cases raises a research question: Is the extended cases' mean of 14 visits, which approximates the same amount beyond the 10-session policy limit as the population mean of 4–6 sessions is below the 10-session limit, a kind of systemic adjustment that arises out of the structuring of the number of visits? That is, are extended cases in any context of limited therapy likely to "adjust" to a mean number of sessions where the mean is the same number of standard deviations above the policy limit as the population mean is below the policy limit? If this is a systems characteristic, any setting of limits might predict the nature of the extended cases vis-à-vis the policy limit. Even though national norms show a mean of about 5 therapy sessions as the most common figure, many clinics extend cases out to 20 or 30 or more sessions. This leads to the question of whether these extensions are a function of policy limits, their absence, or other factors of service delivery. The farther out the extension the more likely individual therapists contribute to this phenomenon; if extensions of sessions are contributed to by all staff members, it may more likely be a systemic feature of the delivery staff. There are many interesting problems in the study of the asymptote; the nature of the extended cases has not been explored heretofore, or even recognized as an issue. The more the service delivery economies and benefits are examined, the more the study of extended cases and the nature of the asymptote come into view. The systemic nature of service delivery is again supported in the questions raised — together with a few leading answers — in regard to the asymptote. Thus far in research, client characteristics or client/therapist features do not add much to our understanding of extended cases (Garfield, 1978). Here, again, the system, qua system, must become the unit of study, not so much individual clients or therapists or even dyads, unless some new perspective can be offered on these types of analysis. This study of the extended cases brings alive some important aspects of the asymptote and points up heuristic leads that require much more examination.

WIDER QUESTIONS REGARDING FLOW OF CASES

The studies reported in this chapter concern the flow of cases within the system. One could, of course, enlarge the notion of flow into, through, and out of the formal system called the clinic, in other ways. Although this larger flow of cases around the boundaries of the system is covered to some extent in other chapters (see Chapters 4, 6, and 7 as well as Chapter 10), there also are a number of ways in which the model of this chapter could be extended. For example, the extended cases could be studied in much greater detail, inasmuch as they, for whatever reason, exceed the boundaries of the present clinical delivery system that attempts to hold to a 10-session limit. Other features of the clients and the therapists should be examined in order to better understand these extended cases. Why some do and others do not go on further in therapy—and whether they might have been referred out at first blush to longer term therapy—and the circumstances surrounding the additional therapy, should be studied in great detail. Also, whether these extended cases—not greatly extended, to be sure, yet quite different in the number of sessions compared to all other in-clinic populations we have at our disposal—get more of what they need or desire later or whether they melt into self-help and community support groups are interesting, practical, and theoretical issues.

The early-on nature of applications to the clinic at the beginning of each semester is an important phenomenon to study more thoroughly. Are there simply pressures from the academic system that promote application to the clinic? Or, are there a number of cases that need to settle in academically and socially before they tackle social/emotional/personal problems? And are these, in turn, related to any particular personality issues or particular problem-status issues (e.g., more crises oriented)? We simply do not know. Further, support groups may define problem areas or need for help more fully and accurately than the individuals can themselves; thus a month or two into the semester may be enough time for this working-out of definitiveness of personal/social/emotional status to be clarified, thereby allowing or encouraging the person to go for formal help. Here, again, the gates are wide open for research. This may be, also, an important issue in service delivery: Clinics on campuses may do more outreach at the start of a new semester in order to provide a catchment for the marginally needy cases for mental health help who need not go into the formal system if they can be helped in more informal, support group ways. The outreach effort might take pressure off intake for the clinic at peak times in the fall and in the spring. The flow of cases through the clinic, the main body of the attrition curve as described herein, may raise many questions about outside support and grass roots help. If some observations alluded to in this book are correct — viz., that multiple sources of informal therapy are with us much of the time (more than is true of formal therapy systems) — then we should look carefully into this matter. Referral systems in residence halls, among professors, from deans' offices, and so forth, may give us a lot of data on how the informal support groups operate — or not — and how some clientele get into the formal system therefrom. If residence hall personnel could keep track of informal support systems, even in a general way, this would give us more information about referral into and out of the formal system than we can imagine now with our too often isolated posture.

Outside the university one could extend these observations to community clinics. Informal support systems exist more often than we might imagine in church groups, among job and vocational groups, in neighborhoods, and in relation to organizations (e.g., recreational settings). We shall have to tap into how these informal community and institutional groups operate, what they do for the mental health of persons, and how they replace, supplement or otherwise influence entrance into and out of the formal mental health system.

6 The Fagan Study of Intake

THE INTAKE SESSION: TERMINATORS AND CONTINUERS

The concern of this chapter is to give more detailed examination to a subpopulation within the 40%–50% of clients who terminate after having had the intake interview. The subpopulation is the 19%–25% of the clients who agree with the intake therapist that they do wish to begin therapy and who, subsequent to the intake interview, unilaterally terminate prior to the first therapy session. The 19%–25% has been widely reported at university counseling centers (Betz & Shullman, 1979; Epperson, 1981; Epperson, Bushway, & Warman, 1983; Rodolfa, Rappaport, & Lee, 1982) but no attrition data on this subpopulation have been reported at other mental health facilities.

What is it that accounts for these clients to "change their minds"? Is the intake session such that it discourages them from pursuing therapy? It would seem that it would be more difficult to show up for the initial contact than a subsequent one. With questions such as these the authors sought to examine a specific subpopulation within the attrition curve.

The data for the present research were available at The George Washington University Counseling Center (GWUCC) and are part of a larger longitudinal study being conducted by Phillips and associates.

Subjects. Prospective clients at GWUCC are identified administratively according to the type of assistance they seek. Three general categories are employed: personal-social therapy, career counseling and testing, and topical groups, e.g., study skills, weight control, and the like. The subjects for the present research were those prospective clients who came to the GWUCC during the fall 1982 and spring 1983 semester excluding:

1. Those whose stated purpose was for other than personal therapy; and
2. Those whose intake session was not during the last calendar month of either semester, i.e., December or April.

The latter condition sought to avoid a confounding factor, i.e., not enough time for a post-intake session prior to the semesters' endings.

Three hundred prospective clients met these initial conditions. There were 121 male clients (40.3%) and 179 female clients (59.7%). This is comparable to the 40–60% male-female differential that GWUCC has had in the past 8 years (Phillips & Fagan, 1982a, 1982b). The average age of the male clients was 22.1 years ($SD = 4.1$) and the female clients averaged 22.6 ($SD = 4.9$) years.

Of the 300 clients who had an intake interview 75 (25%; $N = 33$ males and 42 females) were terminated at intake. A quantifiable description of the reasons for termination was not part of the data kept on the clients. Typical reasons for termination suggested by the present staff were referral to other university departments, e.g., Dean's Office, or to a practitioner/clinic that offered long-term counseling or psychotherapy. The GWUCC offers short-term (10-session limit) behaviorally oriented psychotherapy.

Table 6.1 compares further those who terminated and those who agreed to begin therapy. Among the variables examined no significant difference between the groups was found, although there was a tendency ($p = .0504$) for younger female clients to terminate at intake.

Of central concern to the present study were those clients ($N = 225$) who at the conclusion of the intake interview agreed to begin therapy at GWUCC. Of these 225 clients ($N = 88$ males [39.1%] and 137 females [60.9%]), 44 (19.6%) did not return for the first therapy session although they had requested and had been assigned a therapist. This group was designated as Terminators ($N = 44$). Those who did return for at least one session were labeled Continuers ($N = 181$). A further description of these groups is made in the Results section.

METHOD

The counseling staff at GWUCC consisted of six staff psychologists (three female and three male) and eight master degree level (Ph.D. candidates) externs (five female and three male) in clinical psychology.

TABLE 6.1
Description of Clients Terminated at Intake and Those Assigned a Therapist

Variable	Term. at Intake (N = 75)	Assigned Therapist (N = 225)	p Value
Age of client			
Male ($t(117) = .941$)	21.91 (3.96)	22.71 (4.21)	.349
Female ($t(176) = 1.98$)	21.60 (3.94)	23.09 (5.18)	.0504
Sex of client (chi-sq. (1,300) = .561)			.455
Male	33 (27.27%)	88 (72.73%)	
Female	42 (23.46%)	137 (76.54%)	
Sex of therapist (chi-sq. (1,298) = 1.30)			.255
Male	40 (27.78%)	104 (72.22%)	
Female	34 (22.08%)	120 (77.92%)	
Therapist experience level (chi-sq. (1,300) = 1.60)			.205
Externs	45 (22.73%)	153 (77.27%)	
Senior Staff	30 (29.41%)	72 (70.59%)	
Sex of therapist × sex of client			
Male Therapists (chi-sq. (1,144) = .304)			.582
Male Clients	17 (30.36%)	39 (69.64%)	
Female Clients	23 (26.14%)	65 (73.86%)	
Female Therapists (chi-sq. (1,154) = .118)			.732
Male Clients	15 (23.44%)	49 (76.56%)	
Female Clients	19 (21.11%)	71 (78.89%)	

PROCEDURE

The data were collected by the GWUCC clerical and research staff in two stages: pre-intake and post-intake.

Pre-intake. As part of the standard intake process, clients approaching the GWUCC for personal-social counseling were asked to complete a registration form containing demographic items. Descriptive data were gathered on clients and staff members involved in intake interviews. Among these were age of client, sex of client and therapist, education level of client, experience level of therapist, and major presenting complaint. Clients were informed verbally that the registration form as well as other forms to be completed later would be used for research purposes, that confidentiality would be assured, that participation was voluntary, and that the results of the research would be made available to them upon request. Upon completion of the registration forms the clients returned them to the receptionist.

Post-intake. At the completion of the intake interview the therapist asked the client to complete a six-item Session Scale-Client (SS-C) designed to assess the client's satisfaction with the session, the therapist, and the probability of continuation with therapy (see following). The client was informed that the intake therapist would not see the results of the individual client's rating and responses and that the intake therapist might or might not be assigned to the client as therapist. The forms were completed outside the intake therapist's office and returned to the receptionist. In a similar manner, the therapist completed a six-item Session Scale-Therapist (SS-T) immediately after the session. The items reflected the same content as the SS-C but from the position of the therapist rating the session, the client, and the probability of the client's continuation in therapy.

The intake therapists at GWUCC wrote brief descriptions of the clients and their presenting problems. The descriptions were combined with the demographic data supplied by the clients and used by the Intake Committee to assign the client to a therapist. The Intake Committee was composed of the assistant director of the center, a senior staff member, and two externs. The assignments made by the Intake Committee were not random but were made considering such factors as client need, therapist skill, scheduling, availability of therapist, and training needs of externs. After being informed of a client assignment, the therapist contacted the client by telephone (usually) or, if failing by telephone, by letter to arrange the initial therapy session.[1] The average length of days between the intake interview and the initial therapy session was approximately 2 calendar weeks.

Scale Content and Development.   The SS-C and the SS-T scales are both composed of six Likert-type items (1 = "thoroughly disagree" to 7 = "thoroughly agree"). The content of each item is similar to its corresponding number in the other scale. The six items are:

SS-C	SS-T
1. I found the interview helpful.	1. The interview was helpful to the client.
2. The counselor seemed to understand me in what I discussed.	2. I understood the client in what he or she discussed.
3. The counselor encouraged me to think I can be helped at the Counseling Center.	3. I encouraged the client to think he or she could be helped at the Counseling Center.
4. I liked the counselor.	4. I liked the client.

[1]Data were not available concerning the method of contact employed for each client. It should be noted that the method of patient contact at this point in the process may account for some variance in attrition.

5. I would like to work with this counselor in the matter we discussed.

5. I would like to work with this client in the matter we discussed.

6. Regardless of which counselor works with me, I feel that I will be able to make progress in therapy.

6. Regardless of which counselor works with this client, I feel the client will be able to make progress in therapy.

As noted, the content of the SS-C items reflected those of the SS-T with the obvious difference that the client is the rater and the therapist the rated. They were designed by Phillips and associates to address what they felt to be the salient features of the intake session, i.e., an empathic collaboration by client and therapist in understanding the client's problem and the client's clarification of whether or not therapy would be helpful. In this construct the task of the intake session was to initiate suitable clients into the therapy system. The suitability of the client for therapy is a judgment made ideally by client and intake therapist mutually, only secondarily by the therapist alone.

Reliability. Using the intake interviews ($N = 476$) of the entire 1982–83 academic year as a sample, both the SS-C and the SS-T were tested for reliability. A single factor repeated measures design analysis of variance was employed. The SS-C was found to have a split-halves correlation of .96, a measure of how stable the same thing will be measured over time by the two halves, and a Spearman–Brown reliability coefficient of .98, a measure of how reliable the combination of the two parts is. Correspondingly, the SS-T had a split-halves correlation of .94 and a Spearman–Brown reliability coefficient of .97. With such high reliability coefficients, the variation in observed scores due to errors of measurement was judged to be significantly minimal as to establish the reliability of the scales.

At the time of the administration of the SS-C and SS-T the instruments had only the face validity of each item.

RESULTS

The Terminators and Continuers were compared initially for any significant difference in the variables of age and sex of client, sex of therapist, therapist experience level, and the interaction of sex of therapist and sex of client. As shown in Table 6.2, none of these selected demographic variables showed a significant relationship to termination or continuing on for the first therapy session, although male clients tended ($p = .056$) to have a higher post-intake attrition rate when seen by male intake therapists than when seen by female intake therapists.

TABLE 6.2
Description of Criterion Groups

Variable	Terminators (N = 44)	Continuers (N = 181)	p Value
Age of client			
Male (t(58) = .42)	23.13 (5.25)	22.63 (4.00)	.673
Female (t(134) = .47)	22.69 (5.37)	23.20 (5.15)	.642
Sex of client (chi-sq. (1,225) = .58)			.447
Male	15 (17.05%)	73 (82.95%)	
Female	29 (21.17%)	108 (78.83%)	
Sex of therapist (chi-sq. (1,224) = 2.93)			.087
Male	25 (24.04%)	79 (75.96%)	
Female	18 (15.00%)	102 (85.00%)	
Therapist experience level (chi-sq. (1,225) = .56)			.454
Externs	32 (20.92%)	121 (79.08%)	
Senior Staff	12 (16.69%)	60 (83.33%)	
Sex of client × sex of therapist			
Male Clients (chi-sq. (1,88) = 3.66)			.056
Male Therapists	10 (25.64%)	29 (74.36%)	
Female Therapists	5 (10.20%)	44 (89.80%)	
Female Clients (chi-sq. (1,136) = .47)			.492
Male Therapists	15 (23.08%)	50 (76.92%)	
Female Therapists	13 (18.31%)	58 (81.69%)	

Samples for Hypotheses Testing. Of the 225 clients who agreed at intake to begin therapy and who had the intake session prior to the last month of the semester, 21 (9.3%) either declined to complete the forms or neglected to return the SS-C to the receptionist. Of the 204 SS-Cs returned, 198 were completed. In light of the fact that the SS-C contained only six items, the six incomplete SS-Cs were not included in the analysis of the first and third hypotheses that involved the client ratings.

Therapists returned an identical number (N = 204) of SS-Ts. There were two SS-Ts with missing items and these were not included in the examination of hypotheses 2 and 3 that involved therapists' ratings.

Thus among the 225 subjects of the research there were 44 Terminators (19.6%) and 181 Continuers (80.4%), although in analyzing the three main hypotheses, missing data decreased these groups to 198 (35 Terminators and 163 Continuers) for the first hypothesis, 202 (36 Terminators and 166 Continuers) for the second hypothesis and 196 (34 Terminators and 162 Continuers) for the third hypothesis.

NORMALITY

Two facts about the subjects and the instrumentation suggested that the distribution of the data be examined. First, the sample of subjects was drawn from a student population whose ages were 17–45 years, most of whom clustered around the mean of 22.8 years ($SD = 4.6$). Second, the SS-C and the SS-T were scales that had not been used previously. In light of these two facts, age of client and SS-C and SS-T ratings were examined to determine if these data were normally distributed. Table 6.3 displays the results of examining age of clients and the Likert ratings of the SS-C and the SS-T with the null hypothesis that the data of these variables comes from a normal distribution. Using the Kolomogorov-Smirnov S-statistic the assumption of normal-

TABLE 6.3
Test of Normality of SS-C and SS-T Items

Variable	N	Mean	SD	D:Normal*
SS-C				
1. Client felt interview helpful.	204	6.11	1.11	.240
2. Client felt understood.	204	6.31	1.01	.272
3. Client felt encouraged about help at GWUCC.	202	6.17	1.09	.257
4. Client liked therapist.	204	6.42	1.00	.331
5. Client wanted to work intake therapist.	200	5.78	1.56	.257
6. Client felt able to make progress in therapy.	198	5.54	1.41	.249
SS-T				
1. Therapist felt interview helpful to client.	204	5.41	0.99	.224
2. Therapist felt he/she understood client.	204	5.86	0.98	.302
3. Therapist felt he/she encouraged about help at GWUCC.	203	6.05	1.00	.278
4. Therapist liked client.	204	5.61	1.25	.273
5. Therapist wanted to work with client.	203	5.15	1.60	.180
6. Therapist felt client would progress in therapy.	202	5.33	1.25	.210
Client age	223	22.94	4.82	.181

*all values $p < .01$

ity was rejected ($p < .01$) for age of client and all 12 items of the SS-C and the SS-T.

With normality not a viable assumption for age of client and the SS-C and the SS-T items, it was decided to treat these variables as dichotomous variables with a median split. A decision rule was designed to allow the high-low split to be as close to the median as possible for all 13 variables. The rule was: age of client, SS-C or SS-T Likert rating would be assigned to the low cell if it was below the 55th percentile; if equal to or above the 55th percentile it would be assigned to the high cell. This decision rule resulted in 50.22% of the subjects being assigned to a low age of client group cell and 7 of the 12 SS-C and SS-T Likert ratings being split within 5 percentage points of the 50th percentile. It also allowed for a Likert rating of 6 (maximum = 7) on SS-T 2,3 and 4 to be scored as a high thus avoiding a possible overinterpretation of any score less than the maximum 7 rating as being a "low" rating. The data in Table 6.4 indicates cumulative percentages of SS-C and SS-T ratings assigned to the high-low dichotomous categories.

Demographic Variables.   Corrigan, Dell, Lewis, and Schmidt (1980) have reported that certain client and therapist demographic characteristics may affect the client's ratings of therapist attributes. That these characteristics may also affect therapist ratings of client attributes cannot be discounted. Therefore the item scores for the SS-C and SS-T were examined for differences based on sex of client, client age, sex of therapist and therapist experience level (Ph.D staff and M.A. externs), and the interaction of sex of client and sex of therapist.

In summary, the analyses indicated four significant differences in ratings on the SS-C out of a possible 30 tests. The likelihood of 4 out of 30 tests being significant by chance alone is $p < .05$ (Sadoka, Cohen, & Beall, 1954).

1. Younger clients felt less understood (SS-C 2);
2. Male clients felt less encouraged (SS-C 3);
3. Clients rated senior staff more likable (SS-C 4) and;
4. Clients preferred to work with senior staff therapists (SS-C 5).

Analyses of the SS-T indicated three significant differences out of 30 tests.

1. Senior staff felt they encouraged the client less than did externs (SS-T 3);
2. Externs rated clients lower in likability than did senior staff (SS-T 4); and
3. In one interaction of variables male therapists felt less hopeful about future progress if they had seen male clients rather than female clients (SS-T

TABLE 6.4
Composition of SS-C and SS-T High-Low Categories Following Split

Variable	Likert split	N Low	N High
SS-C 1	6/7	92 (45%)	112 (55%)
SS-C 2	6/7	100 (49%)	104 (51%)
SS-C 3	6/7	105 (52%)	97 (48%)
SS-C 4	6/7	79 (39%)	125 (61%)
SS-C 5	6/7	105 (25%)	95 (48%)
SS-C 6	5/6	75 (38%)	123 (72%)
SS-T 1	5/6	102 (50%)	102 (50%)
SS-T 2	5/6	52 (25%)	152 (75%)
SS-T 3	5/6	41 (20%)	162 (80%)
SS-T 4	5/6	71 (35%)	133 (65%)
SS-T 5	5/6	106 (52%)	97 (48%)
SS-T 6	5/6	100 (49%)	102 (51%)

6). Female therapists indicated no significant difference in ratings of their clients regardless of sex of client.

Thus where hypothesis testing involved SS-C 2,3,4, and 5 or SS-T 2, 3, and 4 the ratings were analyzed separately for the appropriate variables of age of client group, sex of client, therapist experience level, sex of therapist, and the interaction of sex of therapist and sex of client. Table 6.5 shows the SS-C and SS-T items with the demographic groups that were analyzed separately.

Principal Components Analysis.   As a final step in the statistical description of the instruments employed, an exploratory principal components analysis was performed on the raw scores of the 12 items of the SS-C and SS-T. The purpose of this procedure was to identify the latent structural characteristics of the instruments (Green, 1978) as satisfactions scales of two persons, client and therapist, to a shared phenomenon, the intake session. Following Kaiser's (1959) recommendation that only principal components with eigenvalues greater than one be retained, three factors were obtained from the correlation matrix; Factor 1 (eigenvalue = 4.51); Factor 2 (eigenvalue = 2.42); and Factor 3 (eigenvalue = 1.19). Table 6.6 contains a display of the loadings of the SS-C and SS-T items on the three principal factors.

For greater intelligibility, the factors were rotated using a Varimax rotation, and a decision rule of considering only those items loading more than

.49 (rounded) on the rotated factor pattern was employed. The factors were then interpreted as Factor 1 — Response Of Intake Counselor; Factor 2 — Client's Response To Intake Session; Factor 3 — Encouragement Shared And Progress Foreseen By Client. Table 6.7 indicates the rotated loadings of the SS-C and SS-T items on the principle factors with those loadings less than .49 omitted.

Using the obtained standard scoring coefficients, factor scores were calculated for each subject. The factor scores were then used as predictors in an exploratory two group discriminant analysis of an approximate 50% random selection ($N = 117$) of the research sample. The generalized square distance

TABLE 6.5
SS-C and SS-T Items that were Analyzed Separately
by Demographic Groups

Items	Demographic Groups
SS-C	
1. Client felt interview helpful.	
2. Client felt understood.	2. Age of client
3. Client felt encouraged about help at GWUCC.	3. Sex of client
4. Client liked therapist.	4. Experience level of therapist
5. Client wanted to work with intake therapist.	5. Experience level of therapist
6. Client felt able to make progress in therapy.	
SS-T	
1. Therapist felt interview helpful to client.	
2. Therapist felt he or she understood client.	
3. Therapist felt he or she encouraged about help at GWUCC.	3. Experience level of therapist
4. Therapist liked client.	4. Experience level of therapist
5. Therapist wanted to work with client.	
6. Therapist felt client would progress in therapy.	6. Sex of therapist

TABLE 6.6
Principal Components and Factor Pattern of SS-C and SS-T

Variable	Factor 1	Factor 2	Factor 3
SS-C 1	0.652	0.459	−0.077
SS-C 2	0.461	0.601	0.117
SS-C 3	0.471	0.501	0.296
SS-C 4	0.491	0.656	−0.179
SS-C 5	0.525	0.514	−0.415
SS-C 6	0.314	0.296	0.557
SS-T 1	0.691	−0.387	0.153
SS-T 2	0.783	−0.168	−0.051
SS-T 3	0.532	−0.286	0.514
SS-T 4	0.770	−0.345	−0.324
SS-T 5	0.720	−0.466	−0.286
SS-T 6	0.744	−0.465	0.140
Eigenvalue	4.51	2.42	1.19
Difference	2.10	1.30	0.67
Proportion	0.38	0.20	0.09
Cumulative	0.38	0.58	0.67

between the Terminators and Continuers was 0.059. The resulting linear discriminant function was able to predict group membership in Terminators and Continuers at a hit rate of 47% for the Terminators and 66% for the Continuers. This was felt to be so close to chance (.50 prior probability) and considerably less than the predictable 82% hit rate if all cases were assigned to Continuers according to the maximum chance criterion (Huberty, 1984) that further analysis utilizing the linear discriminant function as a predictor on the remaining 50% of the sample was ceased.

Hypothesis 1. There were three major hypotheses of the research. The first hypothesis was to examine whether the client's satisfaction with the intake session would be predictive of attrition. Based on previous research (Zamostny, Corrigan, & Eggert, 1981) who had reported a positive but not significant relationship, it was expected that clients' satisfaction with intake using the SS-C ratings would predict attrition. This hypothesis was examined with each of the six items of the SS-C split into high-low categories as previously described.

A two-group discriminant analysis was performed. In addition to the six items of the SS-C, sex of client, age of client group, and therapist experience level were used as independent dichotomous variables because they had proved to have had significant effect in the SS-C ratings (2,3,4, and 5). The generalized squared distance between the Terminators and the Continuers was .30. The linear discriminant function was able to classify correctly 57.14% ($N = 20$) of the Terminators and 63.80% ($N = 104$) of the Continuers. With an external two-group prior probability of .50 and a potential 82% hit rate of correct classification if all cases were assigned to Continuers, the

TABLE 6.7
Varimax Rotated Factor Pattern of SS-C and SS-T

Variable	Factor 1	Factor 2	Factor 3
SS-C			
1. Client felt interview helpful.		.73	
2. Client felt understood.		.69	
3. Client felt encouraged about help at GWUCC.		.58	.50
4. Client liked therapist.		.83	
5. Client wanted to work with intake therapist.		.81	
6. Client felt able to make progress in therapy.			.67
SS-T			
1. Therapist felt interview helpful to client.	.76		
2. Therapist felt he or she understood client.	.73		
3. Therapist felt he or she encouraged about help at GWUCC.	.53		.58
4. Therapist liked client.	.86		
5. Therapist wanted to work with client.	.89		
6. Therapist felt client would progress in therapy.	.85		
Variance	3.75	2.89	1.41

Final Communality Estimates: Total = 8.05

linear discriminant function produced by the SS-C including client sex and age of client group and therapist experience level was judged too weak in its predictive ability for further statistical analysis.

The six dichotomous ratings of the SS-C were then examined as independent variables using a general linear model multiple regression controlling for client age group, sex of client, and therapist experience level. The dependent variable was established as criterion group membership (Terminators = 0 and Continuers = 1) in a multiple regression for a two-group discrimination (Kerlinger, 1973). The entire model had an R^2 of .04 and was not significant, $(F (9,198) = 0.92, p = .51)$.

A variable was constructed by summing the six items of the SS-C (high = 1, low = 0) for a possible minimum value of 0 creating a range of 0-6. Controlling for age of client, sex of client, and therapist experience level, this sum variable also was used in a multiple regression procedure to predict group membership. The entire model was not significant, $(F (4,198) = 0.91, p = .46)$ and had an $R^2 = .02$. The summed variable was not significant $(F (1,198) = 0.97, p = .33)$ and had an $r = .09$.

Finally the first hypothesis that client satisfaction as measured by the SS-C would not be predictive of return for the first therapy session was examined by the use of a chi-square statistic analyzing separately those client groups shown to have significant differences in ratings for particular SS-C items (Table 6.5). None of the six SS-C items showed a significant effect in the expected direction of Terminators more frequently giving a low rating than Continuers. Only one item approached significance $(p = .068)$ and that was SS-C 6 in which 51.4% of the Terminators and only 35.0% of the Continuers gave a low rating to their *foreseeing progress in future therapy*.

In summary, statistical analysis of the first hypothesis indicated no significant results that would support the hypothesis that clients' reported satisfaction with intake can predict attrition. This finding is consistent with the results of Zamostny et al. (1981) that the clients' ratings after intake are predictive of attrition.

Hypothesis 2.   The second major hypothesis was that therapist satisfaction with the intake interview would predict attrition. The procedures used for the statistical analysis of this hypothesis followed those used for the first hypothesis. The six items of the SS-T were split into high and low categories. A two-group discriminant analysis was performed that included the variables of sex of client, counselor sex, therapist experience level, and were included with the SS-T items as the independent variables. The generalized squared distance between the Terminators and Continuers was 0.49 and the linear discriminant function obtained was able to classify correctly 63.3% of the Continuers and 62.9% of the Terminators. With a .50 prior statistical probability and an 82% clinical probability, this linear discriminant function, as that obtained from the SS-C, was only slightly better than chance and considerably less than clinical predictability. It was considered useless for further attempts at statistical discrimination or prediction.

The two variables, therapist experience level and the interaction of client sex with sex of therapist, that had shown a significant effect on rating the SS-T items 3, 4, and 6 were employed as controls for the six dichotomous SS-T items in a multiple regression procedure. The dependent variable was the criterion group membership (Terminators = 0; Continuers = 1). The entire model was not significant, F (8,201) = 1.09, p = .37 and had an R^2 of .04. However SS-T 4, when added last in the regression model was a significant (F (1,201) = 4.07, p = .045) predictor of attrition in which the clients whom intake therapists rated less likable tended (r = −.004) to terminate before the first therapy session.

An additional multiple regression was performed using the summed variable of the six SS-T items (high = 1; low = 0) and controlling for therapist experience level and the interaction of client sex and sex of therapist. Again the entire model was not significant, (F (4,201) = 0.65, p = .59), and had an R^2 of .01. The summed variable of interest was not significant, (F (1,201) = 0.65, p = .42) and had an R^2 of .07.

A chi-square test of each SS-T item × criterion group (Terminators vs. Continuers) while examining separately therapist experience level on SS-T 3 and sex of therapist × sex of client on SS-T 6 yielded no significant results. However, when asked if they felt the male clients would make progress in therapy, male intake therapists gave lower ratings to 75% of the Terminators (N = 6) and to 30% of the Continuers (N = 8), χ^2 (1,35) = 3.53, p = .058 (adjusted for continuity).

In summary of the statistical analyses of the second hypothesis, there was one significant result amidst many findings of nonsignificance. Only in one instance did therapist giving Terminators lower ratings in "liking" them predict attrition. In the main, SS-T ratings were unable to discriminate between clients who would return for the first therapy session and those who would unilaterally terminate after the intake session. The second main hypothesis that therapist ratings do not predict attrition is not rejected.

Hypothesis 3.   The third major hypothesis was that low congruence between client and therapist's high satisfaction ratings will predict post-intake attrition.

A congruence score (CS) was calculated for each item pair (SS-C 1 + SS-T 1; SS-C 2 + SS-T 2; etc.) by giving a CS of 1 to each pair whose ratings were both in the high half of their splits, i.e., high SS-C item and high SS-T item. All three other combinations (high SS-C + low SS-T; low SS-C + low SS-T; high SS-T + low SS-C) were given a CS of 0. The possible range for each pair's CS was 0 to 6. The CS was then examined with a multiple regression analysis for its ability to predict the dependent variable, criterion group membership (Terminators = 0; Continuers = 1). The selected demographic variables that had shown a significant effect in the SS-C and SS-T ratings were employed as controls. They were age group of client, sex of client, sex intake of therapist, therapist experience level, and the interaction of sex of client and sex of therapist. Analysis indicated that the CS of the subjects did not have a significant effect upon criterion group membership ($r = .07$), ($F (1,195) = 0.41, p = .52$). The entire model had an R^2 of .02 and was not significant, ($F (5,195) = 0.92, p = .47$).

It was decided to test further this hypothesis using discriminant analysis and chi-square statistics. The linear discriminant function produced by the discriminant analysis was able to classify correctly 62.4% of the Continuers and 57.6% of the Terminators, and, as with the previous attempts to predict membership using SS-C and SS-T data, the linear discriminant function was judged too weak for further analysis.

The chi-square statistical analysis examined separately those ratings that had been effected by demographic variables: CS 2 (age of client): CS 3 (sex of client and therapist experience level); CS 4 and CS 5 (therapist experience level); CS 6 (sex of client and sex of therapist). No congruence of item pairs was able to predict attrition.

The statistical testing of the third hypothesis yielded no significant results. Client-therapist congruence in post-intake ratings failed to predict attrition.

RESEARCH HYPOTHESIS

Hypotheses 4 through 12 were designed to examine further certain demographic and process variables and their effect upon membership in the criterion groups, Terminators and Continuers. The SS-C and SS-T ratings were not involved in these hypotheses and so cases eliminated for missing SS-C and SS-T ratings were restored to the sample ($N = 225$). The resulting distribution was 44 Terminators and 181 Continuers.

The fourth hypothesis was that the client's presenting problem as judged by the intake therapist will not predict attrition after intake. To test this hypothesis it was necessary to utilize a categorical schema for the presenting problem. Because no presenting problem checklist was utilized at GWUCC during the time period of the research, the following academic year's categories for presenting problems was used on a random sample ($N = 45$) of the study population. Intake therapists were given copies of their own intake chart notes and client demographics and asked to rate retrospectively the clients whom they had seen. Results of a 7 × 2 chi-square analysis indicated that the presenting problem as perceived by the intake therapist was not significantly related to subsequent attrition, $p = .40$.

The fifth hypothesis was that there will be a significant correlation between failure to complete or return evaluation forms and attrition. A chi-square statistic indicated that 20.5% ($N = 9$) of the Terminators and 9.9% ($N = 18$) of the Continuers did not complete or return the SS-C, χ^2 (1,225) = 3.70, p = .054. When each sex was examined separately there was still no significant relationship between attrition and failure to complete or return forms for male clients, χ^2 (1,88) = 0.93, p = .33, and female clients, χ^2 (1,137) = 2.89, p = .09. Thus no relation between completion or return of evaluation forms and attrition was found.

The sixth hypothesis was that clients who complete their intake interview in the last month of each semester will have a higher attrition rate than those who complete it prior to the last month. There were 27 (11%) clients who had intake interviews in the last 4 weeks of each semester. Using a chi-square statistic these were compared to the 225 (89%) clients who had their intake interview prior to the last 4 months of each semester. Statistical analysis indicated that Terminators were significantly (p = .0001) more likely to have had their intake session within the last month of each semester, χ^2 (1,252) = 20.95, p = .0001.

The seventh hypothesis was that female therapists will have a lower attrition rate than will male therapists regardless of the level of experience. In the initial descriptive statistical analysis of Terminators and Continuers it was found that sex of therapist had no significant effect upon attrition, χ^2 (1,224) = 2.93, p = .087. When therapist experience level was examined separately no difference was found between male and female senior staff therapists, χ^2 (1,72) = 0.01, p = .751, but among externs male therapists had a 29.2% attrition rate and female therapists had 13.8% of their clients in the Terminators, χ^2 (1,152) = 5.46, p = .019. Thus as originally stated, the hypothesis was not supported but upon further examination it was found that male therapists of lesser experience had a higher attrition rate than their female counterparts.

The eighth hypothesis was that clients referred by male intake therapists to other male therapists will be less likely to return than clients seen by and/or referred to female therapists. A chi-square analysis indicated that 60% of the male clients referred by a male therapist at intake to a male therapist were Terminators but only 32.9% of the male Continuers were referred by a male therapist to a male therapist, χ^2 (1,88) = 3.91, p = .048. There were no similar pattern among the female clients seen by male therapists, χ^2 (1,137) = 0.732, p = .392. It was found that male clients seen by and then referred to a male therapist will have a significantly higher attrition rate than either male or female clients seen by or referred to female therapists.

The ninth hypothesis stated that intake therapists with less experience will have a higher attrition rate. Employing a dichotomous split between the externs who were graduate students in clinical psychology and senior staff who had doctoral degrees in psychology, a chi-square analysis indicated that there was no significant effect of therapist experience level upon client membership in Terminators or Continuers groups, χ^2 (1,225) = 0.562, p = .453. No relationship between therapist experience level and attrition was found.

The tenth hypothesis held that clients who were referred to another therapist by the intake therapist will not have an attrition rate higher than those who retain the intake therapist as their therapist. Employing a chi-square statistic indicated that 36.4% of the Terminators and 44.2% of the Continuers retained the same therapist for therapy as they had had in the intake interview. This was not a large enough difference for a significant effect of referral/retention patterns upon attrition, χ^2 (1,225) = 0.89, p = .346. When sex of client groups were analyzed separately, no significant effect was found for either male, χ^2 (1,88) = 0.075, p = .785, or female clients, χ^2 (1,137) = 0.929, p = .335. Thus no significant difference on attrition was seen between clients who were retained as counselees by the intake therapist and those referred to another therapist.

The eleventh hypothesis stated that clients will not rate same-sex intake therapists higher than opposite sex therapists. A chi-square analysis was performed on the 95 sex-matched dyads and 103 opposite dyads. The demographic variables that had a significant effect upon the ratings were examined separately for those SS-C items that had been effected. There was one significant finding. Sex-matched externs were rated more likable (χ^2 (1,137) = 7.05, p = .008) than opposite sex externs. All five other items showed no effect of sex-matches on the SS-C ratings. In light of the fact that 10 different chi-square analyses were performed to examine this hypothesis and but 1 was significant, it was concluded that there was no difference in the ratings of clients with same-sex or opposite-sex therapists.

The twelfth and final hypothesis stated that elapsed time between intake and first therapy session will predict a subsequent higher attrition rate. The Terminators were excluded from this hypothesis testing because, by definition, they had no first therapy session. The analysis of a random sample (N = 87) of Continuers was performed, therefore, using the total number of subsequent therapy sessions as the dependent variable and the elapsed number of days between intake and first therapy session as the independent variable in a multiple regression, controlling for sex of client, sex of assigned therapist, experience level of assigned therapist, and the interaction sex of client and sex of assigned therapist. The entire regression model including the control variables had an R^2 of .11 and was not significant in its ability to predict number of sessions, (F (6,87) = 1.57, p = .17). Entered as the last variable in the stepwise regression time between intake interview and the first therapy session was not a significant predictor of the total number of sessions the Continuers eventually had, (F (1,87) = 1.71, p = .20).

A correlation matrix of all the variables of interest is available.

DISCUSSION

There are four areas to discuss concerning the statistical analyses: (1) the descriptive statistics of the GWUCC population and research sample; (2) the SS-C and SS-T as instruments to rate post-intake satisfaction of client and therapist; (3) the three major hypotheses; and lastly, (4) the nine research hypotheses. Each of these four areas is discussed and the clinical and research implications of each is suggested as it is treated.

Before these four areas are discussed, however, it might be helpful to recall that the present research can be described generically as evaluation of mental health delivery systems research. As such it has examined one counseling center and is limited by data available at that center. During evaluation research it often becomes apparent that the data available are insufficient to answer some questions and test hypotheses about the local mental health delivery system. The realization that other client, therapist and systems data are desirable for future research is intrinsic to evaluation research. A feedback loop is created in a particular system whereby the system's data base can be expanded or improved to include variables that address the new questions and hypotheses. This process has been called "iterative enhancement" in the database management field (Byers, 1982). Such was the case during the present research. It is hoped that the data bases at GWUCC and similar mental health centers will be continuously improved by the efforts of evaluation research as was attempted here.

GWUCC Population and Research Sample.   The GWUCC serves a private urban university community whose student body comes largely from the middle Atlantic states. The demographic data and attrition rates of the present research were comparable to those of the 8 previous years at GWUCC (Phillips & Fagan, 1982a, 1982b). It is necessary to replicate the results in different settings, e.g., a state university or a small rural college, and possibly community mental health clinics, before generalizing the findings widely to university and community mental health centers. This is because the SS-C and SS-T have not been standardized with a normative population, and because of other demographic considerations found in clinics serving widely different populations.

It was observed that among the 300 persons who sought therapy at the GWUCC during the period of research, there were no significant differences in sex of client, age of client, sex of therapist, and therapist experience level between those who terminated at the conclusion of the intake session and those who agreed to begin counseling at GWUCC and were assigned to a therapist. Only younger female clients showed a tendency ($p = .0504$) to terminate at intake.

When these same demographic variables were examined on the 225 clients who agreed to begin therapy at GWUCC and thereby comprised the research sample, no significant differences were found between the Terminators and the Continuers. Thus as in the majority of studies done previously on attrition using demographic and descriptive variables, it was concluded that the variance explaining attrition lay elsewhere.

There are two questions for future research that are raised by the analyses of the present sample. The first concerns the demographic variables of age and sex of client; the second concerns the decision to terminate made in collaboration with the therapist during the intake session.

First, to explore further the tendency of younger female clients to terminate at intake, efforts should be made to identify and test the intervening variables within the sex of client and age of client interaction. One such hypothesis following a social influence model (Strong, 1968) is that younger female clients have their needs (reassurance, direct suggestion about problem solving) met by the therapist in the one-session intake interview. If this hypothesis were supported, the clinical implications are that intake therapists might be expected to modify the tasks and the time of the intake interview to allow the dyadic interaction to become (as many are) a single consultation session — especially for their younger female clients.

An initial research design to examine this hypothesis might include pre- and post-intake interview measurement of the client's expectations of therapy in interaction with two intake treatments. The experimental group would have a 50-minute interview designed to be a problem-solving consultation (although open to beginning therapy if clinically indicated). The control group would be given an intake session designed not to problem solve but to initiate the prospective client into therapy. It is hypothesized that termination after intake will be at a higher rate for clients whose expectations of therapy are to problem solve and are in the experimental group. It also is hypothesized that younger female clients will be represented at a significantly higher rate among those whose expectations are that the intake therapist will engage in problem solving.

The second research question concerns the 75 clients (25%) who reached a decision to terminate at intake. It is recalled that these 75 are distinguished from the criterion group Terminators ($N = 44$) in that the Terminators agreed to begin therapy at the intake interview. Previous research (Phillips & Fagan, 1982b) has indicated that up to 60% of these terminations involved therapist collaboration. The exact nature of that collaboration was not reported. However, observation of staff discussion at GWUCC indicates that the usual procedure is that a "clinical judgment" is made by the therapist to the effect that this person is not an appropriate candidate for the type of treatment being given at GWUCC. Presently, research is being conducted at GWUCC to identify more precise descriptions of the norms intake therapists use to collaborate in a decision to terminate at intake with or without a referral to another agency. The identification of these norms might prove more heuristic than further analyses of demographic variables in attempting to account for the termination at intake phenomenon.

The SS-C and SS-T as Rating Instruments.   Satisfaction ratings of mental health delivery systems have been consistently reported to be very high (Balch, Ireland, McWilliams, & Lewis, 1977; Edwards, Yarvis, Mueller, & Langsley, 1978). Despite this fact, satisfaction-rating instruments employing a Likert scale are frequently assumed to be interval and to yield data that are normal. The present research did not assume normality for its Likert scales on the SS-C and SS-T. Once examined, normality was rejected ($p < .01$) for both rating instruments. The data were treated consequently as dichotomous data. The present results suggest that Likert ratings in client satisfaction scales be subjected routinely to tests of normality before parametrical statistical analyses are performed.

An additional advantage of treating Likert ratings categorically is that significant differences may be identified in the 1st and 4th quartiles. This was not done in the present research; but with samples of sufficiently large number such techniques could be employed to examine the hypothesis that a truly "not good enough" intake experience will predict attrition.

The question arises concerning the content of items in the SS-C and SS-T that are predictive of attrition. The principal components analysis of the 12 items of the two instruments yielded three factors. Factors 1 and 2 were the global satisfaction ratings of the intake therapist and client respectively. Factor 3, identified as Encouragement Shared and Progress Foreseen by Client, had as its three highest loading items SS-C 3,6 and SS-T 6. SS-C 6 ($p = .068$) and SS-T 6 tended ($p = .058$) to suggest that client and therapist concern about the likelihood of future progress may be the content of rating scales most able to predict attrition.

It is regrettable that there were not more items on the SS-C and SS-T to amplify the content of Factor 3. Several hypotheses about the content of Factor 3 are possible. Encouragement shared and concern about future progress in therapy might reflect an optimism trait in the client which he or she brings to *any* new undertaking. There might also be present an interpersonal sensitivity to encouragement cues from others. Conversely, concern about future progress might reflect a reactive or endogenous depression in the prospective client. Increasing the number of items relating to future progress in therapy and comparing them to independent measure of optimism trait or depression are necessary to establish the content and criterion validity of the third factor of the SS-C and SS-T. In any case, item 6 of the SS-C and in a lesser degree item 6 of the SS-T are distinct from the other five items, which rate satisfaction with an event just completed. Further research into the emotional or cognitive set regarding future tasks that the client brings to the intake interview is necessary. In this regard the Health Beliefs Model (Rosenstock, 1974), in which the clients' attitudes toward severity of distress, cost involved in treatment, and likelihood of amelioration through treatment are examined as predictors of treatment compliance, might be an appropriate construct to be applied to attrition research.

Lastly, the SS-C and SS-T were examined to see whether the variables of sex of client, age of client group, sex of therapist, therapist experience level and the interaction of sex of client and sex of therapist significantly affected the ratings. Three variables and one interaction indicated a significant effect on the categorical (high-low) ratings. The experience level of the intake therapist was implicated in 4 of the 12 items. On the SS-C, externs were less likable to clients and less desirable as assigned therapists. On the SS-T, externs felt they encouraged clients more than senior staff rated their own efforts; externs also rated the clients less likable than did senior staff members.

Results such as this rating discrepancy toward and by the externs evoke at least one intuitive explanation in the author. It is that the externs' relative inexperience causes them a higher degree of anxiety, which interferes with their establishing an affective rapport with the client at intake. They compensate for this by making extra efforts to encourage the client. Certainly this intuitive explanation or hypothesis can and should be examined. It will be necessary to establish that the externs are, in fact, more anxious and that, secondarily, to determine whether anxiety is negatively correlated with, curvilinearly related to, or not related at all to affective rapport between therapist and client.

The primary use of the result is rating differences between evaluation data. As such it can be utilized in the local setting, in this instance GWUCC, as a training device to explore with externs the skill needed and stresses encountered in an intake interview. Having data that describe them or their colleagues of former years makes supervision more pertinent. It also allows the training itself to be evaluated by observing pre- and post-training session ratings of externs.

Similar hypothesis generation and training utilization can be made from the other SS-C and SS-T items that were significantly effected by age of client, sex of client, and the interaction of sex of client and sex of therapist. Because the SS-C and SS-T items were all significantly ($p < .01$) correlated and no one demographic variable effected more than one third of the items, it does not seem necessary to sort SS-C or SS-T scores according to any demographic group in future use.

In summary, analyses of the SS-C and SS-T as satisfaction rating instruments give evidence that (1) the test for normality is both necessary and heuristic when using Likert rating scales; (2) future research into the criterion validity of Factor 3, Encouragement Shared and Progress Foreseen, is required; and lastly, (3) although variables that have a significant effect upon individual items may provide some grounds for future research, they need not be employed as controls for the entire rating scales.

Three Major Hypotheses

None of the three major hypotheses was supported. As measured by the SS-C and SS-T neither client, therapist, or congruence of client and therapist ratings predicted post-intake attrition. It was expected that client ratings would not be predictive (Zamostny et al., 1981). It was, however, hypothesized that therapist ratings and the congruence of client ratings with high therapist ratings would be predictive of attrition.

These results can be understood either as the failure of the instruments employed to be reliable and valid or that post-intake attrition is accounted for by variable other than satisfaction with intake. The reliability and validity of the SS-C and SS-T have been discussed previously and are felt to be sufficient to state that satisfaction with the intake interview has been reliably measured by the SS-C and SS-T in the present study. What is concluded here is the second explanation, namely, that satisfaction with the intake session and intake therapist does not account for a significant portion of the variance in attrition.

As an event recalled and reported by both client and therapist, the intake interview is for the most part a "good enough" experience not to deter the client from seeking further therapy if desired. There may, of course, be some "not good enough" intake experiences at the lowest percentile of SS-C and SS-T ratings that do cause premature termination on the part of the client. The present research, however, suggests that satisfaction of client and therapist with the intake interview is generally such that it neither predicts nor causes unilateral post-intake termination by the client. Intake sessions are, in the main, good enough experiences for the client to begin therapy.

Other factors, still unspecified, appear to be responsible for the 19.6% of clients who indicated they wanted to begin therapy and then did not. A step toward specification of this variance may be found in the data of SS-C 6 and SS-T 6. Both items rated how future progress in therapy was foreseen and tended ($p < .07$) to suggest that Terminators were marked by lower ratings on these two items. As was observed previously, these two items loaded highly on Factor 3, which was distinct from the other two factors, composed the satisfaction ratings of the therapist (Factor 1; SS-T 1–6) and those of the client (SS-C 1–5). The tendency of these two items to predict attrition indicates that the client's concerns about future therapy may be more predictive of attrition than his or her satisfaction with the completed intake interview. From a conjectural viewpoint, the client's needs during an intake session are not only that the session itself be sufficiently satisfactory but more importantly that it address issues of *whether or not therapy is warranted*. This is a finding not previously reported in the attrition literature and invites replication to examine the attrition variance explained by the suggested difference between the client's orientation toward the pending question of beginning therapy. As Ajzen and Fishbein (1980) have suggested, the more behaviorally specific an attitudinal item is the more predictive it will be of that behavior. Item 6 of the SS-C and SS-T asked the client and therapist about the behavior of making progress in therapy. As such it appears to have elicited responses that tend to predict attrition behavior in the client.

Both research and clinical implications are found here. The research implications are, as have been suggested, a further identification of the client's concerns about beginning therapy. This type of research is presently in progress at GWUCC. It seeks to gather from a semi-structured post-intake interview the reservations that clients have about beginning therapy. Phillips (in press) has reported that 80% of clients are able to cite one or more factors that would dissuade them from therapy. Once a representative list of these items is obtained it will be examined to see what reservations/problems are most correlated with post-intake attrition. Research might be designed whereby therapists in an experimental group actively solicit and explore clients' hesitations and reservations whereas the control group therapists treat them only if they are mentioned by the client.

The clinical implications of the suggestion that concern about future progress in therapy is a significant factor in attrition is that the task and structure of the intake interview may have to be altered. Generally the task of the intake interview is seen by the therapist to involve (a) a greeting of the client, (b) understanding the presenting problem, (c) obtaining a personal history of the client, and (d) explaining the services offered and parameters expected by the local mental health center. What is omitted from this design is an exploration of the client's concerns about initiating the process of therapy. The purpose of the exploration is not to "sell" psychotherapy (although the metaphor is not entirely inappropriate); but to assist the client to make an advised decision about whether or not to begin therapy.

If such explorations were part of the general structure of intake interview then more time would have to be allowed. The benefit is that in addressing the prospective client's concerns the therapist is not only talking *about* a problem of the client but is recognizing and tending to doubts and anxieties that are the grist of the therapy process itself. In this way, the intake interview becomes a *de facto* initiation into the collaboration of therapy—the task that is central to the intake interview.

Before discussing the results of the research hypotheses there was one finding of significance in the examination of the second hypothesis. In a multiple regression analysis, clients who were liked less by the intake therapist were more likely ($p = .045$) to become Terminators. Although the variance explained in the criterion group membership by this item (SS-T 4) is minute (r

$= -.004$), the finding does replicate an earlier one suggesting (Fagan, 1982a) that clients who are less liked are more likely to terminate prematurely. As only one of nine separate analyses that were conducted on the second hypothesis, the finding is not felt to support the hypothesis that therapist ratings are predictive of attrition.

Research Hypotheses.   There were four significant results among the nine research hypotheses that were examined:

1. Terminators were significantly ($p = .0001$) more likely to have had their intake session within the last month of the two semesters under study;
2. Male intake therapists who were also externs had a significantly ($p = .02$) higher post-intake attrition rate than their female counterparts;
3. Male clients seen by and then referred to a male therapist had a significantly ($p = .048$) higher attrition rate than those seen in intake by or referred to female therapists;
4. Clients rated sex-matched extern therapists more likable ($p = .007$).

That clients who come for intake in the last months of an academic semester are more likely to become Terminators suggests several explanations. Student distress over examinations, concerns about returning to the family over semester break, the benefits of change of environment over vacation — all speak to the fact that intake clients are more likeky to be "intake only" when they approach a counseling center in the last 4 weeks of a semester.

It is important that the academic counseling center recognize that there may not be a homogeneity in the needs of the population it serves across different time periods in the semesters. As suggested earlier, some clients may be served more efficiently by one session. It seems likely that clients coming at the end of a semester often fit in such a category. If such be the case, intake therapists can alter their typical intake protocol whose principal aim is that of initiating the client into the counseling center program by using the intake as a one-time "crisis" intervention. Future research might examine more closely the nature of the presenting problems of the university community to see if they do reflect a significant heterogeneity across different time periods of the academic year (see Chapter 5).

Along these lines the present study attempted in the fourth research hypothesis to examine any effect the chief complaint or presenting problem had on attrition. No significant finding emerged. However, the analysis of this hypothesis was limited by several factors: (1) therapists rated the client's presenting problem/diagnosis retrospectively (10 to 19 months); (2) the design of the categories used by the GWUCC has not been examined for reliability or validity. Future research that compares the *DSM III* diagnostic categories with a more problem/complaint design for its ability to predict attrition in a college population is suggested.

Male therapists were implicated in two findings of significantly higher attrition. In one case, male therapists who were externs were identified as distinct from the female externs and the male senior staff. In view of the facts that (a) the number of male therapists involved in the present study is small (Senior staff = 3, externs = 4), (b) externs do most of the intake work, and (c) sex of therapist alone has not been a consistent predictor of attrition, the present findings are better seen as local evaluation data rather than as results to be readily generalized. Were the research findings available at the time, the supervisors of the four male externs might be alerted to the results and the skills and tasks of intake counseling reviewed.

Externs were rated more likeable by same-sex clients than by opposite-sex clients. This may suggest that within a university population prospective clients may prefer opposite-sex therapists to be significantly older than they are. One of the oft-voiced concerns of novice therapists is that they are the same age or younger than their clients. The result of clients giving higher ratings for same-sex therapists who were externs and thereby younger than senior staff may reflect the same concern from the client's perspective. If so, it may imply an intervening variable of age rather than experience level. Should further research be done in this area, ages of clients (more representative than found in a college sample) and therapists should be examined for relationships to ratings of sex-matched dyads.

For the most part, however, the analyses of the research hypotheses confirm the impression widely held (Garfield, 1978) that demographic data, especially as broad as age and sex variables, do not provide consistent variance explaining attrition from counseling and psychotherapy. What they do provide are data for evaluation of the local mental health system and, in the case of the clients who come late in the semester, an opportunity for exploration into the heterogeneity of presenting problems (therefore needs) across different time periods in the academic year.

CONCLUSION

The study was an attempt to see if two brief rating scales, of comparable item content, given to clients and intake therapists immediately after the intake session could predict subsequent attrition. Given the transformation of the ratings scales into median split categorical data, clients and therapists alike gave indication of attitudes that later were manifested in the behavior of the client not returning for a first therapy session. The rating items that tended to predict attrition concerned the client's and therapist's estimation of progress being made by future counseling. Where less progress is foreseen, the likelihood of attrition increases.

The clinical implications suggested are:

1. Expanding the task of the intake interview to include treating the client's concerns about beginning the counseling process,

2. Encouraging flexibility to use the intake as a one-time "crisis" intervention (as many do) and lastly,

3. Utilizing ongoing statistical analysis of the demographic and attrition pattern involved as evaluation tools for the local university counseling center.

Future research directions and hypotheses suggested are:

1. Identification of the norms intake therapists use in a particular setting in the decision that a prospective client should terminate at intake (with or without a referral);

2. That those clients who desire reassurance/direct suggestions about problem solving will more often terminate at or after intake because their needs have been met;

3. That a "not good enough" intake experience will be reflected by the 1st quartile of client satisfaction ratings and will predict post-intake attrition;

4. That the prospective client's attitudes toward severity of distress, cost of treatment and the likelihood of amelioration through treatment are predictors of post-intake attrition;

5. That anxiety in the intake therapist is negatively correlated with the establishment of an affective bond with the client;

6. That intake therapists who actively elicit and explore the prospective clients' concerns about beginning therapy will have a higher return rate than those who do not elicit and explore such concerns.

7. That a presenting problem scale is more predictive of attrition among perspective clients at a university counseling ceenter than are *DSM III* diagnostic categories predictive.

8. That there is a significant difference of presenting problems/clinical diagnoses across different time periods in the academic year.

It is hoped that the present research contributes to understanding the phenomenon of 19%–25% post-intake attrition by finding no evidence that client or therapist dissatisfaction with the intake session accounts for the premature terminations. Other sources of variance, in particular concerns about future progress, have been suggested as areas to be investigated. In light of the fact that the modal number of sessions in most mental health systems is one, the more that is known about the intake session, the more efficiently will mental health resources be used and clients needs be served.

7 The Kaiser Study of Attrition in Alcoholic Outpatients

As part of a more intensive look at the attrition matter among both first and second admissions, an outpatient alcoholic clinic was utilized for several studies.[1] These data came under the purview of one of us (MBK) — among the several represented in this book — and constituted the basis for a more complete report than can be given here (Kaiser, 1984; also see portions of Chapter 2). This report is based on attempts to find predictor variables relevant to alcoholic patients remaining in therapy.

Research into the problem of attrition among alcoholic patients has received considerable study (Krasnoff, 1977; McWilliams & Brown, 1977; Miller, Porkony, & Hanson, 1968; O'Leary, Calsyn, Chaney, & Freeman, 1977; O'Leary, Robsenow, & Chaney, 1979), all of these researchers pursuing MMPI patterns to predict dropping out from alcoholic treatment. Studies using the Rotter Locus of Control Scale (Bowen, Tremlow, & Stuart, 1978; O'Leary et al. 1977; Schofield, 1978), all found mixed results, as did the researchers on the MMPI, when it came to predicting attrition from alcoholic treatment on an outpatient basis.

Considerations of therapist variables in relation to client attrition from treatment of alcoholic patients also failed to come up with consistent results (Betz & Shullman, 1979; Fiester, 1977; Frank, Gliedman, Imber, Nash, & Stone, 1957; Linn, 1978; Tantam & Klerman, 1979). Examining different

---

[1]We are indebted to the Reverend Paul H. Sandusky and the entire staff of the Fayette County, Pa., Drug and Alcohol Commission for data found in this chapter; conclusions drawn are the responsibility of the present authors and do not reflect policies or opinions of the Commission.

therapist-related variables did not turn up very consonant contributions to therapist influences on alcoholic patients leaving therapy before mutual termination. However, some factors such as changing therapist and general interactions sometimes played a role in this respect.

Demographic variables such as age, sex, marital status, economic stability, familial alcoholism, and drinking history also present a mixed picture of influence on the attrition rate. Demographic variables and the ease with which they may be obtained fared somewhat better than the more subtle interpersonal variables relating to client and therapist characteristics (Altman, Evenson, & Cho, 1978; Baekeland & Lundwall, 1975; Baekeland, Lundwall, & Shanahan, 1973; Hahn & King, 1982; Smart & Gray, 1978; Wilkinson, Prado, Williams, & Schnadt, 1971; among other researchers).

Although little if any research has attempted to predict no-show rate, it is common knowledge that alcoholic outpatients miss between 20% and 60% of scheduled appointments. In addition to the interruption in treatment, these missed appointments cost clinics a considerable amount of money at a time when federal funds also are being cut, as well as representing poor use of therapist time when therapy hours are left open.

The present study was an attempt to develop a regression equation using demographic variables and drinking history variables in order to predict no-show rates, premature dropout from treatment, and total sessions attended.

The subjects for this study were 417 alcoholic outpatients (72% males), admitted and discharged between March, 1979, and December, 1982, from a County Drug and Alcohol Commission in Pennsylvania. Age range was 12–80, mean age = 33.8 years, 90% white, with 73% admitted into treatment for the first time. Thirty-four percent were fully employed, 5% part-time, and 61% were unemployed or retired; 49% were high school graduates, 14% had some college and 33% had less than high school education; 41% were married, 27% separated/divorced, the remainder single.

This patient population had a mean of 7.79 sessions ($SD = 8.15$), and a range of 1–59 sessions; average number of months in treatment was 2.75 ($SD = 3.20$), thus they came close to one session per week for treatment. Of the total treated, 19% were discharged having satisfactorily completed treatment, 19% transferred, were jailed or died, and 62% left against facility advice. Missing data amounted to less than 5% for all variables included in this study.

Several demographic variables and drinking history variables that have been shown in previous studies to correlate with dropout were investigated. These included age, sex, race, marital status, employment status, education, previous treatment history, length of alcohol/drug problem, pattern of drug use, and several others. A multiple correlation procedure was used to determine which variables correlated with total sessions attended, the no-show rate, and the disposition at discharge.

As can be seen in Table 7.1, several variables were significantly correlated with the dependent variables ($p < .01$) although the amount of variance accounted for by these variables ranged from 2% to 19%.

The dependent variable Sessions Attended was positively correlated with Highest Grade Completed, the Number of Months Employed in the 2 years prior to admission, and the Reason for Treatment. Being in treatment for reasons other than one's own personal alcohol/drug problems tended to correlate positively with Sessions Attended. Employment Status at Discharge and Pattern of Drug Use were negatively correlated with Sessions Attended. That is to say, patients who were employed at the time of discharge tended to stay in treatment for more sessions than those who were unemployed. In terms of the Pattern of Drug Use, patients who used alcohol/drugs more frequently tended to stay in treatment for fewer sessions than occasional users and individuals who had been sober for at least 30 days prior to admission.

The dependent variable Show Rate was positively correlated with Age and negatively correlated with Pattern of Drug Use. Older patients tended to miss fewer appointments than did younger patients. Again, increased frequency of use tended to result in a higher no-show rate.

TABLE 7.1
Significant Correlations ($p < .01$)

Independent Variables	Sessions Attended
Why treatment	.17
Highest grade completed	.16
Months employed in the two years prior to admission	.16
Pattern of drug use	− .16
Employment status at discharge	− .20
	Show Rate
Age	.14
Pattern of drug use	− .15
	Reason for Discharge
Previous treatment	.13
Employment status at admission	.17
Months in treatment	− .37
Pattern of drug use	.44
Employment status at discharge	.18

The dependent variable Reason for Discharge was positively correlated with Previous Treatment, Employment Status, and Pattern of Drug Use, but it was negatively correlated with Months in Treatment. That is, individuals who were employed, had previous treatment, and were frequent alcohol/drug users tended to be discharged for non-compliance. The negative correlation between Months in Treatment and Reason for Discharge suggests that patients who stayed in treatment longer tended to be discharged having completed treatment.

A stepwise regression was run for each of the dependent variables using the variables from Table 7.1, which were significantly correlated with each of the dependent variables. The best four-variable model for Sessions Attended involved the variables Reason for Treatment, Highest Grade Completed, Months Employed in the 2 years prior to admission, and Pattern of Drug Use and resulted in an r of .077 and $F (4,362) = 7.63$, $p < .01$. The best two-variable model for the Show Rate included the variables Age and Pattern of Drug Use and resulted in an r of .024 and $F (1,365) = 9.08$, $p < .01$. Finally, for the variable Reason for Discharge, the best four-variable model included the variables Previous Treatment, Employment Status, Months in Treatment, and Pattern of Drug Use and resulted in an r of .297 and $F (4,373) = 39.46$, $p < .01$.

As the variable Pattern of Drug Use appeared to be the only one correlated with all three dependent variables, a series of analyses of variance was used to examine the relationship between Pattern of Drug Use, Sessions Attended, and Show Rate. There was a highly significant relationship between Sessions Attended and the Pattern of Drug Use, $F (7,359) = 7.23$, $p < .01$. Duncan's Multiple Range Test was used to locate the significant differences. Patients who were sober for 30 days prior to admission attended an average of 11.6 sessions, which was significantly more than for patients whose frequency of drug/alcohol use was several times a week or more. The average Show Rate ranged from 66% for individuals who used alcohol/drugs once a day to 81%, for individuals who used alcohol/drugs less than once a week. The Show Rate did not differ significantly between these groups.

A series of analyses of variance was used to examine the variables of Sex, Marital Status, First Scheduled Appointment Attended, and Counselor Also Did Intake with each of the dependent variables. The only significant F value resulted from the comparison between First Scheduled Appointment Attended and the Show Rate. The average show rate for patients who attended the first session was 74% ($SD = 20\%$), compared to an average show rate of 71% ($SD = 21\%$) for those individuals who did not attend the first session.

One final analysis of variance was performed as part of the analysis of Reason for Discharge, after it was discovered that patients who were discharged having completed treatment attended an average of 13.88 sessions compared to an average of 5.80 sessions for patients who were discharged under unfavorable conditions. This difference was highly significant, F (1,393) = 46.45, $p < .01$.

DISCUSSION

Overall, attempts to develop equations to predict the number of sessions attended, the no-show rate, and whether or not patients successfully completed treatment using demographic variables and drinking history variables were largely unsuccessful. The only significant regression model involved the attempt to predict the Reason for Discharge. It was quite impressive that this model was able to account for 30% of the variance with only four variables in the model. The Reason for Discharge in many ways is a highly subjective variable. From a practical standpoint this model may be much more useful in helping us begin to understand the criteria used by therapists in making a final disposition than in predicting who will complete treatment successfully. The study did lend some support to the idea that "social stability" may be related to longer treatment and fewer missed appointments. That is to say, patients with more stable work histories, more years of formal education, and a less chronic pattern of drug/alcohol use tended to stay in treatment longer. Older patients tended to be more responsible in terms of fewer missed appointments.

The patient's pattern of drug and alcohol use was the only variable that correlated significantly with all three dependent variables. Results were consistent with what one might expect. That is, patients who were drinking or using drugs several times a week immediately prior to admission tended to stay in treatment for shorter periods of time, miss more appointments, and be terminated under less favorable conditions than patients who used alcohol or drugs less frequently. This finding provides further support for the idea that outpatient counseling may indeed be more successful with individuals who are sober for a period of time prior to admission. Individuals who had been abstinent for at least 30 days prior to admission stayed for considerably more sessions and were more likely to be discharged having satisfactorily completed treatment. In many cases these individuals had probably been discharged from inpatient rehabilitation programs prior to admission for outpatient counseling, which would account for the 30 days of sobriety. It may be helpful indeed to take a look more closely at the circumstances under which individuals seek outpatient counseling after being sober for extended periods of time. On the other hand, this study suggests the possibility that outpatient counseling for individuals who are drinking several times a week or more may not be the most appropriate form of initial treatment. Even with a 3-to-5 day hospitalization for detoxification, patients still may need to be sober for an extended period of time before outpatient counseling can be expected to have a significant impact.

One other important finding was the fact that subjects who completed treatment attended significantly more sessions than subjects who dropped out or who were discharged for non-compliance. Although there are no data available on long-term follow-up, this finding does support other research that suggests that longer treatment may be better for chronic problems such as alcoholism. The need for adequate follow-up in order to determine the success of clients who have "completed treatment" is clear, and also what therapists mean when using this term.

Finally, this study suggests the need for new directions in approaching the problem of patient attrition. Perhaps it is time to spend more energy investigating pragmatic techniques to increase participation rather than trying to predict attrition, particularly using demographic variables. Treatment of alcoholic patients is often singularly medical or psychological (psychotherapy) but often it is a combination of medical and psychological treatment. Bridging over from this population to general patient (medical) compliance in the interest of possibly finding attritional data, the two following research reports are offered as a tentative move toward understanding attrition in this field of service and research.

PATIENT (MEDICAL) COMPLIANCE

Once the attritional matters have been described for outpatient psychotherapy, it is at once suggested that similar patterns of attrition might occur with medical treatment; this is usually called "patient compliance" (Bergman & Werner, 1963; DiMatteo & DiNicola, 1982; Marcus, Reeder, Jordan, & Seeman, 1980; Pothier, 1975). Most of this literature — although registering the large number of dropouts from physicians' prescribed treatment regimens — fails to aggregate the data in ways allowing for the systematic study of attrition. Combining the literature and perusing several general reviews of patient compliance (or adherence) yielded only two articles that came close to aggregating data in a way affording a test of the attritional hypothesis (Bergman & Werner, 1963; Marcus et al., 1980). Two figures are presented herewith (Figs. 7.1 and 7.2) displaying the attrition (service delivery, medical compliance) results.

Figure 7.1 shows the completion rates for Los Angeles Health Surveys, 1974 and 1977 (Ns = 1,592 and 1,512 cases, respectively); both dates are shown in one figure with the hatch marks identifying the 1974 data (replotted). Some explanation of this figure in relation to attrition is warranted. These respondents "complied" with a health-related matter; the survey has to do with actual or potential treatment, and the responses are to medical serv-

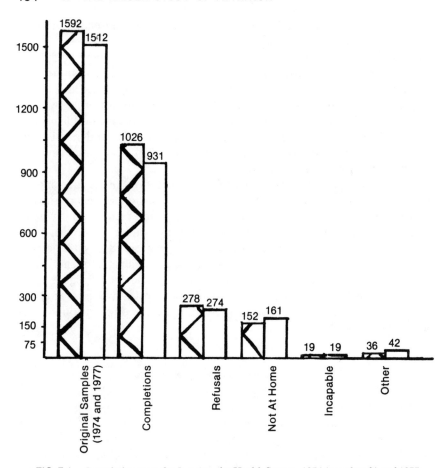

FIG. 7.1   Completion rates for Los Angeles Health Survey, 1974 (crosshatch) and 1977; based on various degrees of compliance with survey. (Marcus et al., 1980; adapted from Table 1, p. 253)

ices. Although the role of the physician or a therapist, and the attritional time-frame are not directly involved, the category of possible treatment is the basis for enlisting the help of the respondents. The respondent's behavior can be viewed, tentatively, and in part, as examples of responses to and use of services. In this figure an N of 81 cases (1974 data) was subtracted from the original 1,592 cases (referring to "ineligible" cases occasioned by incorrect or vacant addresses), which, in turn, accounts for the differences between the net eligible cases and the dispositions and conditions of replies (completions, refusals, etc.). The same "eligible" category applies to the 1977 survey where the adjusted eligible sample N was 1,427. The declining curves show the causes of the loss of patient responses to the survey beginning with the difference between the total number surveyed (1974, 1977), the ones completing the survey, refusals, and so on. The resultant curves are similar to psychotherapy attrition curves in that varying degrees of compliance with a regimen are displayed. How reliable a medical compliance/adherence curve would be over different settings, diagnoses, and conditions is yet to be established.

The next report, Fig. 7.2, shows actual treatment compliance by parents of children with streptococcal infections, involving both administering penicillin by mouth and procuring urine samples. Data are presented in Fig. 7.2 for days 3, 6, and 9 of the treatment regimen, but not for the intervening days (Bergman & Werner, 1963). This sparsity of data reporting, although useful for some initial purposes, fails to give the full information needed to have confidence in the attritional matter where medical compliance is concerned, and how gradually compliance is reduced session by session, day by day, from an initial point out to an asymptote. It is not now known what an asymptote would look like among medically treated cases similar to these; possibly the asymptote would be much shorter than in psychotherapy since the

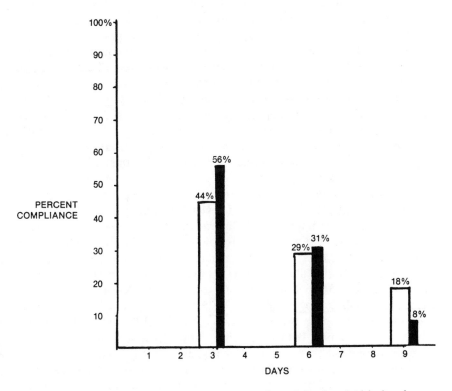

FIG. 7.2   Showing percent patient (medical) compliance following physician's orders; streptoccal infection among children, treated by penicillin pills (open bar graph; $N = 59$), and urine test ($N = 41$ of above 59 cases). Adapted from: Bergman & Werner, 1963; also see general review article on compliance: Marston, 1970, p. 315.

definitiveness of the medical regimen, and knowledge of results, would be clearer and usually shorter than for psychotherapy. Other matters related to the characteristic attrition curve found with psychotherapy might also differ among medical regimens, a useful topic for much exploratory research.

If we observe widely the decline in compliance among medical treatment cases, we would have the start of an attritional description for various diagnoses and treatment regimens — a matter yet to be researched. As the importance of psychotherapy attrition gains recognition, analogies with medical compliance will doubtless arise and serve as a guide to improved treatment delivery services and outcomes.

ALCOHOLIC PATIENT REFERRALS IN A SINGLE COUNTY

Noting that the attrition picture for alcoholic outpatients is similar to that found among other mental health cases (see Chapter 2), we considered next how patients in this diagnostic category would utilize a variety of clinics offering five different treatment programs within the same county — Drug and Alcohol treatment, Mental Health Clinic treatment, Detoxification Center treatment, Rehabilitation Center treatment, and Halfway Houses treatment. One question asked was how the point of entry into treatment affects the overall flow of patients through the system. That is, do clients who first become involved in treatment through outpatient therapy, hospital detoxification, and the like, differ in terms of their overall utilization of different treatment services? In addition, one might ask whether the frequency distribution of previous treatment experiences is consistent with the attrition curve, which has been well-documented in previous chapters.

The mean number and the standard deviations of individual treatment experiences, depending upon point of entry, for the five treatment regimens and the number thus served are as follows: Drug and Alcohol Outpatient Centers (N = 139; Mean number of treatment experiences = 3.68, and SD = 2.19); Mental Health Clinics (N = 115; Mean number of treatment experiences = 3.22, and SD = 1.49); Detox Centers (N = 91; Mean = 3.45, SD = 1.82); and Rehabilitation Centers (N = 25; Mean = 3.56, SD = 2.35); and only one case reported in the county records for the present time period (March, 1979, to April, 1984) for Halfway House treatment. Thus, where the alcoholic outpatient enters the treatment system appears to make very little difference in the average number of treatments that follow. How these figures relate to subsequent sobriety goals is not now known in this treatment framework.

Pursuant to the flow of cases entering the county treatment system through any of the five treatment programs cited above, we see in Fig. 7.3 how the patients are distributed among the entire system.

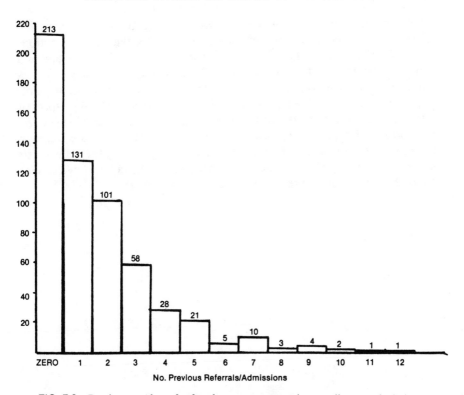

FIG. 7.3   Previous number of referrals to treatment regimens, all types, alcohol patients; March 1979 to April 1984; $N = 586$ Admissions. (Missing: $N = 8$)

With a total N of 586 cases surveyed, 213 cases had had zero previous referral to treatment, 131 had had 1 previous referral to treatment, and so on to an asymptote out to 15 previous referrals. The asymptote is reached at about 7 previous treatment referrals, and remains very low (one to five cases) being referred out as many as 15 previous times. The worth of these referrals in terms of sobriety is not accounted for in these data but remains an important issue for further research.

It will be noted that Fig. 7.3 closely resembles the characteristic attrition curve we have previously described so abundantly. It is remarkable that the help-seeking distributes itself in the same manner as the attrition curve describing the number of sessions engaged in by a population of clients or patients. Is help-seeking behavior, then, a kind of independent state of affairs that obtains more or less similarly among three or more classes of clients/patients: those seeking help in a given clinical facility in terms of the number of sessions; those moving from one facility to another (on referral or on their own, a kind of compliance or help-seeking in its own right); and those observed under some medical treatment program in relation to patient compliance. Surely this is a rich area for study, with a host of practical, training, research and economic and policy problems all crying for enlightenment and testing. One of the most available areas for studying the enlarged notions arising from attrition is that of the alcoholism clinics found in our states and counties throughout the United States. These clinics, ready-made for research because so many are run by and through local and state data accounting systems, are available testing grounds for studying almost any aspect of attrition one might want to investigate. Because a large number of ways to refine old research problems, plus defining new research areas, are found in this report, it is hoped that researchers will be willing to study the many facets of intriguing problems still remaining. The cost/benefit value related to such study should be a strong recommendation to researchers.

8

Outcome Studies: Satisfaction and Behavioral Problem Solving (Clients and Therapists Evaluate Each Other)

Traditionally, psychotherapy results have been evaluated by the therapist (Bergin & Lambert, 1978; Brammer & Shostrom, 1982; Garfield, 1978; Luborsky & Spence, 1978; Mandel, 1981; Parloff et al., 1978; Strupp, 1978). It was the therapist who was presumed to know the patient and his or her problems, especially the patient's "defenses"; hence the therapist's evaluations were more professional, unbiased, clinically based, and so forth. In the more traditional literature and until recently (Lambert et al., 1983; Parloff et al., 1978; Strupp, 1978) clients or patients were seldom asked what they thought about their therapy experience. Follow-up studies of client/patient reactions to therapy may have been carried out, but because only a small percentage of clients were available for such assessment (see the first three chapters of this book), little stock could be taken in client reactions. If a person was not "fully analyzed" or if he or she left therapy "prematurely," little weight could be given such an opinion base.

As a result of this pervasive reaction to the client's appraisals of therapy — except for more recent studies — not much research was done on client reactions. The vast literature on client follow-up questionnaire research (Bergin & Lambert, 1978; Garfield, 1978; Parloff et al., 1978), however interesting and valuable in a limited research sense, never got incorporated very ably in the whole literature on psychotherapy theory and research. The leading theorists of psychotherapy (Corsini, 1981; Ellis, 1962; Patterson, 1980; Shostrom, 1966) seldom bothered to do systematic research on therapy outcome, save for occasional illustrative articles, to look at how therapist and client viewed the upcoming psychotherapy at the outset, during the process, or at the end point, whether the end point was at the last interview or after some follow-up point months or years later. It is fair to say that psychotherapy publications have been more a means of forwarding the interests of the therapist/theorist, albeit in the name of science and clinical acumen, than serving a set of consumer needs and interests (Fiske, Cartwright, & Kirtner, 1964; Frank, 1979).

Until recently, the nearly total absence of a general data base for psychotherapy delivery over a substantial period of time, from a single clinic, amply supports this generalization. When sizable data bases have been reported, they have included scant statistics and have seldom been neutral in the larger, demographic scientific sense. Most clinics do not keep overall statistics of the type this volume avers important; most of the data bases are on average number of client sessions with some demographic breakdown such as age, sex, and socio-economic variables occasionally included. Not until this résumé of the flow of cases in the home counseling center of the present authors or in the reworked data bases from the literature (see Chapters 1 and 2) has there been a pulling together of needed data that would allow for the proper juxtaposition of most research issues, other than those touching only briefly or scantily on attrition and its importance. No marvel, then, that client attitudes have been neglected, and that the focusing on client and therapist attitudes at the same therapeutic junctures has been eschewed with amazing regularity. The present chapter is a beginning attempt to rectify some of the neglect found in the client-therapist attitude literature, at least for walk-in, self-initiated therapy. Behavioral researchers studying limited or focused change, and analogue studies (despite their limitations) have done a better job of keeping account of agreed-upon client/therapist objective, data-based incremental changes (weight loss, smoking cessation, etc.); yet these studies, however useful, do not go very far in filling in the larger picture of client/ therapist evaluations of psychotherapy or behavior change. And the general issue of the considerable differences in client/therapist attitude has not been dealt with very satisfactorily, save for a few studies (Bergin & Lambert, 1978; Garfield, 1978). Few if any studies of client/therapist attitude differences have fed back into the therapeutic delivery system framework and influenced later research or practice.

ACKNOWLEDGING THE CLIENT MORE FULLY

Even though we may fail to recognize it at times, client satisfaction is a compelling matter. Therapists in essence depend upon their services and skills being appreciated. Like any other skilled professional, satisfaction with one's performance is a powerful reinforcer, more powerful if it comes from others. However, one would scarcely ever recognize this dependence on client evaluations if one paid attention only to the literature. Therapists have tended to be more occupied with their own versions of therapy, with the client's psychopathology, and with the nature of therapy; less so seeing their own roles more clearly or using client feedback constructively.

Recently the opportunity arose to ask attendees at an APA session on psychotherapy why they thought clients dropped out of therapy (this term was used to elicit generous replies, not because it was considered a valid notion). Over 70% of the replies among 50 attendees placed the blame on clients: not motivated, not anxious enough (or too anxious), resistance, apprehension, and so on; a few involved the therapist directly and some referred to a poor match between therapist and client.

Following case discussions by mature clinicians and fledgling therapists, it has been observed that most comments about the conduct of therapy hinged on therapists reporting on how the client was handled in a way suggesting the therapist was dealing with a recalcitrant horse in training. Therapists credit themselves with wisdom, compassion, and patience, but tend to ascribe opposite features on these continua to clients. Most negative comments in such discourse are aimed at the client; the therapist's responsibility, sometimes perplexity, are often given short shrift. We commiserate with clients, recognize their extensive psychopathology, and allege it is too strong to allow the therapist to achieve his or her goals with the client.

LEARNING FROM CLIENT RESPONSES

The more the staff at the GWU Counseling Center grappled with the problem of client follow-up evaluation, the more we realized the client was far more the center of attention than we had supposed. When soliciting client follow-up evaluations we are not simply asking them, as in a political opinion poll—although there is doubtless some of this motive present—what they think about the therapy, the intake process, the clinic and its policies, and so on; we are trying to learn something of value from them. The wider picture of follow-up concern—in the earnest effort to try to get people to reply at all to inquiry—has been neglected in much evaluative research. We always have answers, as clinicians, concerning why clients do not fare better in therapy, but we shun much of what this set of problems implies for us as therapists. This criticism does not mean that clients are always right, but they are "right" from their own vantage point; if we are to improve in their eyes—our consumers—we shall have to do better than just try to "sell" them a new brand of therapy, like the latest "hit" record in the popular music domain.

With these somewhat skeptical and questioning remarks on clinician behavior, we now embark on several studies of a follow-up nature—studies that have begun to challenge our previous thinking in several aspects.

FOLLOW-UP QUESTIONNAIRE RESULTS, 1975–1981

Beginning in 1975 a systematic effort was made to gain follow-up ratings from clients approximately 3–4 months after therapy termination. Follow-up is almost always fraught with difficulties. The first report on these findings — repeated in part here — was done by Phillips and Fagan (1982a). Continued revision of questionnaires is still with us, each effort telling us more about how to pursue this difficult but rewarding labor.

During the 1975–1981 period three somewhat different questionnaires were utilized, each one an attempt — through staff discussion — to improve upon previous ones. However, many of the changes made in the questionnaires were hip pocket changes because until recently we lacked the feedback of rapid results afforded by computer help; intuition was our guide for changes for a long time, a less helpful associate than objective computer printouts.

Results for the three questionnaires, Forms A (1975–1976), B (1976–1979) and C (1979–1981) are found in Table 8.1 It can be seen from Table 8.1 that for Form A (N = 117) of the follow-up questionnaire, Factors 1 and 2 account for about 71% of the variance. These items related to feelings/relationships/thinking/decision-making changes on the one hand; on the other hand to productivity, and to reported changes of others toward the client. General satisfaction and approval of counselor roles loaded not heavily but appreciably on Factor 1. Factor 2 loaded more heavily on trust, empathy, and satisfaction with the counselor; the latter factor was appreciably less determining of results than Factor 1. We summarize these by saying they related to client satisfaction, feelings change, and behavior change.

Form B (1976–1979) (N = 289) also produced two factors accounting for 59% of the variance, a less robust finding than for Form A. All items of these forms are not included in these results, only those items loading appreciably on one or the other factor. With Form B results we see Factor 1 loading heavily on satisfaction, counselor approval, and a global rating; less robustly on items relating to information, skill, and conflict resolution. Factor 2 accounts for the decidedly smaller percentage of the variance and finally centers on trust, physical features of the center (a surprising outcome!) and good treatment as a client. Thesè findings appear to revolve around self-appraisal changes, approval of the general therapeutic effort offered the client, and overall satisfaction (global rating), a consistent finding.

Form C, utilized in 1979–1981 (N = 179), contains all the 11 items used. Two factors account for nearly 70% of the variance. Factor 1 clearly loads on counselor trust/understanding, self-changes (conflict resolution, self-awareness, confidence), and both behavioral and feelings changes. Global rating of satisfaction loads heavily for the third time. Factor 2 relates most robustly to feelings change, improving problem-status, and self-improvement.

The accumulation of these findings in the direction of self-changes (feelings, etc.) and behavior change led to the development of the most recently used questionnaire, Form D. This questionnaire contains 22 items and is reproduced in Table 8.2.

Having evidence for placing confidence in the global ratings found in Forms A, B, and C, we included (in Form D) three such global ratings; we separated behavior and feeling change, and both of them from the overall rating of the therapy experience. This subdivision proved to be heuristic. There is some support for this view of the global rating in the literature (Frank, 1974).

Form D of the follow-up questionnaire has been used for 2 years, 1982–83 and 1983–84. The results for the most recent year include about 8 months only, with data intake cut-off the end of April, 1984; this means that many clients seen the second semester, 1983–84, have not had time to finish therapy, especially if therapy began mid- or late semester. We expect fairly good returns about 3–4 months after therapy completion, a date that would, for 1983–84, put us into the fall or early winter of 1984 for more complete returns.

Table 8.3 presents data from this questionnaire on how the 22 items loaded on five factors (1982–1983; $N = 78$). These are discussed in turn.

The five factors account for about 72% of the variance. Factors 1 and 2 may be viewed together: feeling better; working on specific problems; "handling" and "dealing" with problems, all load .50 or higher on Factor 1; clients reporting their friends observed client "feeling" and "behaving" better/differently, also loaded on Factor 1; and global rating loaded .63 on feeling change (with global ratings of behavior change and the counseling center experience much lower on Factor 1).

Factor 2 shows robust loadings for attitude toward therapist and learning to deal with problems; along with "behavior change . . . lasting longer than feeling change." Global rating on Factor 2, "behavior change" loaded strongly (.83), compared to a loading of .63, Factor 1, on "feeling change." Many other items contrasts between behavior and feeling change can be noted in the item listings under Factors 1 and 2 columns in Table 8.3.

Very favorable ratings of therapist behavior are found in the Factor 3 portion of Table 8.3, revealing five item loadings from .51 to .87 on such items related to therapist behavior as: "understanding problems," "giving attention to feelings," "helping to identify problems," "suggesting approaches," and "relating well." Client ratings gave about .50 loadings for Factor 2 on "specific problems" and on global ratings of the counseling center experience.

Quite interesting client-reported ratings occur with Factor 4: Feeling better about themselves being greater than problem solving yielded a − .54 loading (Item 10), whereas solving problems rated higher than feeling better as to therapy outcome (.74) (Item 11) − a matter likely to be found as

TABLE 8.1
Varimax Rotated Factor Patterns: Various Follow-Up Questionnaires: Forms A, B, & C;
1975–76, 1976–79, 1979–81, respectively; Ns = 117, 289, 179, respectively

	Varimax Rotated Factor Pattern			
Item	*Content*	*Factor I*	*Factor II*	*MEAN¹ (SD)*
2A	Feelings changed	.85	.23	2.14 (1.09)
2B	Relationship(s) changed	.82	.28	2.39 (1.09)
2C	Productivity changed	.85	.11	2.51 (1.00)
2D	Decision making changed	.87	.04	2.41 (1.00)
2E	Thinking clearly changed	.86	.18	2.28 (1.06)
2F	Others behavior toward subject changed	.83	.09	2.60 (1.12)
3	General satisfaction	.71	.56	2.04 (1.04)
4B	Trust in confidentiality	– 0.09	.69	1.25 (0.49)
7	Empathy of counselor	.29	.79	1.41 (0.66)
8	Counselor helpful in problem resolution	.55	.59	1.62 (0.82)
Variance explained		5.18 (51.8%)	1.94 (19.4%)	

Cut-off point = 1.0 eigenvalue
Suggested Factor Names:

I – Concern with behavior change resulting from counseling (Outcome)
II – Satisfaction with counselor

¹Range 2A – 3 is 1 through 4]
    4B – 8 is 1 through 3] 1 is most favorable

Form B (1976–1979)   (N = 289)
Varimax Rotated Factor Pattern

Item	*Content*	*Factor I*	*Factor II*	*MEAN¹ (SD)*
9	Gained *information* about self	.76	.14	3.94 (1.04)
11	Resolved *conflict* within self	.72	.11	3.52 (1.21)
13	Remedied lack of *skill*	.47	.49	3.17 (1.26)
15	Trust in confidentiality	.14	.65	4.83 (0.48)
17	Overall rating of experience (satisfaction)	.90	.13	4.17 (0.99)
19	Helpfulness of counselor	.88	.14	4.30 (0.98)
22	Physical facilities of Center	.08	.71	3.86 (1.03)

TABLE 8.1 (continued)

Item	Content	Factor I	Factor II	MEAN[1] (SD)
23	Self-perception as a client	.03	.56	3.92 (1.06)
24	Global rating	.90	.11	4.16 (0.93)
Variance explained		3.74 (41.6%)	1.57 (17.4%)	

Suggested Factor Names:

I – Satisfaction with Counseling Process and Insight Outcome
II – Perception of Counseling Process

[1]Range 1 – 5; 5 is most favorable

Form C (1979–1981)   (*N* = 179)
Varimax Rotated Factor Pattern

Item	Content	Factor I	Factor II	MEAN[1] (SD)
1	Clarification of conflicts and concerns	.72	.40	4.20 (0.98)
2	*Trust* in counselor	.82	.07	4.52 (0.88)
3	Increase in *confidence*	.52	.66	3.78 (1.04)
4	More effective expression of feelings	.54	.60	3.58 (1.10)
5	Therapist showed *understanding*	.84	.23	4.39 (0.99)
6	Gained awareness of strengths and weaknesses	.65	.43	. 4.08 (0.98)
7	Interpersonal *relationships* improved	.37	.67	3.60 (1.13)
8	Made progress in presenting *problems*	.14	.86	3.84 (0.93)
9	Increased potential for *fulfilling aspirations*	.21	.83	3.90 (0.92)
10	Would recommend Center to a friend	.73	.38	4.44 (0.94)
11	Global rating	.79	.46	4.25 (0.98)
Variance explained		4.24 (38.5%)	3.43 (31.2%)	

I – Satisfaction with Counseling Process
II – Outcome rating of behavior change

[1]Range 1 – 5; 5 is most favorable

TABLE 8.2
George Washington University 22-Item Follow-Up Questionnaire, Form D, 1982--

This is a follow-up questionnaire on the services you received at the GWU Counseling Center. Your answers will help us improve our services, and they will be held in confidence. Please answer all items and return the questionnaire in the addressed, stamped envelope.

Age ____ Sex ____ Academic Major _____ No. sessions: Individual ____ Group ____.
Class: Fresh. ____ Soph. ____ Jr. ____ Sr. ____ Grad . ____ Other (explain) _____

Circle your response.	*Very Little*				*Very Much*	*NA*
1. My therapist *understood* my problem(s).	1	2	3	4	5	☐
2. My therapist gave attention to my *feelings*.	1	2	3	4	5	☐
3. My therapist helped me identify *specific problems*.	1	2	3	4	5	☐
4. My therapist suggested *useful approaches* to solving my problems.	1	2	3	4	5	☐
5. I felt I *related well* with my therapist.	1	2	3	4	5	☐
6. I *felt better* at the end of therapy compared to the start.	1	2	3	4	5	☐
7. I worked on *specific problems* during therapy.	1	2	3	4	5	☐
8. I was able to handle better one (or more) problem(s) *during* therapy.	1	2	3	4	5	☐
9. What I learned in therapy helped me deal with some problems *after therapy* was over.	1	2	3	4	5	☐
10. *Feeling better* about myself was more important than solving problems.	1	2	3	4	5	☐
11. *Solving problems* for myself was more important than feeling better.	1	2	3	4	5	☐
12. Solving problems for me came *before feeling better* in therapy.	1	2	3	4	5	☐
13. Solving problems for me came *after feeling better* in therapy.	1	2	3	4	5	☐
14. Behavior change with therapy *lasts longer* than a feeling change.	1	2	3	4	5	☐
15. Friends noticed I *felt better* during (or after) therapy.	1	2	3	4	5	☐
16. Friends noticed I *behaved differently* during (or after) therapy.	1	2	3	4	5	☐
17. My *overall rating of feeling change* through therapy:	1	2	3	4	5	
18. My *overall rating of behavior change* through therapy:	1	2	3	4	5	
19. My overall rating of my counseling experience:	1	2	3	4	5	

TABLE 8.2 (continued)

Circle your response.	Very Little				Very Much	NA
20. I would undertake therapy again if I *felt* I needed it.	1	2	3	4	5	
21. If I noticed I was having difficulty solving problems, I would enter therapy again.	1	2	3	4	5	
22. I would recommend a friend to seek counseling at the GWU Counseling Center.	1	2	3	4	5	

On the reverse side, feel free to comment on any of the above questions or any other aspect of your therapy.   (4/83)

counterintuitive to the assumptions and conventions of most psychotherapists. The last two appreciably high loadings on this factor came with positive attitudes about returning to the clinic again, if the need arose, and being willing to tackle problems.

Factor 5 has one significant finding, the comparison between Items 12 and 13, with the former stated, in essence, as "solving problems *before* feeling better," showing an .82 loading; whereas Item 13 — "solving problems *after* feeling better" — yielded a negative loading (− .65)! This finding, together with some items from Factor 4, puts a considerable emphasis on the behavior change aspects coming prior to feeling change, as clients so report, separating these aspects very clearly, with problem solving coming before feeling better on both items. From the cognitive viewpoin and from traditional depth psychotherapy, it is stated that thinking/feeling comes prior to behavior change, as leading the way, so to speak; but these data show that clients endorse the opposite route to change (or what they report about change based on the questions posed). This is a result all therapists should pause on, because the short-term effort to produce an effective psychotherapy appears to begin with, emphasize throughout, and end with a behavior change momentum (all the while giving proper attention to and respect for feeling change).

It was necessary to check out these findings during the 1983–1984 period and the results follow. Also, these findings should be checked further among clients other than college or university students.

COMBINING 1982–83 AND 1983–84 POPULATIONS

Results from the 22-item follow-up questionnaire to clients were available through April, 1984, thus permitting combining the findings previously cited for 1982–1983 with about 80% of the expected 1983–1984 questionnaire replies from clients. The combined N now becomes 157 (89 + 68), thereby

TABLE 8.3

Varimax Rotated Factor Pattern, Form D, 1982–1983, 22-Item Follow-Up Questionnaire, Client Ratings ($N = 89$)

		Factor 1	Factor 2	Factor 3	Factor 4	Factors
Item 1	Therapists understood problem	0.13506	0.64568	0.58084	-0.08737	-0.02420
Item 2	Therapist gave attention to feelings	0.22355	0.65199	0.51255	0.06038	-0.18738
Item 3	Therapist helped identify problems	0.41486	0.26654	0.61286	0.28625	-0.02333
Item 4	Therapist suggested approaches	0.10370	0.08506	0.86689	0.26592	0.08326
Item 5	Client related well with therapist	0.21046	0.32970	0.73768	-0.11404	-0.06291
Item 6	Client felt better at end of therapy	0.67940	0.13793	0.34029	0.27356	0.04215
Item 7	Client worked on specific problems	0.52966	0.10350	0.51391	0.14656	0.41214
Item 8	Client able to handle problems better	0.67565	0.49090	0.21093	0.24180	0.05951
Item 9	Client learned to deal with problems	0.68546	0.57994	0.03215	0.13007	-0.03474
Item 10	Feeling better about self > than prob	0.32589	-0.15435	0.24374	-0.54270	-0.37470
Item 11	Solving prob > than feeling better	0.14383	0.31039	0.05467	0.74344	0.33844
Item 12	Solving problems before feeling better	0.17731	0.22293	0.06452	0.01284	0.82155
Item 13	Solving problems after feeling better	0.45781	0.33257	0.06740	-0.25508	-0.64998
Item 14	Beh change longer than feeling change	0.20225	0.78301	0.19263	0.12921	0.22415
Item 15	Friends noticed client felt better	0.82905	0.01510	0.14754	-0.07650	0.04391
Item 16	Friends noticed client beh differently	0.60527	0.33781	0.28082	-0.20079	0.02430
Item 17	Global rating of feeling change	0.63534	0.39726	0.12250	-0.05878	-0.12250
Item 18	Global rating of behavior change	0.30163	0.83773	0.18881	0.14534	0.15724
Item 19	Global rating of cnsctr experience	0.43634	0.53022	0.52200	0.03808	0.18630
Item 20	Client would undertake therapy again	0.04221	0.16600	0.19172	0.71586	-0.05771
Item 21	With problems he/she would come again	0.01254	-0.19772	0.19743	0.78128	-0.00418
Item 22	Would recommend a friend to CC	0.15435	0.40871	0.37063	0.28591	-0.07375

making the factorial results more stable. The resulting variance Rotated Factor Pattern with 66% of the variance explained is as follows.

Five factors were delineated showing eigenvalues of 1.0 or more; the total amount of variance accounted for was 68% (Table 8.4). Factor 1 loaded heavily on items relating to positive attitudes toward the therapist (Items 1 through 5), plus a .70 loading on global rating of the Counseling Center experience; all showed close similarity to Factor 3 previously cited for the one year period, 1982–1983.

Factor 2 loaded on items relating to feeling better at end of therapy, to behavior and feeling change (the latter slightly more robust; compare Items 15 and 16, and 17 and 18 in this regard), thereby showing some inconsistency with the ratings from the first year of the study, previously cited. However, Factor 3 returns somewhat to the distinction between feeling change and behavior change: Note the − .67 for Item 10 (Feeling better about myself was more important than solving problems), compared to the .72 loading on Item 11 (Solving problems for myself more important than feeling better). Likewise, note that Item 12 loaded .81 (Solving problems . . . before feeling better) versus Item 13 (the latter with a loading of − .78), which stated that solving problems came after feeling better. This marked difference, comparable as it is on two pairs of contrasting items and on the 1982–1983 data, requires long and hard scrutiny.

Factor 4 shows two robust loadings — Items 20 and 21 — showing, respectively, positive attitudes toward undertaking therapy, or coming to the Counseling Center again, should the occasion occur (with .83 and .84 loadings, respectively). Factor 5 shows Item 14 (Behavior change with therapy lasting longer than feeling change) loading .81, and 15 and 16 showing some differential loadings on friends noting the reporting client showed feeling change and behavior change (.46 and .53, respectively, for these two items).

It seems reasonable to conclude that satisfaction and behavior change (problem solving) are the two main generalizations we can extract from these findings, the satisfaction aspect relating to therapist, to clinic and to the therapy itself. Behavior change/problem solving seems to weigh more heavily than feeling change in nearly all comparisons of these ratings. Because the intuitive notion is that feeling change is more important, perhaps more reliable, and seems to many to come before behavior change, this order of things and corresponding ratings by clients over a 2-year period suggest the need to reexamine our notions about therapy. These findings point, as well, to many needed areas of research, especially the matter of extending these findings to populations other than university students.

CLIENT-THERAPIST MATCHED PAIRS RATINGS

The opportunity was seized in the fall of 1983 to begin research on comparing client-therapist ratings on therapy outcome, using the same 22-item

TABLE 8.4

Varimax Rotated Factor Pattern, 22-Item Follow-Up Questionnaire, 1982–1984, Form D, Client Responses.
Combined N = 157

Item #		Factor 1	Factor 2	Factor 3	Factor 4	Factor 5
1	Therapists understood problem	0.76485	0.12861	-0.03816	0.19477	0.08868
2	Therapist gave attention to feelings	0.76447	0.15748	-0.01565	0.04743	0.20948
3	Therapist helped identity problems	0.72039	0.27002	0.06972	-0.09075	0.17146
4	Therapist suggested approaches	0.66143	0.17527	-0.07356	0.32660	0.07726
5	Client related well with therapist	0.79242	0.27165	-0.08508	0.01453	0.05296
6	Client felt better at end of therapy	0.28982	0.72396	0.00390	0.14624	-0.06167
7	Client worked on specific problems	0.47335	0.24968	0.00631	0.14421	0.53760
8	Client able to handle problems better	0.39023	0.48553	0.18433	0.07926	0.24781
9	Client learned to deal with problems	0.29227	0.71701	0.07226	0.17787	0.19983
10	Feeling better about self > than prob	0.07004	0.04962	-0.67358	-0.08338	-0.04850
11	Solving prob > than feeling better	0.08778	0.22373	0.72654	-0.04283	0.07771
12	Solving problems before feeling better	0.02768	0.08350	0.81153	-0.11681	0.11285
13	Solving problems after feeling better	0.17931	0.30085	-0.78657	-0.01111	0.17182
14	Beh change longer than feeling change	0.16619	0.07232	0.14105	0.07288	0.80911
15	Friends noticed client felt better	0.08260	0.67431	-0.14072	0.03645	0.46398
16	Friends noticed client beh differently	0.13618	0.53787	-0.01617	-0.06044	0.53032
17	Global rating of feeling change	0.37680	0.77518	-0.13471	0.08403	-0.01086
18	Global rating of behavior change	0.30884	0.60441	0.27490	0.19422	0.27355
19	Global rating of cnsctr experience	0.70110	0.47087	-0.03611	0.25046	0.07159
20	Client would undertake therapy again	0.17549	0.16108	-0.07399	0.83012	0.12523
21	With problems he/she would come again	0.06160	0.09509	0.01614	0.84177	0.02573
22	Would recommend a friend to CC	0.38477	0.38536	0.01689	0.46155	-0.07437

questionnaire (Form D) reported on above. Near the end of the 1983–1984 school year, all client follow-up ratings were collated for purposes of independent ratings being obtained on these same persons by the corresponding therapists. The total study N was between 69 and 78, differences arising because some respondents did not answer all items. The main question posed was whether clients and therapists, although admittedly having somewhat different vantage points, would assess the shared therapeutic experience to a high degree of correspondence. Table 8.5 summarizes these findings, among which only 8 of the 22 items lack significant difference (t test) between the

TABLE 8.5

Summarizing "t" test and Significance For Mean Follow-Up Ratings, Client-Therapist Matched Pairs, 22-Item Questionnaire (Ns = 69 – 78 Pairs)

Item #	Items	Significance	
1	Therapists understood problem	0.0070	
2	Therapist gave attention to feelings	0.0001	
3	Therapist helped identify problems	0.0003	
4	Therapist suggested approaches	0.0233	
5	Client related well with therapist	0.1756	N.S.
6	Client felt better at end of therapy	0.0017	
7	Client worked on specific problems	0.0154	
8	Client able to handle problems better	0.0001	
9	Client learned to deal with problems	0.0001	
10	Feeling better about self > than prob	0.6007	N.S.
11	Solving prob > than feeling better	0.2325	"
12	Solving problems before feeling better	0.7137	"
13	Solving problems after feeling better	0.1569	"
14	Beh change longer than feeling change	0.0004	
15	Friends noticed client felt better	0.9186	N.S.
16	Friends noticed client beh differently	0.2206	"
17	Global rating of feeling change	0.0436	
18	Global rating of behavior change	0.0767	N.S.
19	Global rating of cnsctr experience	0.0250	
20	Client would undertake therapy again	0.0001	
21	With problems he/she would come again	0.0225	
22	Would recommend a friend to CC	0.0024	

means, suggesting that client-therapist ratings at follow-up are considerably different. Noting the items on which nonsignificant differences in mean ratings occur, we observe that agreements were reached on how client related to therapist (Item 5); items relating to feeling and behavior change and their order were concurred in (Items 10–13, inclusively), the noting of reported feeling and behavior by observation of friends (evidently mentioned in the therapy hours, otherwise therapists would not know about these changes), and the global rating of behavior change, probably present because it could be somewhat easily observed by the therapist. The items showing significant differences between clients and therapists may simply be more difficult for therapists to rate, or they may react to considerably different perspectives on the referents to the items. Item analyses of these and other items may indicate some core issues on which therapists and clients can usually agree, leading to possibly basing change efforts or therapeutic emphasis on such items, following by giving more (or less?) therapeutic attention to those item areas (from a self-report standpoint) on which agreement is less. Over time the latter differences might be cleared up, or considered less important, if both client and therapist are refractory to change in judging such items. Also, a questionnaire of this type might be used to assess therapy at the mid-point or perhaps several times during the course of therapy, then goals realigned to suit the resultant ratings, aiming for greater concurrence between therapist and client.

RESEARCH ON ATTEMPTS TO ALTER THE THERAPY COURSE

We have said elsewhere that there are probably three ways to experiment with the course of therapy into, through, and out of the formal system known as the clinic. One way is to alter the intake process; some ways have already been suggested for this research (also see Chapter 6 on the Intake Interview by Fagan). A second way is to attempt to alter the attritional curve features by interposing contracts on the number of therapy sessions, such as limiting therapy to 3, 5, 8, 10, or more sessions and see if this attempt meets with success, and/or changes the nature of the distribution of cases (including means and standard deviations). A third way is to set end-of-therapy or asymptotic limits and, of course, to study those cases that go out three or more standard deviations beyond the mean of the distribution (Phillips & DePalma, 1983). In the present research an attempt was made to alter the course of therapy, in relation to the number of visits, by setting up three contract conditions.

After some discussion with the staff, it was decided to set three contract conditions on the number of therapy sessions: a 5-session limit because that was the closest figure to the actual number we have observed over the years as a baseline. A second limit was to be therapist-determined (T-D), set at the first or second interview upon the accumulation of a reasonable amount of information about the client, with consensus between client and therapist that a given number of sessions was likely to be satisfactory. The third condition for contracting for the number of therapy sessions was a control condition — 10 sessions — which was already established as the outer "control" limit (sometimes exceeded as above reports indicate — see Chapter 4), with one third of the cases being assigned to this condition. Each client up for therapy assignment went, in order, to 5, T-D, or control conditions. Clients knew that the clinic had a 10-session limit from earlier information received. When the therapist who was assigned the case received the folder on the client, a form was included that identified which condition that particular client was assigned to; the therapist followed this contractual assignment but later had the option of changing it for good and ample reasons, which were recorded on the pink sheet for later reference if needed. Table 8.6 presents the means and standard deviations for each of these three contractual conditions, plus data on the actual number of sessions the clients were seen.

Table 8.6 shows that the intake therapist's estimate of the number of sessions the client would need showed a mean of 7.24, significantly above the standard mean over the years and reliably higher than the presently obtained empirical mean (5.08). When the client was seen by the assigned therapist, the mean number of estimated sessions the client would need was 6.97, also significantly higher than the empirical mean. In the instances in which the therapist and client saw fit to change the contractual number of sessions, the 22 cases of revised therapy contracts averaged 7.82 sessions. Thus it appeared that each time the therapist was involved in some estimate of sessions needed or in some change of venue, so to speak, the mean figures went upward. The three contract conditions, then, did not influence the overall flow of cases through the system in a way that changed the actual mean number of ses-

TABLE 8.6

Summarizing Data on Three Contractual Conditions for Number of Therapy Sessions (5-Session Limit; Therapist-Determined Limit (T-D); and Control (10-Sessions)

N	Contract	Mean No. Sessions	SD
296	Intake Estimate of N/Sessions Needed	7.24	2.70
112	Therapist N/Sessions Actually Set	6.97	2.74
22	Revised Therapist Contract	7.82	3.17
104	Actual N/Sessions	5.08	3.99

sions. It is always possible that later data coming in will change these figures but it is not likely.

Comparisons between these three sets of therapy contractual conditions failed to show significant differences. The actual number of sessions (mean = 5.08), broken down for the three conditions are as follows: 37 T-D (Therapist-Determined) cases versus 5-session limit cases, with means of 5.13 and 4.47, respectively, by t test showed a p value of .47; 29 control cases (mean 5.79 sessions) versus 5-session limit (38 cases; mean, 4.47), netted ap value of .14; and the twenty-nine 10-session limit cases (controls) versus the 37 T-D cases, with means of 5.79 and 5.14, respectively, also failed to show a significant difference by t test (p = .55). Thus, the 10-session control cases and the 5-session contractual cases both had means between 5 and 6 sessions, showing that the widest contractual limits failed to produce significantly different means regarding the number of sessions.

Everywhere we have looked at the issue of therapist versus client estimates of what is needed in therapy, and also in regard to their ratings of outcome, it has been repeatedly shown that therapists tend to be more pessimistic about the number of sessions needed (or are they more realistic in some hypothetical "big picture"?) and tend to be less favorable than clients in giving final evaluations.

As far as these results go, they appear to have both positive and negative implications. The implications are positive insofar as the attrition curve findings are concerned: The three contractual groups failed to produce significant variations from the characteristic 5-session means for total populations over several years. This stability is apparently high and efforts to influence the delivery of services in the form of changing the number of sessions will have to be based either on more salient interventions and/or on improved methods for handling therapist practices in relation to contractual obligations. How therapists decide what a client "needs" remains largely a mystery, a research problem requiring much study but one which we did not have the time to investigate in this series of reports.

Also, the findings are positive in pointing to other new research possibilities. If the mean number of sessions is clearly about 5 in these studies and in populations reported on in Chapters 1 and 2, then the whole nature of preparing therapists for short-term therapy must be put up front early on in their training. The real issue in therapy among outpatient clinics, at least, is how to do truly effective short-term therapy, because a short time is all most therapists are going to have.

Negatively speaking, this research is a bit discouraging in showing how persistent therapists are in devaluing client capacity to change insofar as therapist estimates of the needed number of sessions and outcome are concerned. Locating variables in the "psyche" is one contributing factor in this misfiring, even in the short-term, time-limited framework. Of course, if these findings were compared to private practice therapist and/or to practices in clinics where larger numbers of sessions, and much longer asymptotes were the case, then the small differences found here would loom much larger. Again, this is a compelling reason for promoting cooperative, programmatic research where a very wide basis for investigations of the type reported here—plus many, many more—can be carried out over time. The "Mom and Pop/ Corner Grocery Store" nature of most research on psychotherapy will have to give way to a larger data base, and to examining greater variation in clinic practices. Far more work on client attitudes and evaluations, with more openness and readiness on the part of therapists to be flexible in what they do, also requires consideration and study.

THERAPISTS' "AVERAGE SUCCESSFUL" CLIENTS

One hundred two therapists in the Washington, DC, area graciously agreed to cooperate with the author in providing responses to the 22-item follow-up questionnaire (reported on above). They were given the following instruction: "Answer these questions as you think they would be answered by an "average, successful client." The total number of respondents from several counseling centers in the metropolitan area was 102. Results are shown in Table 8.7.

Table 8.7 shows that the factorial study of these 102 therapist replies netted seven factors. Factor 1 loaded primarily on Items 7 (client worked on specific problems) and 8 (client better able to handle problems during therapy), and on Items 3 and 4 (referring to the therapist role). These items and loadings are a bit less robust than those obtained by client ratings, shown previously.

Factor 2 looks a bit like Factor 1 client ratings in that reported therapist understanding and giving attention to client feelings loom relatively large. Overall ratings of feelings, behavior and Counseling Center experience, none of which are robust here, show the last-named loading the highest (.51); and with feeling change slightly higher than reported behavior change loadings as therapists see hypothetical client change (Items 17 and 18 with .36 and .30 ratings, respectively).

Factor 3 emphasizes item loadings dealing with feelings and relating well (Items 10 and 5, respectively, showing some robustness); with overall feeling change (Item 17) loading higher than overall behavior change or overall rating of Counseling Center experience. These results are consonant with therapist reporting how hypothetically successful clients would emphasize feelings and relatedness; but they show some inconsistency insofar as Item 12 (solving problems before feeling better) ranks higher than Item 13 (solving problems after feeling better) (with .38 and .07 loadings, respectively, assigned to these opinions, neither of which is very convincing).

TABLE 8.7

Varimax Rotated Factor Pattern for 102 Therapists (including Interns/Externs) on 22-Item F-U Questionnaire, D.C. Area Counseling Centers, Under Instructions "How Hypothetically Successful Client Would Respond"

Item #		Factor 1	Factor 2	Factor 3	Factor 4	Factor 5	Factor 6	Factor 7
1	Understood	0.18725	0.79417	0.11812	0.04689	0.19401	-0.11037	0.08638
2	Feelings	0.22942	0.82111	0.13534	0.05482	-0.07797	0.06164	0.18045
3	Therapist specific problems	0.74757	0.26692	0.08618	0.04718	0.02561	0.10258	-0.00901
4	Useful approaches	0.68017	0.22821	0.09423	0.14015	0.27181	-0.12839	0.19710
5	Related well	0.05874	0.45097	0.52324	0.15521	0.02939	0.12465	0.08738
6	Felt better	0.02105	0.11904	0.46331	0.18381	0.29975	0.16365	0.53395
7	Client worked on specific problems	0.72611	0.08897	0.17291	0.35762	0.24205	0.07111	0.14596
8	During therapy	0.64405	0.05509	0.01193	0.12843	-0.01684	0.55659	0.01462
9	After therapy	0.36094	0.49354	0.26403	0.23387	0.05448	0.34232	-0.05550
10	Client feeling better	0.14440	0.02909	0.86760	-0.12665	-0.13809	-0.04789	0.12515
11	Solving problems	0.07621	-0.01388	-0.14417	0.05771	0.74164	-0.14944	0.08805
12	Solve prob before feeling better	0.44417	-0.13258	0.38375	-0.03419	0.39002	-0.29507	-0.40969
13	Solve prob after feeling better	0.14486	0.11334	0.07235	-0.02202	-0.05423	-0.04090	0.85709
14	Lasts longer	0.39103	0.14860	-0.10556	-0.07134	0.29785	-0.55439	0.13726
15	Friends noticed felt better	0.13893	0.07630	0.06335	-0.11802	0.14644	0.81141	0.09088
16	Friends noticed behaved differently	0.30606	0.18649	0.13023	0.09393	0.67037	0.29754	-0.09179
17	Overall rat feeling change	0.14135	0.36029	0.66081	0.19883	-0.01129	0.17304	-0.00428
18	Overall rat behavior change	0.42789	0.29661	0.10542	0.34750	0.48172	0.08544	-0.18577
19	Overall rat of center exper	-0.01294	0.50888	0.49515	0.30083	0.28995	0.20920	-0.08339
20	Undertake ther again if needed	0.16058	0.22668	0.24901	0.41279	-0.22106	0.40560	0.02485
21	Solving prob enter ther again	0.07682	0.14670	-0.00831	0.77233	0.17977	0.01472	0.14788

A slightly higher loading on Item 18 (overall rating of behavior change) compared to Item 17 (overall feeling change), neither of which is strong, is part of the findings for Factor 4. More significant for this factor, however, is willingness to enter therapy again if difficulty in solving problems occurred (Item 21, with .77 loading); and Item 22, willingness to recommend a friend to the Counseling Center (.81 loading). Both therapists and clients agree that this is an item worthy of high rating.

Factor 5 nets interesting results given the tendency for therapists to rate feelings-related items higher than do clients. Therapists hypothesized clients would rate higher the notion that friends observed their behavior change, Item 16 (in contrast to their feelings change, Item 15) in therapy, with a loading of .67 versus .15. And, although neither Item 17 nor 18 is robust, overall behavior change is much higher than overall feeling change loading (.48 and − .01, respectively). Item 11 is also very interesting in this context, with solving problems (.74 loading) judged more important than feeling better, Item 10 with − .13 loadiing.

Factor 6 appears to reverse some of the feelings versus behavior change aspects of therapy inasmuch as Item 15 (friends noticed client felt better) received a .81 loading whereas Item 16 (friends noticed client behaved differently) produced a loading of .30. Other items appear not to differentiate importantly in regard to this factor. Behavior change seen as lasting longer (Item 14) shows a − .55 loading.

The last factor to receive a 1.0 or higher eigenvalue showed only one robust loading: .86 on Item 13 (solving problems came after feeling better) reemphasizing the therapist-related tendency to rate feeling items higher than behavior change or problem-solving items and to differ with clients in this respect. Otherwise, Item 6 was the only other item loading above .50.(.53 on feeling better at the end of therapy).

Essentially, then, therapists (including externs and interns usually with 3–4 years of therapy experience in these five settings) tend to slant their ratings in the direction of saying clients experience feeling change over behavior or problem-solving change; to produce more factors than clients; and to produce generally less robust loadings on items than do clients. However, the hypothetical nature of the directions may have diminished the precision and differential character of staff ratings. More comparisons of therapists − staff and interns/externs − on a matched pair basis with clients, as previously cited, are needed for better understanding of the apparent tendencies of therapists to veer off in several ways from client evaluations. Also, as has been previously stated, carrying this research to other than university populations is powerfully suggested.

CLIENT-THERAPIST CORRELATIONS,
MATCHED PAIRS

Another small study of how therapists and clients rated the client's therapy experiences was carried out on the home (GWU) Counseling Center population, 1983–1984. From among the 75 client replies to the 22-Item Follow-Up Questionnaire, Form D, received by late April, 1984, matched ratings from the staff (including externs) were submitted to a correlational analysis. The matched-pairs numbers varied between 55 and 73 owing to all respondents not answering all questions. Results are as follows:

Item # 1, $r =$	.12 (73)	Item # 12, $r =$	.03 (61)
2, $r =$	.22 (73)	13, $r =$	.04 (61)
3, $r =$	.11 (73)	14, $r =$	$-.12$ (58)
4, $r =$	$-.01$ (73)	15, $r =$	.08 (55)
5, $r =$	.10 (72)	16, $r =$	$-.08$ (57)
6, $r =$	.10 (72)	17, $r =$	.17 (71)
7, $r =$	.24 (71)	18, $r =$	.05 (70)
8, $r =$	.07 (70)	19, $r =$	.12 (73)
9, $r =$	.18 (64)	20, $r =$	$-.05$ (69)
10, $r =$	.19 (68)	21, $r =$	.03 (71)
11, $r =$	.09 (72)	22, $r =$	.08 (73)

Of these 22 items, only one (Item 7, "client worked on specific problems") showed a significant correlation (.24, $p = .0407$), thus showing overall marked absence of agreement between client and therapist on this series of questions. All client-rated means were higher than those for therapists, except for small mean differences on Items 11, 12, and 16.

The evidence here matches that reported above in other contexts, viz., that client and therapist are noticeably apart in evaluating many aspects of psychotherapy, from inception, through the process, and out to final evaluation. All of the practical and theoretical implications of these discrepancies are not well-known, and some are hardly recognized, but all call for more careful examination if we are to improve not only short-term psychotherapy but all therapy.

Surely there are a number of lessons for therapists in these findings. Too often therapists and clients are discrepant in their ratings and therapists often lack understanding of these discrepancies. It appears that therapists may be too doctrinaire in their evaluations, that they impose on, or attribute to, the clients some or many values, preferences, and experiences that relate primarily or only to the therapist's perspective; and as a result the consumer (client) viewpoint is played down.

Many students of psychotherapy have remarked on the absence of re-search—and a lack of interest in same—by therapists (and clinicians in general)—a matter that has seemingly resulted in clinicians taking their cues for practice and knowledge on other than data-based evidence. Most thera-pists learn their skills through imitating their mentors, not from doing re-search on the many fascinating problems that confront them and their cli-ents. Perhaps that is one major reason why therapists and clients appear somewhat far apart with many therapy evaluations. Research should work, however, not to prove who is right or wrong—that would be even less egalitarian—but to find ways to bring client and therapist closer together in their joint enterprise, some of which may have been elucidated here.

9 Conflict Theory: Psychotherapy and Micro Processes

The notion of conflict is a well-tenured one in psychotherapy and psychopathology (Hull, 1943; Miller, 1971; Miller & Dollard, 1950). It was used loosely and frequently by Freud, has had an active experimental life in the work of Miller and associates (Miller, 1971), as well as in the works of Anderson and Parmenter (1939); Brown (1948); Gantt (1944); Guthrie (1938); Hovland and Sears (1938); Maier (1939); Masserman (1943); and more recently, Seligman (1975); Solomon (1964).

Miller (1971) says "Conflicts can distract, delay, and fatigue the individual and force him to make maladaptive compromise responses" (p. 3). It is also recognized that conflict can spread (or generalize) to numerous areas of one's life if the central or most salient areas of conflict are not handled gainfully by the individual.

Conflict derives from reinforcement principles, most clearly articulated by Hull, Miller, and their associates. Although clinicians have tended to use the term conflict loosely—in a kind of intuitive, commonsense way—the concept is amenable to experimental verification and description. Space is not available to go into the notion of conflict thoroughly; suffice it to say that conflict is made up of approach tendencies (toward a goal) and avoidance tendencies (away from a goal area). Conflict is present in our lives daily; most conflicts are easily resolved and elicit no serious personality or behavioral consequences for persons. In a more profound and far-reaching sense, however, conflict can be serious. It can paralyze the person, lead to or accompany depression, and may be the precipitant to extreme withdrawal from social life and/or suicide. When conflict is intense and long-lasting, it so debilitates the organism (animals as well as mankind) that the natural repertoire of the organism is so constricted that life is almost unlivable.

THE APPROACH-AVOIDANCE GRADIENT

Quantitatively, conflict may be described in terms of an *avoidance gradient* (how the organism's movement away from a goal area is described, most likely related to fear, escape, pain provocation); and an *approach gradient* (Miller, 1971, pp. 4–16). Approaching a goal area is gradual; avoidance gradients are steep (see Fig. 9.1) for examples of hypothetical approach-avoidance gradients).

What does the gradient mean? It means there is a gradualness to the approach and avoidance tendencies, as Fig. 9.1 shows. The steepness of the avoidance gradient indicates that we leave a feared or aversive situation posthaste: the burning building, the sinking ship, the precipitous stairs, predatory animals, the aversive social situation, and so on. We get away as fast as possible. When patients indicate strong disapproval, escape, fear, apprehension regarding a place, situation, or another person, one can be sure the general stimulus condition there (a complex of stimulation) is dangerous, foreboding or extremely unwelcome. On the other hand, the gradualness of approaching a liked social situation, a trip to an art gallery, meeting a respected or loved person, and so forth, are characterized by relishing the approach, savoring the experience all along the way. Approach tendencies are usually not hurried or precipitous.

When the same situation becomes endowed with both approach and avoidance tendencies, trouble brews. It is probably impossible to conceive of tur-

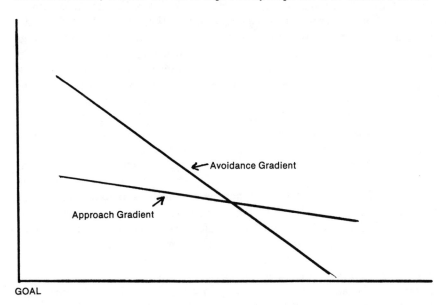

FIG. 9.1   Showing approach avoidance gradients in the conflict paradigm. (Adapted from Miller, 1971, Fig. 1, p. 6)

moil, psychopathology, abnormal behavior (not organically or structurally produced) without conflict. Conflict is the *sine qua non* of psychopathology or abnormality. No conflict, no psychopathology. However, due to the degree of conflict, the opposite is not true: conflict, per se, does not mean psychopathology; it may mean minor annoyance, or even a relished encounter, a test of strength and skill (as in taking a difficult examination, or meeting a challenging opponent).

CONFLICT IS EVER PRESENT

Clinically, the therapist can assume that if a person comes for psychotherapy there is conflict present in the person's life, in the person's relationship with his or her environment (including, of course, other people). In extreme phobic cases, however, the conflict may be between crossing the street or not, between handling an ordinary utensil (a knife, e.g.) or not and so on; conditioned, likely, in relationship to experiences with other people but with the particulars (street, knife) carrying the burden, so to say, of the conflict. In such cases as severe phobias (or obsessional states), the client and therapist will sooner or later get around to discussing the client's interpersonal settings, the client's anger and/or fear in relationship to certain people, and so on (Emmelkamp, 1982). The client, probably lacking assertiveness, has never or scarcely ever, handled conflicts with others well, even simple conflicts such as expressing one's feelings about a commonly experienced matter, and has as a result harbored resentments, even anger, at the other person. Lacking even a modicum degree of resolution, the client continues on with strong feelings concerning the "unfinished business" of conflict resolution and appears "ready" to be emotional — to withdraw, to be angry, to express strong fear — regarding certain classes of experience with other people, or with situations involving others. For example, one patient became irate at the mention of the name of a cousin who was about to get married because the client felt "obliged" (actually, he felt *compelled* by his parents) to appear at the cousin's wedding when he had no desire whatsoever to attend the affair. Not coping directly with the issues involved, feeling hopeless, resentful — even passionately angry as he dwelt on the issue — set up profound dislike for the cousin and her wedding, when the cousin, herself, had nothing to do with the client's attending the wedding or not (it was the parental pressures that were the focus of the conflict). The client felt unable to confront the parents with his feelings and be honest and straightforward about the conflict involved.

It really matters less what the conflict is about than the fact that conflict is present in such cases, or, indeed, in any debilitating psychological problem. In terms of therapeutic tactics, it is very advantageous to interact with the client on "conflict terms" (that is, holding up the notion that conflict is uppermost in the client's life and, as such, get on with discovering and discussing it). This straightforwardness makes for a more economical therapy and puts the right issues forward at the outset. The micro theories — about the individual, in contrast to the macro way the whole clinical delivery system operates — is the focus in this case; however, as these cases multiply in the course of the clinic's operation, how such phobic (or extreme anger) cases are handled — whether judiciously and parsimoniously, or in terms of assumed long-range therapy — does affect the overall delivery system. What we call the more "serious" or "difficult" cases may often be simply those cases where we have trouble locating the conflict, or when we tend to think there is a nucleus of experience to "explain" the symptom (or syndrome) rather than searching with the client for coping behaviors of use to the client. Although the attritional curve would likely be the same in overall slope in any instance, we could treat a population of clients as very formidable cases requiring long-term help, or we could treat them in terms of finding and resolving the conflicts forthwith. In the first situation, the clients might have a mean number of sessions in the 50+ range, with a standard deviation of (say) 12 or 15 sessions, whereas the latter treatment posture might well come under the purview of short-term help as documented herein with a mean of 5–10 sessions and a standard deviation of about the same amount. (As the mean number of sessions increases — say up around 50 or more — the standard deviations would not keep pace with the means, but would show a very long asymptote, possibly 5–10 standard deviations beyond the mean. See Zilbergeld, 1983, p. 293, where he reports finding that the average number of analytically oriented therapy was about 290 sessions, whereas "full-scale psychoanalysis" averaged 835 hours; what the standard deviations would be in these cases might surprise one.) The point is that, given the nature of shorter term psychotherapy, the micro problem based on proper attention to conflict and conflict resolution in the client's life (Phillips, 1984) would lead to a more heuristic psychotherapy with the vast majority of cases (see Fig. 9.1).

LINKING MICRO AND MACRO CONDITIONS

The link, then, is that in the micro condition the therapist does as much as possible to structure therapy and to move toward effective problem solving while keeping in mind that "satisfaction" with the therapeutic encounter appears to be very important to the client and is one of the main avenues of assessment by which the client judges the efficacy of therapy (see Chapter 8). The question can always be raised by the clinician: "So what if the attrition curve is as described — how does that influence what *I do* in the therapy hour?" Of course, there are not now clear and certain connections between the micro situation (the clinical and therapeutic situations) and the overall delivery system. These are matters for more empirical study. However, given the importance — especially in the first four chapters — placed on the intake, getting as much accomplished there as possible may bode as well as any one event for successful outcome and for controlling the length of therapy.

Another possible connection between the micro and the macro considerations is based on the whole curve and the flow of cases. Although this is considered the macro event of all events, there are presumably a number of things the clinician or the clinic as an administrative unit can do to capitalize on the relevance of the attritional curve. For one thing, insofar as can now be told, all clinics with reasonably good data show the characteristic attritional curve; but some show larger drops after intake, some smaller drops, some with the major drop after two or three sessions (see Chapters 1 and 2). Whether these are matters of therapeutic effectiveness (or its absence) is not now known; improving therapy at the individual or small group level through more structured effort to identify and help solve client problems — keeping the satisfaction issue uppermost, as well — may help to shorten the overall flow of cases through the system (reduce the mean and standard deviation and shorten the length of the asymptote). We may not be able to alter the slope of the attrition curve as far as we now know, but we may make the whole curve less lengthy. If the number of visits is the "bottom line" in evaluating psychotherapy — insofar as quality of therapy is not sacrificed — then efforts at the micro level that led to this economy are to be valued and enhanced. In short, the activities of the therapist working with the client to increase macro efficiency are likely to be of greatest value for the training of therapist, as a basis of research, for understanding the entire flow of cases through the delivery system and for flexibly meeting exigencies in the lives of people seeking psychological help.

CONFLICT THEORY AND CONTENT-FREE THERAPY

Although the assertion cannot be empirically supported at this time, it appears reasonable and likely that conflict is basic to any need for psychotherapy, and that solving conflict does not, in turn, depend upon any particular psychotherapeutic formulation or diagnosis (Colby & Spar, 1983). All therapist/theorists speak about conflict, whether or not they make it explicit. Gestalt therapists attempt to resolve conflicts between the individual's roles that lead to candidness, honesty, and sincerity; Ellis's (1962) position refers to conflicts between what one wants from others on the one hand and the "awfulness" of not receiving the kudos on the other hand, plus all the psychological gyrations that go with the play between these two tendencies, aiming for realistic, rational outcomes from the struggles. It is not difficult to apply conflict theory to all the systems of psychotherapy found in Corsini (1981),

Patterson (1966), and others. This does not mean that the therapists/ theorists themselves identify and grapple with conflict-related variables — most of them never mention the possibility explicitly save for a few (Phillips, 1984), but one does not have to read far between the lines to come again and again upon at least implied conflict.

IS CONTENT IMPORTANT FOR THEORY?

If most, or all, psychotherapy theories can be reduced to conflict theory terms, what then is the importance of the particular content of a theory of therapy? It may have an appeal to prospective clients. A client may present himself or herself as "needing to be more assertive" (or, alternately, "overcoming shyness" or the like); or he or she may need to deal with depression (which may, in part, be viewed as a kind of stalemate arising from opposing approach and avoidance tendencies that have been intense enough to deplete the energies of the person). With depression, inactivity and loss of reinforcement potential are the resultant conditions. In dealing therapeutically with patients/clients who present Gestalt-like, Ellis-like, depressive-like (perhaps Beck-depressive-like) problems, one would look for the areas of conflict, openly discuss conflict with the client, and attempt appropriate problem solving.

Emphasizing Coping Behavior. One important aspect of looking at micro events of a clinical/therapeutic nature this way is that it helps get the person started with coping procedures. The word "coping" may be more palatable with most clients; problem solving may sound too formidable; others may, semantically speaking, prefer other terminology. Clinicians need to be aware of semantic matters in communicating with clients; it is important in most settings not to "pathologize" the client's behavior. Yet, sometimes, too, one encounters clients who want to feel they are formidable cases, as this may add to their notion of their own worth, their uniqueness ("My therapist says she or he has never seen a case quite like mine — I must be something for the books!"). A lot of therapeutic communication, especially at the outset (the importance, again, of the intake) has to hinge on appropriate references to emotional events in the lives of persons. There is usually more emotion and less fact and circumstance and condition revealed by the client in the opening passages of therapy. However, one cannot easily employ the ABC's notion — antecedent conditions, behavior itself, and consequences — at the outset. A good therapist doesn't tell the client all he or she (the therapist) is doing at the outset; that comes out gradually as the context is prepared and the statements are meaningful to the client; otherwise the client is being talked "over" and may be resentful if not simply perplexed.

Let the context features come forth as the content of the conflict is revealed is a better guide. Diagnosis is really putting the proper names, emotionally speaking, on some of the client's reported feelings/behavior/attitudes; it is not putting on a label in the formal diagnostic sense. "I think I hear you saying you have some trouble in making up your mind, pro or con, about Elizabeth," might be very appropriate in a number of ways: It is loosely diagnostic insofar as it specifies conflict in the relationship; it identifies a person (perhaps, also, circumstance) with the mention of the name of the person the client has referred to; and it incorporates a lot of data the client has already produced. If more content is needed it will — or may — appear. It takes the openness of the therapist to see that similar conflicts may — among other possibilities — characterize other relationships with women, among the client's office mates or among other friends, relatives, and so on. A number of events are almost always readily appropriate and available for the discussions between therapist and client in such cases.

Staying on Same Frequency as the Client. Another matter of clinical parsimony at the micro level is that of responding directly to the client's statements, and not ignoring them because the therapist is thinking something quite different from what the client is reporting. Some remark by the client about his brother does not need to arouse thoughts in the therapist (which are likely not mentioned to the client) about sibling rivalry; or comments about the mother leading to therapist thoughts about Oedipal striving, thereby neglecting to meet the client on his or her terms. Many therapists as they interact with the client spend a lot of time reaching "diagnostic opinions." Two channels of communication are not better than one in such a case. In reviewing tapes made by fledgling therapists, it has come up often that a therapist fails to respond to a matter introduced by the client because the therapist identifies the client statement as belonging to a (usually diagnostic) category different from what the client is asserting. When asking the fledgling therapist why the client comment was not picked up and reacted to, the typical reply was that the therapist was "assuming" the client was remarking on some different topic than the apparent (or obvious) one. This tack on the therapist's part takes the therapy away from the main line of discourse or stifles fluency about the channel of thought introduced by the client, and may fail to come to grips with salient issues. Continuing with this tactic (or it may even be a ploy on the therapist's part) tends to introduce irrelevancies into the therapy exchange and lengthen or postpone the matter of getting down to the pertinent issues. Therapists come to therapy matters filled with hypotheses about content gleaned from their training, most of which are often irrelevant to the issues at hand and are actually hindrances to effective therapy. Adhering strongly to content often blinds the therapist to saliency in the here-and-now statements of the client. As and when content is important, it will show itself, so to say; we need not introduce it *ex cathedra* at the outset, or impose it — following our theoretical fads and fashions — from the beginning in order to convince the client and ourselves as therapists that a particular content is "the thing." A given content may be important and sometimes this is realized early on, but it should arise naturally. The matter of referring to potential suicide or thoughts of same by the client is a case in point. The moment some clients remark they feel depressed or discouraged, some therapists want to introduce questions about suicide: "Have you thought (much) about suicide?" "Are you preoccupied with suicide?" "Have you tried it, or have you made any plans for suicide?" All these questions without considering the possibility that many people feel discouraged and even hopeless at times with nary a (serious) thought of suicide. Why introduce this formidable topic before it has any known saliency? It arises, it seems, from therapist preoccupations with certain notions they have about suicide, what leads to suicide, and so on. Moreover, the excursion into questions about suicide obfuscates the real problem of how events accumulate in ways discouraging to the client, and what manner of coping has been tried to what ends. And so on. . . . These excursions into pet theories of therapists, guesses about what the content must be arising from client expressions, may be more distracting than anything else; and they hinder access to more important information and to more important considerations about how learning coping behaviors may reduce the conflicts involved.

Listening Carefully: Clients will Tell You Their Problems. Consonant with a parsimonious attitude toward client problems at the micro level is the observation that client statements, sometimes very succinct and pointed, will let you in on what their problem(s) are. One client, after talking several minutes about "feeling badly about relationships," stated that she had a terrible time trying to control her temper when even mildly provoked. This statement turned out to be a highly important one, introduced during the first 5 minutes of the intake interview. The statement about temper control ramified into a number of areas of her life and showed how most friendships were lost owing to this tendency, several jobs terminated by her bosses following outbursts, and so on. This one topic proved to be the most seminal in her whole series of therapy sessions, seven in all. Another client said, also early on in the first session, "I think I am too vain abut myself and this turns off others." Therapists quick to see the core statement for what it is can usually bring the client into discussions that get to the heart of the matter in short order. The proof of the pudding, however, is not the therapist's opinion that detects the potential relevance of the client's statement in such instances, but in where the core statement leads and how much behavioral relevance in life-outside-the-therapy-session it provokes. In supervising tyro therapists one of the main instructional efforts by the supervisor stems from examples of early client statements about definitive problems; supervisees in seminars ask one another: "Has the client told you his or her problem yet?" when the first interview (intake) is being discussed from taped recordings.

The skill of early recognition of client statement of the problem is an important one, although therapists with little experience are often hesitant to take the risk of pointing out such salient client statements. The prevailing attitude among trainees (and among experienced therapists, as well) is that the problem is long-ago-and-far-away; not waiting for it to somehow come out of its cocoon is considered risky business. Quite the opposite: Not picking up on the client's cogency is a waste of time, a possible loss in rapport, and may encourage an excursion into less important topics. The micro worker — the clinician — has always to keep an eye on the macro results. To do otherwise is to risk being inefficient and ineffective, because the clinician is beholden to and a product of the system; to ignore this, or not to be mindful of the structure of the delivery system is unrealistic. Anything the clinician can do that is contributory to — or a proper challenge to — the overall delivery system is a high cause; the clinician failing to see this relationship is working to some extent in the dark.

ANXIETY

The most commonly used clinical term is *anxiety*. It has more meanings than any other term and fewer referents. The greatest non-contribution to clinical work is to single out anxiety as "the problem" or to build diagnosis and treatment on it. Although anxiety in some way is ubiquitous in the person's conflict status, anxiety cannot be regarded as the problem or as a core issue; it is a by-product of conflict, which is another way of pointing up the importance of conflict as the basis of psychopathology and the raison d'être for psychotherapy of any type. Why is anxiety regarded as a secondary issue when so many think it is *the* issue?

If conflict is the *sine qua non* of psychopathology and psychotherapy, anxiety by this definition is *derived*. There is no anxiety without conflict. Anxiety in this view becomes the condition observable by the individual (and often by others) and is a signal that the person, the client, is caught, as it were, in the intersection of the approach and avoidance conflict gradients. One may, of course, experience anxiety by the spread of effect — to use the time-honored phrase — outward from the core conflict setting. One may have high anxiety at the point of giving a speech or engaging in some other public performance. The anxiety does not occur just at the point of the activation of the performance; it begins as and when the individual discriminates cues related to the core issue, the actual presentation. We often call this "anticipatory anxiety" and consider it a generalization from the central performance issue itself.

This anticipatory condition is in evidence when upon awakening in the morning, one remembers that the speech is to be given at 10 a.m. There are many cues related to dressing, eating breakfast, having extra coffee to blur the anxiety, motoring to the office, preparing for the actual presentation, and so on, that are "anticipatory." What is significant here is that as one moves toward the moment of performance, one's anxiety appears to increase. We lack the instrumentation now to record all the physiological signs — sweating palms, "butterflies in the stomach," hesitant speech, poor voice control, and the like — that signal the actual performance anxiety and the anticipatory stages; but we shall have them some day. The increase in felt (reported) anxiety stems from the fact that one is moving up on the conflict gradients, both approach and avoidance. What would relieve the anxiety? To have the speech or presentation cancelled. Failing this event, the individual is caught in an apparently ever-increasing anxiety level; sometimes, however, when the speech begins, the actual behavior — the speaking, the content of the speech, and so on — take over and anxiety abates. When one is ushered into actual performance of the task itself, anxiety tends to subside; the moving toward the event without access to the performance behavior — the speech, the acting, the playing of the musical instrument — is the most crucial part for feeling anxious. One has the feeling at the time — one says to one's self or to a friend — "I wish this were *over!*" "I'd do anything to get out of this!" And so forth. Where is the problem in this formulation?

The problem lies in the intersection of the approach and avoidance gradients. If one had no concern about the speech, one would do it just as matter-of-factly as putting on one's socks and shoes. It is the aversive, fearful, disapproving, standard-setting aspects of the performance that give it its negative or avoidance aspects. The person feels and may say to himself or herself, or to others, "I am afraid I'll do poorly, or look silly." Or equivalent statements. If one is fully confident in the performance, or if the performance is of no great value, then one enters into the arena with composure and performs as well as the situation allows. No issue is present. Or, conversely, if the situation to be avoided is not one a person wishes or needs to engage in, he or she simply avoids the potentially provocative situation. We do not hesitate much when there is only an escape alternative present, where one does not have to approach the goal area. Straightforward approach or avoidance, each uncomplicated by the other, raises no issue for us; it is the presence of the incompatible alternative that raises anxiety.

Addressing the condition of anxiety then is a matter for therapists to clarify. Do we dwell in conversation with the client on the anxiety matter? Or do we pay increasingly more attention — once the occasion for anxiety has been named and somewhat described — to the approach/avoidance issues? Why is the speech or performance so everlastingly important? What is at stake? A history of reinforcement, probably on an intermittent schedule — thereby making extinction more difficult — is probably present for the person. One can deal infinitely with the background experiences that made the performance so important; or one can, therapeutically, look to alternative ways to make the performance, and the approach to it, more comfortable by successive approximation routes, and so forth. On many occasions the present writer has had the anxious speech-giver rehearse the speech aloud, give the speech before selected others, practice in the same setting (if possible) where the speech is to be given, record on tape and listen for cues that will aid performance, and so on. Most people do not go through these corrective steps, but suffer in silence, wondering why they feel as they do; they concentrate on the misery and not on the solution. Extinction of the fear in the usual sense of extinction is likely not feasible; there is not enough time, and anyhow one would have to recreate the initial situations wherein the anxiety was initially learned, so one might as well create the real situation vicariously and develop competent alternatives to the anxiety; the latter is the shorter, more productive route. One should not — and the therapist should not — concentrate on the anxiety per se but on alternatives. Of course, this is true for any behavior change, especially the more refractory concerns people have, but we tend to think that anxiety is a whole problem in its own right, whereas it is the by-product of a more general condition with discernible features that we tackle.

One of the contributors to long-term therapy is the supposition that anxiety is, itself, a formidable problem and that it takes a long time to remedy. Problem is, longer term therapy does not remedy the anxiety issue any better — as far as we know — than short-term therapy where the latter is pivoted on developing alternative behaviors rather than pursuing the anxiety condition in its own right, as if it were the core problem. Seeing anxiety in the more formidable terms, then, increases the macro problem, sends clients out into the asymptote that describes longer term therapy when, in fact, this devotion to the longer term work on the anxiety issue may be due to the absence of appropriate therapeutic techniques at the micro level.

The same arguments and alternative proposals for engaging the problems may be made for conflicts related to depression, hysteria, suicidal tendencies, and so on. One should not be naive here, however; some problems are formidable, not because of the diagnosis, but because the environmental conditions are not present or properly arrangeable in ways conducive to effective therapy in a short time. As we learn more about effective therapy we will discern how we can arrange the environment of clients — with their help and understanding, of course — in ways that promote therapeutic change. The task that clinicians face is not that of inventing ever more therapies — the 250 + varieties, so-called (Herink, 1980) are quite enough! — but of developing alternative approaches to the problems heretofore practiced by the clients and testing out the consequences in the research ways adumbrated in this book (plus others, of course, that will be invented as we tackle the problem of therapeutic change more realistically).

ASSERTIVENESS AND SOCIAL SKILLS TRAINING

It has been implied in much of the discussion of the micro situation faced by the clinician in therapy that one is reeducating the client to better ways of coping and living. Pursuant to these objectives is an emphasis on assertiveness and generally on social skills (Bellack & Hersen, 1979; Curran & Monti, 1982; Hargie, Sanders, & Dickson, 1981; Phillips, 1978; Singleton, Spurgeon, & Stammers, 1980; Trower, Bryant, & Argyle, 1978; Weeks & L'Abate, 1982; Wine & Smye, 1981). It is at once apparent upon consulting research and writing on social skills that this area is made up largely of assertiveness dimensions, that each is compatible with a short-term problem-solving emphasis in psychotherapy, and that through these connections the micro situation blends noticeably into the macro one. One of the bridges of importance between clinical skills (micro) and the client learning better to function in his or her natural environment comes about through assertiveness improvement leading to more general social competence. Mental health from this viewpoint is a matter of social skills in the broad sense of the term (Phillips, 1978). Looking, as well, at the actual operations performed by the clinician, one sees a considerable emphasis on interpersonal relationships which are, basically, social skills. The reason the social skills movement has had such currency the past decade or so (Weeks & L'Abate, 1984) is not because social skills have lately been discovered, but because the behavioral movement has moved into broader social issues, well beyond the confines of the laboratory where it had its beginning and even well beyond classroom and hospital work with retarded and other handicapped children and adults (Eysenck, 1960; Haring & Phillips, 1962, 1972). This movement has also encompassed in a more scientific, objective and researchable sense the social and interpersonal emphasis from psychiatry seen in the work of H. S. Sullivan, Karen Horney, Eric Fromm, and others. It is one thing to talk loosely about social influences in the lives of patients/clients and quite another thing to build a body of testable knowledge that can be more than a "point of view" for the clinician. Moving the activities of the clinician from the individual, psychic framework, which has dominated clinical and psychotherapeutic practice to these many decades, into a viable social framework is quite an accomplishment, although the movement is new and hesitant in many ways. The description of the attrition curve as a function of how the delivery system, as a system, works is one important way to bring in the social matrix. At the micro level, the teaching of social skills and the conceptual framework of social competence and social functioning as the proper setting for clinical activities is another important facet of this overall conceptualization. Just as medicine is moving into a "wellness" framework, with emphasis on holistic functioning as contrasted with arriving late in the development of the person's illness with an armamentarium of gadgets, drugs, and nostrums, so is psychotherapy moving into a "social wellness" framework. The preventive emphasis is, of course, apparent in both revolutionary systems.

ALIGNING MICRO AND MACRO PROCESSES INFLUENCING PSYCHOTHERAPY

It is relatively easy to speak of micro processes in one breath and macro considerations in another breath; what is difficult is smoothing the transition between them. This is, of course, a problem for all science; psychology is no different from chemistry and physics, physics and engineering, or micro and macro economics, in this respect. However, it is important to struggle with some micro/macro integration, at least as a rough guide to the study of psychotherapy, our present concern.

Micro processes (variables) define the fundamental nature of the phenomena under study, the lawfulness involved. It is implied that some units are relatively self-contained, such as learning principles, especially the operant viewpoint regarding stimulus control and reinforcement contingencies. The micro processes and variables set the smaller limits on studying phenomena, those from which larger units of study are derivable, and state what is necessary for the regulation and control of macro processes, although the latter may often appear to be independent of the former.

On the other hand, macro processing is composed of combinatory rules and principles based on micro findings. In order to make psychotherapy delivery systems work efficiently and effectively, therapy must be structured in a way that to some extent simulates a laboratory study of learning or behavior change. Participants in a sense must stay within the confines of the pertinent micro processes that fundamentally define the conditions for change: Unwanted behavior is not reinforced; the desired or goal-related behaviors are reinforced (in the laboratory more to the investigator's liking, in the clinic more to the client's objectives); and the control of stimulus contexts must be maintained if the purposes of the therapy or behavior change are to be realized. The chapter on macro processes (Chapter 10) displays a number of conceptual leads that purport to clarify and simplify salient macro considerations related to psychotherapy. In part, at the macro level this means moving away from considering the individual as an entity to seeing the person in a (social) matrix of variables, some actually—some potentially—available to bring about and support change. The *needed* (desired, goal set) behavior is focused on in the clinic, a kind of dependent variable, comparable to the same operation under study in the laboratory; operations performed by the clinician and the experimentalist may be more alike than different.

The workings at the macro level should not violate any micro principals. If the therapist/client interaction is efficient and effective, therapy should be moved through with dispatch, and, in turn, emphasis should be placed on making the macro process efficient and effective in ways parallel to the salient macro processes. (Or ways should be sought after that direct the therapist and client into larger environmental considerations, sometime prosthetic manipulations, if the immediate dyadic ones are not potent enough.) Said another way, long-term therapy that probes for alleged origins of present difficulties are fruitless ways to proceed; emphasis, instead, should be placed in the present context for either new solutions or for readjusting and reapplying older solutions to current problems. Any restructuring or realigning of variables for change perforce takes place in the present, and requires only the tests of social adequacy, broadly considered, in the present and forseeable future — not a validation of the present problem(s) based on their facsimiles from the past.

Macro processes should always be under scrutiny, by looking them over for possible flaws in utilizing micro principles, with the test of the macro products hammered out in the social context.

We move on now to a more direct consideration of macro processes and practices.

10 Toward a Conceptual Integration — Macro Level

Research on short-term psychotherapy has been around a long time. Research on longer term psychotherapy has amounted to relatively far less, although a plethora of articles has always been in evidence. Much of the research on psychotherapy of all kinds, except for the behavioral movement of the past two or more decades, has been considered indifferent in its effects on practice; some has been leading and heuristic, such as the work of Rogers and his students who helped break open the ironclad psychoanalytic mold so long in command of theory and practice. The psychoanalytic model was considered to be the "real" therapy with other forms simply palliative. Still other research on psychotherapy has led to useful hypothesis testing and/or to models for validating notions about therapy and its effects (counseling psychologist, 1982).

Most of the large-scale books that review progress in psychotherapy (Garfield & Bergin, 1978; Lambert, Christensen, & DeJulio, 1983) and the comprehensive books on psychotherapy theory (Corsini, 1981; Patterson, 1980), although interesting and informative about the state of the art, tell us in only limited ways about the broader nature of psychotherapy and behavior change. Such review books may also point up, sometimes unintentionally, the redundacy of psychotherapy theories. Although dozens, even hundreds, of psychotherapy theories, so-called, are touted (Herink, 1980), the case can be strongly made that there are basically only two types of psychotherapy theories — those that locate the variables in the person-environment interaction and those that place the significant variables in the "psyche." The latter seems to take on more and more varieties as therapists/theorists play semantic games with their data and their experiential accounts of their roles in psychotherapy, almost entirely centered on a one-to-one (or dyadic) basis.

Main Movements in Psychotherapy. In the present writer's opinion there have been only four important and influential movements in the history of psychotherapy. The first is the original work of Freud, wherein he stated many of the problems of psychotherapy and pointed up the significance of the "talking cure" (which incidentally is of only limited accuracy, inasmuch as therapy can take place without verbal exchange, and the interpersonal nature of psychotherapy was yet to be understood), and the proposal of an array of conceptual tools that have been the guide to the theorizing of many therapists for several decades. These "tools" were, however, located in the "psyche" because Freud had neither the empirical data nor the scientific/conceptual armamentarium available to develop a solid basis for what he observed. The unfortunate result of much of Freud's thinking, although seminal at his time, has been its "hardening" into a rigid structure that has brooked only minor modifications by his stalwart followers and has ramified into literature, the arts, theater, and general "common sense" about human behavior to an extent that is now detrimental to better understanding of human social and individual behavior.

The second most important series of events in the development of psychotherapy came from the dissenters from Freud. These followers/dissenters — except for Jung — left behind, relatively speaking, some of the more rigid aspects of Freud's theorizing and pointed more and more to interpersonal processes that went beyond the "psyche," although none of them fully abandoned the whole range of Freudian concepts. Even though some of the dissenters from Freud put more emphasis on social variables, most of the theorizing went from the individual to society rather than from society to the individual, as the source of influence on individual behavior.

It took Rogers (1951) — representing the third most important influence in the development of psychotherapy theory and practice — to break with the psychoanalytic "depth" model. Although Rogers located some of his variables in the person, qua person — he did not have enough data of the right sort to do otherwise — he did put enough emphasis on the role of the therapist to later stimulate theorists, therapists, and researchers to develop their positions more deliberately in the interpersonal direction. Rogers' work has proved heuristic in many ways and has loosened our thinking about psychotherapy far more than did Freud or any of his followers or dissenters, even though many of Rogers' specific interpersonal hypotheses have not proved themselves (Lambert, DeJulio, & Stein, 1978).

The behavioral movement of the past 25 years as it has applied to and influenced psychotherapy — and, of course, more broadly, behavior change in general — is the fourth most significant movement. Its broad and long bases are accounted for in other publications (Kalish, 1981; Kazdin, 1978; Krasner, 1973) and need not concern us here. Suffice it to say, however, that for the first time, psychotherapy and its "parent" (behavior change) began to put psychotherapy on a more solid scientific footing, offering far stronger empirical bases for the conceptual aspects. The conceptual aspects were just that – conceptual – not theories in the grander sense, often attempted by psychologists/psychotherapists in emulation of the more developed physical sciences (Kalish, 1981; Kendler, 1981; Meehl, 1978).

THE CONTINUA OF CHANGE

Several examples of continua of change are represented in the development of psychotherapy. These are discussed at this point.

The "Psyche." It has already been mentioned that the predominant position in psychotherapy theory and, to some extent, in practice (although it is really not known just how much theorists/therapists actually follow their own theoretical pronouncements) has been the tendency to locate the variables in the "psyche." There are a lot of historical reasons for this tendency. First and foremost, Freud and his followers – and even the more socially oriented dissenters from the mid-40s movement by Fromm, Horney, Sullivan, and others – simply did not have good empirical support for their socially oriented theories (or, for *any* theories, for that matter!). They fell back at crucial junctures on the psyche, and failed to develop the logical consequences of their departures. Second, these clinicians met people one by one. How could they have had a perspective on the flow of cases into and through institutions (clinics) in the sense possible today? They dealt with the material they had at hand, a wise and practical thing to do. But as long as therapy was to be studied primarily in the dyad context – and even much of group therapy, later to develop, was dyad-oriented, the only real exception to this tendency coming with the advent of family therapy – no alternative of a conceptual nature was likely to arise. A third possible reason for the dominance of the individual/clinical view of psychotherapy arises in relation to the absence of *social* data that would lend itself, or even suggest itself, to the clinical situation. Even the influence of Mead (1934, 1938) was meager, although to view mind in social terms was, at his time, a very radical and far-reaching viewpoint, not yet fully appreciated today. (We are now looking for "mind" in terms of neurophysiology and neuropsychology, and doubtless this will be fruitful, but where is "mind" in the social/behavioral sense?)

We can illustrate this tendency to locate the significant variables in the psyche as follows:

| Psyche | Psycho-social with causality coming from the psyche and | The social matrix as the central concern of psychotherapy deliv- |

shaping the social fac-   ery efforts.
tors.

vs.

A slowly developing
tendency in the oppo-
site direction.

The direction of data gathering and conceptualization of findings in this book follows fairly closely on this progression. Data on individual opinions, "expectations," and other characteristics of potential clients are not able to explain much of the variance of psychotherapy outcome, nor the number of sessions, nor the process characteristics of within-therapy phenomena. As we are better able to develop a hold on more significant social matrix variables, we will presumably be able to improve upon our prediction efforts regarding psychotherapy and also to develop newer and more efficient and effective methods for psychotherapy.

The Individual as the Unit of Study.   Parallel to the above discussion is the tendency in psychotherapy over the decades to hold the individual as the unit of study. This view has been modified slightly in group therapy and by attempting in individual therapy to bring in the role of the therapist; but by and large the greatest amount of research is still done on the client, not on the therapist. Therapists seem to conduct and think about therapy in particular ways that enhance their own notions of what they are doing, and seldom take as seriously the vantage point of the client. The notion of the dyad — therapist and client — is abundantly in evidence in the literature and, with some modifications, we hear about the alliance, and the like. But none of these modifications give us much new data and none of it seems to influence practice (Barlow et al., 1984; Dowds & Fontana, 1977; Friedman & DiMatteo, 1982; Janis, 1982; Jones, 1980, 1982; Karasu, Stein, & Charles, 1979; Keithley, Samples, & Strupp, 1980; Lambert et al., 1978; Martin, 1977a & 1977b; Martin, Moore, Sterne, & McNairy, 1977; Martini, 1978; Patterson & Heilbron, 1978; Peake, 1979).

The above discussion might be depicted as follows, although the trend toward the right side of the page is only feebly present at this time.

Individual behavior   Clinical assessment   Social behavior as
                       giving way to experi-   frame of reference in
                       mental assessment as   relation to how the de-
                       in analogue studies.   livery system operates.

This characterization of the role of the individual in psychotherapy theory, research, and practice is, of course, an approximation of the truth; but the overall trends are seen by the writer to be as depicted; small changes are in evidence in the right-hand side of the paper, a topic with which this book is greatly concerned.

The Location of Variables. Somewhat of a corollary to the above point, one could characterize the change in conceptualization of psychotherapy in terms of the location of variables that are posed as predictors of therapy outcome (more often, "satisfaction" ratings of outcome plus some references to behavior change, as we have seen in Chapter 5). We have traditionally asked questions about client characteristics that would predict their staying in therapy and completing the course. Despite strong evidence that clients on the average have only a small number of psychotherapy interviews in most mental health settings, therapists/theorists have ignored this and have proceeded to theorize without regard to the array of facts available. The theorizing and researching have centered on trying to identify the client characteristics that will tell us who, what, and when about continuing in therapy and gaining benefit therewith. We have centered our efforts on the following:

Pre-therapy research on clients	Variables initiated by the system not in evidence in a prior state.	The system becomes the matrix within which the client identifies what to "expect" to a considerable extent. Outcome results follow therefrom.

In this conceptualization, the greater amount of the variance influencing various notions of outcome are contributed by the manner in which the system works, not so much on how the individual, qua individual, functions or what his or her "perceptions" are. If the latter were important, then the attrition curve would never have come into being.

Change the Individual Versus the System. Notions of how to promote client change have begun a new direction. We have centered traditionally on changing the individual in therapy; this idea is bolstered by a large number of clichés about therapy. The individual is regarded, in a sense, as his own — and the only — change agency; no other change agents are posed as important in much psychotherapeutic writing. Just how this "bootstrap" operation is supposed to function has not been clearly enunciated. Reference is made, of course, to the psyche, to the will, to internal motivational states, and to perception, with almost complete disregard for the fact that one could not even discern that therapy was needed without feedback from others (albeit more often indirect than direct). This notion of total responsibility in the individual is shown, along with some changes now in progress, in the following:

Individual change only.	Individual is one of several "pivots" in a family setting; change individual by altering family interactions.	Change the larger context in order to embrace many individuals, without onus on one individual as patient.
	Generalizes to office, workshop, corporations, as systems.	

Altering the Size of the Change Unit.   As the literature on stress builds up, more and more recognition of the salience of this formulation becomes possible. We cannot reduce stress in the individual to as great an extent by working, alone, on the individual as we can by working by and through the system in the larger sense. The exact size of the unit of analysis and influence in a system is, of course, a moot point, and one yet to be examined in detail; however, units larger than the individual are paramount in importance (Phillips, 1982; Selya, 1974; Terkel, 1974). In fact, one of the important heuristics in a systemic way of thinking about changing behavior generally (including psychotherapy in particular) is the search for the size of unit to tackle for most salient, reliable, and economical change. In a family, to put everyone in individual therapy is probably wasteful; to look upon the stress-related problems among individuals in an office as a series of individual therapy problems would be too time consuming and expensive; and so on throughout a whole range of problems. If psychotherapy is sufficiently practical and flexible, those problems approached through the social matrix could reasonably well be expected to encompass the "other" problems a person has in his or her life outside the family, school, the work setting, and so on (Acosta, Yamamoto, & Evans, 1982; Blocher & Biggs, 1983; Goldring, 1980; Grayson, 1979; Insel, 1980). This is not said to pronounce problem solving in the individual as a pro forma process, or to discount individual differences or complexities, but to engender the idea of comparability of change in one setting with change in another, then ferret out the inconsistencies and special problems as one moves along the most economical route possible from the start. Parsimony is the hallmark of efficient therapy as well as science in general.

From Dropout to Attrition to Flow of Cases to Help-Seeking.   The most important and far-reaching aspect of this book now comes into view: the traditional tendency to call clients "dropouts" when they have not continued on with therapy in the manner envisioned by therapists. The term *dropout* occurs more frequently in the literature than the term *attrition,* which gives clear testimony to the biased viewpoint contained therein. The interesting point here is that although dropouts, so-called, have occurred since data have been kept on psychotherapy (and other treatment regimens as well), no one has put together the whole of the attrition phenomena until now. Attrition — as the name of the phenomena of how patients utilize and systematically leave therapy — has been ignored or summarily set aside. We have left behind untilled, fertile research soil. The term dropout has been so negative that not only has little research been done on the subject, it has been dismissed so thoroughly that even the interesting term attrition has been eschewed. Hence, attrition, as a perfectly legitimate phenomenon, has been lying fallow in the literature and in the potential for research for over 50 years! It is no exaggeration to say that the eschewing of attrition is not only the neglect of the ages in psychotherapy, it is also the single most important problem in the whole range of psychotherapeutic study.

But there is much, much more to the story than just dropping out or even attrition. We have, also, to move on beyond the notion of attrition, important as it is as a description of the negatively accelerating, declining ("decay") curve, following the Poisson distribution. We encounter next the notion of the flow of cases through the system. This flow from intake to asymptote does, indeed, follow the negatively accelerating declining curve, but if we look at the pre-intake phenomenon (as was done in Chapter 5), it is immediately evident that it is suggestive of an increasing frequency (a positively accelerating curve) or movement from outside the system toward the intake as a formal step. Through ambivalence and other considerations, the individual moves from his or her *informal* (or, possibly, from previous formal) sources of help and support into the more formal features of the clinic as a delivery system. The pre-intake phenomenon, although not very well understood — we have only recently described it in our data from the GWU Counseling Center, and similar data seem to be nonexistent in the literature — suggests enlarging the notion of attrition to the *flow of cases* into and out of the formal therapeutic system. (The same might be true of hospitals and other medically related delivery systems; an introduction to examining this possibility is seen below.) (See Fig. 10.1.) The flow of cases idea, then, embraces the pre-intake juncture, the intake and subsequent therapy delivery throughout the number of sessions, out to the asymptote and beyond — back into the informal support systems a person utilizes. The flow of cases notion can be extended to include people seeking conjunctive or parallel therapy from another source (or system) while principally engaged in a "home system" (although this has scarcely even been recognized, much less focused on). And it can, moreover, begin to encompass the fact that some people move

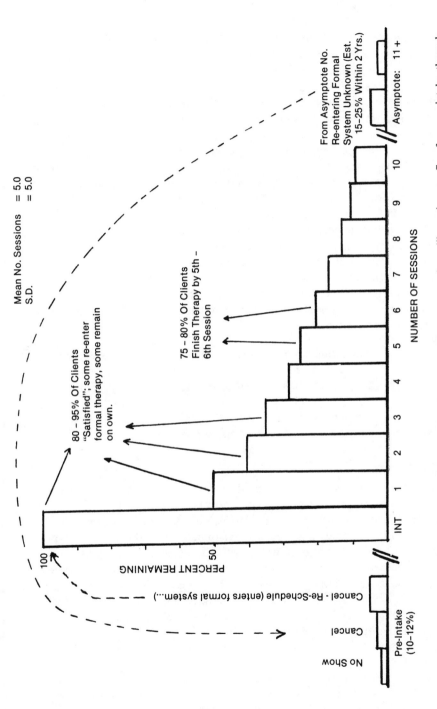

Mean No. Sessions = 5.0
S.D. = 5.0

80 – 95% Of Clients
"Satisfied"; some re-enter
formal therapy, some remain
on own.

75 – 80% Of Clients
Finish Therapy by 5th –
6th Session

From Asymptote No.
Re-entering Formal
System Unknown (Est.
15–25% Within 2 Yrs.)

Asymptote: 11 +

NUMBER OF SESSIONS

PERCENT REMAINING

Cancel - Re-Schedule (enters formal system...)

Cancel

No Show

Pre-Intake
(10–12%)

FIG. 10.1   Hypothetical smoothed attritional distribution: one year, 500 cases, outpatients, illustrating case flow from pre-intake, through intake, to asymptote, with suggested projections on clients leaving formal systems, returning to the community, etc.

from one source of help to another over time; the exact nature of the flow has never been described in the literature (although it is under study by the present research group; see Chapter 8).

This larger sense of flow of cases might well be described as "help-seeking behavior." It appears to apply well to seeking psychotherapeutic help, especially when we recognize that the potential clients are moving from their natural social orbits wherein they experience informal sources of help, to a formal system, and even while participating in a given formal delivery system may also approach another (i.e., move from a short-term clinic into a longer term one, or vice versa, or into group therapy in the same or another clinic, and so on for a variety of clinic-sampling possibilities). Add to this mixing and melding of formal and informal partaking of psychotherapy the evidence that some people go more or less systematically from one clinic to another and that this progress from one formal delivery system to another is probably also of the negatively accelerating, declining ("decay") type, a Poisson distribution itself (see Chapter 7).

Thus we have the following progression from the extremely limited and biased notion of "dropout" to the notion of "help-seeking" behavior as indicated in the above discussion:

Dropout	Attritional curve and related descriptive matters, highly stable in its characteristics.	Flow of cases into, through and out of the formal delivery system (including informal support as well).	Help-seeking behavior that encompasses all the foregoing and possibly other delivery systems, as well as between-systems behavior.

Although these strictures have been developed primarily in the self-initiated, walk-in, outpatient psychotherapy context, they appear to apply to analogue studies as well (DiLoreto, 1971). The exact nature of the dropout/attrition/flow-of-cases/help-seeking phenomena from the analogue type of treatment/study has not been well described, although an attempt has been made herein to approach this complex set of data (see Chapter 3). As we learn to appreciate the whole phenomena of help-seeking behavior, we will not only gain a better perspective on the analogue type of intervention—together with its possibilities for improvement (see Chapter 3)—we will have increased our expertise on how to view the individual more ably in his or her social context and how to improve that context for purposes of both formal and informal help-seeking behavior.

Egoism in Therapy.   Some would say we have just passed through the period of the "me generation." The self-centeredness of the self-improvement cults has been apparent to everyone, from philosophers through therapists out to newspaper columnists. An unfortunate prostitution of the highly salient notion of *assertiveness* has been witnessed in the wake of the proliferation of the me-generation pronouncements and practices. That psychology, along with psychiatry and social work and even the ministry, has collaborated with this egoistic emphasis seems patently true. Psychologists are now beginning to conceptualize some aspects of this movement (Wallach & Wallach, 1983). American psychotherapy is in strong contrast to Japanese psychotherapy in this respect (Reynolds, 1976, 1980, 1983). Reynolds points out how much therapy in Japan attempts to tie the individual sufferer to his or her social/familial responsibilities; general neuroses, known as *shinkeishitsu,* are said to submit to general therapy procedures that emphasize responsibility. *Shinkeishitsu* includes what we would call "ordinary neuresthenic states," "obsessive-compulsive behavior" and "anxiety states" (Reynolds, 1976, pp. 12–13). Moreover, it is held that Western versions of the neuroses involving the heavy-laden notions of Freudian psychology would hardly ever be expected to gain a foothold in Japan (Reynolds, 1980, esp. pp. 113–132, an "Afterward" by George DeVos). American psychology and psychotherapy with its strong emphasis on the individual tend to separate the person from the social context. We are told we, as individuals, can do anything we want if we want to badly enough and if we try hard enough, from overcoming intractible illness or pain to becoming president of the United States. We are a full-speed-ahead-damn-the-torpedoes culture. This type of culture doubtless helps account for many of our assets, but it also has some liabilities inasmuch as it separates the individual not only from his or her social context in the scientific and objective sense, but from the social responsibility context. Little wonder, then—if this observation is true—that there has been a proliferation of psychotherapies in the United States, almost none of which emphasize social responsibility except in the very loose sense referred to via psychic states. It has taken the grassroots movement and self-help groups to emphasize the presence of strong support by others in informal ways. Not knowing how to anchor or relate important concepts concerning the individual to the social matrix (a field of inquiry sorely in need of research), we tend to fall back on what we think we know best: the psyche. When we fall back on the psyche, we eschew the most heuristic leads possible, viz., those relating the individual to the social setting. We invent more and more intra-psychic concepts and slosh around in them interminably, all the while failing to relate the individual to almost any social context (save for standard variables such as social class and occupational/educational levels). The recently burgeoning emphasis on minority and ethnic populations has modified somewhat this tendency. If we allow ourselves to pursue only the psyche of the individual, trying to find all "meaning" there, we run the great risk of overlooking alternative environmental notions that might be both scientifically leading and therapeutically productive. Egoism, then, abounds in American psychology and psychotherapy and part of the movement away from it, as represented in this book, might look like the following:

Egoism: locating variables in the psyche is the individual's prerogative.	Seeing individual "choice" in relation to the social context, a beginning trend.	Discovering social variables that are needed to understand individual behavior; and to see how therapy is itself a kind of institutionalization of extremely limited notions of the individual moving toward the social matrix.

We will, in time, overcome the very limiting aspects of this view of human individual behavior and of the tasks of psychotherapy, but in order to do so we shall have to have better notions than are now provided by the emphasis on the psyche. We will have to connect what we observe in ourselves in the naive, introspective, subjective ways to the social context, and also relate what we actually do in therapy to the social context of the delivery system purporting to change individual behavior.

Theory Versus Practice.   The social context of the psychological service delivery system is, itself, a kind of offshoot of the notions we have about how to change behavior and what is important in human functioning. The disparity here is that theories of psychotherapy are notoriously impervious to the inclusion of the social matrix; thus we have a set of principles, beliefs, and practices known as psychotherapy theory, on the one hand, and the very different actuality of how psychotherapy is delivered via clinics on the other hand. The latter, in fact, has almost nothing to do with the former, and this disparity has encrusted us as therapists in a cloudy glass jar that is very hard to see out of and even harder to escape from. The notions we hold about psychotherapy, beginning with the triparte division of the mind via Freud, out to the cognitive array of states and styles and concepts, is a world unto itself. The way therapy actually works, in situ, is considerably different.

We may depict this regrettable mishmash of theory and fact thus:

Individual probing of the psyche.	Seeing more the family context, the school, etc. as a framework.	Observing the way the delivery system operates almost entirely unrelated to the former.

Diagnosis.   It is more or less apparent that we do not have the traditional need for diagnosis in the context of the present discussion. The labors going into the *DSM-II* and *DSM-III* encyclopedias net us very little except for administrative purposes. Little research exists that ties diagnosis with a preferred therapeutic regimen, save for a few small, statistical differences favoring behavior therapy with some neuroses (Smith et al., 1980). What is needed at the front end of the therapeutic system is not diagnosis of the individual in the traditional sense but a system of investigating how conflict dominates the individual (egoism versus social responsibility, assertiveness versus passivity and ambivalence, wish/desire versus effective approach behaviors, and so on) and more effective *interrelating* between therapist and client in ways that introduce the client to more effective problem solving, arising out of the social possibilities that exist for the person (or that can, prosthetically speaking, be invented, designed, arranged, etc.). The task of the therapist is as much a prosthetic one, speaking broadly, as it is anything else, with an emphasis on the *possible* (or, more modestly, on the likely). The important question clients seem to ask is, "What will I get *from* therapy?" Not, "How ready am I *for* (the ordeal of) therapy?" And not, "What is *wrong* with me?" What comes *from* is a social/interactional matter; what arises in the diagnostic past formulations is backward looking and without inventiveness, without considering the possible (or likely), without heuristics, ingenuities, discoveries, and the like. A very important difference!

Traditional therapy: What happened to me? Why am I this way? What's my diagnosis?	A functional view of conflictual interacting forces.	Arranging the possible so that conflicts are solved, reduced, new opportunities envisioned.

There is no necessary prologue in the individual historical sense to therapy. The context that arouses opportunity for change is the only viable prerequisite.

Clinician's Style.   For the want of a better term the clinician's style (and prerogatives, one might add) is an important consideration for understanding the relationship between micro and macro processes. The clinician works almost in secret; no one knows what goes on behind the clinician's office door except the client and the clinician — that is, unless video or audio tapes are made. This access is not as common as might be expected. Many clinicians feel their and the client's privacy is being invaded if tapes are made, and when some clinicians yield to allowing an account of their therapeutic work, they choose the most responsive patient possible, not showing a crossrun of their

typical activities in the consulting office. For years, I have found it difficult
to get regular senior staff members to make tapes of their therapy sessions to
be played to tyro therapists only, not to other experienced therapists. People
I know who have taught didactic courses on psychotherapy for years have
never played a therapy tape of their own to their students. What
prerogatives!

Rules, laws, and practices concerning privacy and confidentiality buttress
the clinician's attitude about the prerogatives of the therapy hour. Although
some of this attitude is good for clients, if not overdone, it is not a framework
in which science can flourish. Even if one learns what a clinician does in the
therapy hour, and even if one points up important alternative ways and considerations to what is heard on the tape, one is often put off by references to
the "clinician's style" and other dodges, altogether inimical to objective scrutiny about what the clinician is doing, why, how, and so forth. The isolation
in which the clinician works is not conducive to objective study of psychotherapy; and this tendency will have to be challenged and materially reduced
if more people are to study psychotherapy processes objectively. All of these
problems are well known by those who study the scientist-practitioner model
(Barlow et al., 1984). Typically, the clinician is reinforced by his or her client-
related work and by his or her own "kicks," not very much by clinical peers,
research findings, or clinic policies. Not only is the day-to-day study of psychotherapy processes hindered by the clinician's style and assumed prerogatives, but the accumulation of knowledge and educational and training practices with fledgling therapists are reduced in value, and clinicians walk away
from the therapy hour with impunity. As a result, students of psychotherapy
learn what they learn from their mentors in a craft sense; their teachings are
not data based. Barlow et al. (1984), in discussing different persuasions and
procedures more recently associated with psychotherapy such as
biofeedback, cognitive therapy, and so on, say "the popularity of these procedures with clinicians, to the extent that it exists, is most often due to convincing clinical demonstrations or persuasive communications, rather than
data" (p. 36). One can hardly differ with this observation. Graduate students
seem to spend more time going to short workshops and seeing and hearing
"clinical demonstrations" of all kinds of phenomena than they do learning on
a day-to-day basis in clinics and in seminars and case presentations. "Education by workshop" is the model for much graduate training in clinical psychology and psychotherapy today, rather than the more steady methods of
clinical experience and practice honed on a variety of cases calling for no specialized techniques. Most of these workshop presentations are hortatory and
lack data as well as perspective. Few workshops – and many books for that
matter – offer the basis for critical examination of what we do; they seem primarily to offer new wares and to excite practitioners into trying ever newer
techniques with this or that clinical group without either conceptual clarity or
research data on what is being "sold."

As a result of all these tendencies — not wholly true but largely true — clinic policy suffers as well. It is difficult to get clinicians to consider changing policies, say, even for practices based on such a substantial data base as that underlying short-term psychotherapy (Barlow et al., 1984; Bloom, 1981; Budman, 1981; Garfield, 1978; Gelso & Johnson, 1983). One clinic the writer knows of espouses dynamic, long-term psychotherapy; the best data available from this clinic indicate that their 2-year mean number of therapy sessions was about eight. What clinicians do, what they say about what they do, and how they develop clinic policies based on what they do are sometimes so disparate that one wonders why they do not submit to schizophrenia.

Summing these observations, we conclude that,

| Individual clinicians hold to policies and practices idiosyncratically learned and followed, buttressed by "clinician's choice" and similar notions | Some yielding to clinical reality in carrying therapy to focused groups, outreach activities and short-term therapy; some recording via audio and video tape | New frontiers now developing based on data that influence wide-ranging practices and clinic policies, leading to flexible clinical practice. |

Not all psychological clinicians are subject to this severe criticism; some are truly interested in knowledge, do research, and espouse theories with a strong responsibility to conceptual clarity rather than simply selling their wares on the clinical street corners of the world.

Complexity of Therapeutic Task.   Understandably there is much disputation about the nature and complexity of the therapeutic task faced by client and therapist. Much of the naming of the problem arises from the clinician's thinking, especially where diagnosis in the traditional sense is concerned. However, if we leave aside the conventional diagnostic categories and focus on the presenting complaints and how they are worked on, through their ramifications, we come to a much more concrete notion of what ails people. Also, we have maintained that, in essence, the client will tell the therapist early on what is wrong. This tendency to "tell what's wrong" is not a profound rendition of the problem(s), but a focal area of concern that needs at first to be accepted at face value; then teased out more fully with its implications and ramifications noted. The test is always the extent to which the named problem(s) lead the client into gainful change outside therapy. Diagnosis in the traditional sense states neither how the change could take place, nor how the categorization embraces the salient issues of the person's problem status.

How the therapist responds to the client and works with the client for sake of change depends in part on what exactly the therapist can do as an instigator and supporter of change. It is held here that the therapist has only a few things he or she can do. What are these? The therapist can simply reflect what the client has said, in the Rogerian sense. The therapist can ask a few questions: for more detail, for how the client felt about the event or events cited, and for the pre- and post-circumstances related to the significant event (or person/event complex); this might be thought of as the behavioral "ABCs" of change, viz., the antecedent circumstances, the behavior itself and the consequences. The therapist can suggest ways the client can react to significant events, or other actions the client might take. Pointing out the similarities and differences in client-reported events over a series of events, or over time, can lead to a conceptual tying up of significance for the client in both practical and larger ways. Giving attention, concern, and support in a variety of ways via stance, body language, and so on, are also ways of responding, usually making up a class of events called rapport.

Not much work of the sort that identifies therapist's response categories has been done, and what has been done appears not to be very heuristic (Gottschalk, Winget, & Glaser, 1969). It might be useful to take almost a simple-minded tact for a while until a research door is opened for studying client/therapist interactions with a view to describing the very finite number of things the therapist can actually do. If this limitation is as severe as it seems to be, the complexity of interactions between client and therapist may be overemphasized, leading to an exaggeration of the complexity of the client's problem status and to an underestimation of what the therapist can do that is active, supportive and suggestive, preferably all in one bundle. Shortening therapy would seem to pivot in some important ways in the therapist's knowing fully his or her limitations and in using these limited choices wisely in order to bring about client change. Centering attention on such an array of client/therapist interactions would go some distance in providing a crisper, moving, testable set of interactions leading to client independence and self-directed change. The emphasis here might look like the following:

| Client problems exacerbated and made more a puzzle than is indicated. | Therapist takes a too passive role leaving too much interaction vague and unable to capitalize on probable leads of value to client change. | Therapist appreciating his/her limitations and capitalizing actively on available skills and techniques in a supportive way, promoting client self-initiated and self-directed change. |

Although some may argue that it is unwise and/or inaccurate to diminish the importance of client suffering, the above remarks should not be construed in that context. Actually, the therapist in this version of client/ therapist interaction is appreciating his or her own limitations and respecting the client's strengths and prerogatives.

Were it not for this condition, national norms would not support the fact that most psychotherapy ranges from a mean of four to six or seven visits, and as far as we can now tell, variance in the same amount. Such a baseline has to lead to more searching study of how much the therapist can, in fact, do.

Content-Free Theories.   All therapists at our present stage of development of the art/science of therapy must be *content free.* Culturally speaking, content will — and does — arise in the course of therapy, but the dimensions of conflict (that give rise to the content in particular settings) are the important consideration, not the content. If we start therapy off with a necessary content — in the Freudian sense, or in any sense whatsoever — we will constrict our flexibility and overlook possibilities that are summarily dismissed before they are tried out. Thus:

"Givens" in the individual's make-up (e.g., Oedipal).	Conflict as a functional condition.	Assertive, social skills building, connecting the person with environmental heuristics; overcoming conflict by changing relationships in the social matrix.

The final point in this array of strictures regarding a more functional view of psychotherapy — ultimately tied down to the way the delivery system operates, which is, of course, a social matrix matter — is that of building a science of behavior change. I happen to believe we have a beginning of this scientific endeavor in the micro sense in the behavioral movement, especially the contributions of Skinner and his students. I would have to include Cybernetics here, too, for reasons too ramifying for consideration now. The Skinnerian revolution — we certainly can call it that — has shown how concepts, experiments, operations at the experimental/laboratory level can be built upon at the clinical level; how the laboratory work stands as important baselines, a bedrock taken as the foundation for other research and practice. The important work of Miller and others on conflict stands high on the list of "baseline" knowledge (Miller, 1971). Meehl (1978) laments the state of "soft" psychology in not being able to make contributions to the *building* of a science in ways already exemplified in the foundation sciences and in genetics and some aspects of biology. Meehl says, "Theories in 'soft' psychology lack the cumulative character of scientific knowledge" (p. 306). He goes on to say that theories in the soft areas – clinical, counseling, social, personality, community, school – are not scientifically (conceptually) useful and are technically without much value. I heartily agree. One might say existing theories lead nowhere; they are not building blocks. They proliferate like fashions and fads, and they may exist more to enlarge the pocketbooks of theorists who are lucky enough to get a public following. Some theorists encourage small contributions to scientific work by a few – very few in number – who attempt to do research on their theories. The lack of scientific rigor plays immediately into the hands of faddists and temporizers and leads to the kinds of observations cited by Kilbourne and Richardson (1984) and by Zilbergeld (1983). Sorely needed are baselines for describing psychotherapy in as many ways as possible, largely devoid of existing theories, and a willingness to develop wide-ranging, cooperative research among groups of clinics and counseling centers on shared problems, eventually arriving at data bases worthy of the name, from which, in due time, *meaningful theories may be derived.* At the macro level, likely none of the present array of existing psychotherapy theories will survive; but at the micro level, as herein argued, empirical bases in the work of behaviorists such as Skinner and Miller will form the bedrock of empirical knowledge. However, many challenging problems exist in regard to how the micro and macro levels can be melded, as is true also of economics and other sciences working at various levels of complexity.

Apropos of the scientific neglect found in present-day clinical and other psychology at the macro (or "soft") levels is a concern for the training of psychotherapists. There is little doubt that clinical training is more a hodgepodge than a concerted attempt to follow the avowed scientist practitioner mode (Barlow et al., 1984). Most clinicians after even 20 or 30 years of professional activity fail to do research or publish (Barlow et al., 1984; Kelly, Goldberg, Fiske, & Kilkowski, 1978). What interest patterns do clinicians have that renders research so unimportant and why do so many clinicians feel they have little or nothing to learn from research? Doubtless there are many complex answers to these questions. One important answer is that research is not emphasized in clinical graduate training and/or in clinics and hospitals where interns and externs do their preparatory clinical work and wherein they might become sensitive to and participate in clinical research. Perhaps all along the way, from selection of candidates for training in clinical (and counseling) psychology through the graduate training years and into professional practice, the emphasis is on service and not on the accumulation of knowledge from research. Clinical psychology and its brethren, counseling psychology, social work, and psychiatry are personal contact areas, not scientific or research areas of knowledge and practice. Most clinicians I have observed seldom ask research questions; they take clinical reports at face value as long as they espouse the preferred theory of the observers. Conceptual levels of thinking and organizing the data about subjects under discussion in clinical roundtables seldom reach more than a descriptive level, mostly based on invoking notions about "depth" theory psychopathology and the like. It is interesting to observe how redundant are clinical reports – oral or written – on patients or clients; one can tell at the outset what the clinician will say given knowledge of his or her theoretical vantage point. There are no surprises.

What would remedy the lack of interest in research among clinicians, especially psychotherapists? This question does not submit to an easy answer. New plans are needed at every stage of the clinician's training. Suggestions might include the following.

Accept for clinical training only those students who have strong indications of research interest and productivity (albeit part of a team or directly under the guidance of a senior researcher) while undergraduates. Coupled with this would be specification of broad areas of research interest and some statements about how the candidate would go about following up on the research potential mentioned. This approach would take the place of the graduate student candidate writing 4–6 pages about why he or she wants to be a clinical psychologist, most of which is personal and, although interesting, has little bearing on graduate training for research or practice, as far as we know.

The entering graduate student would work first at the animal level on simple projects that may relate to how psychopathology is developed in experimental regimens and how the animals are taught to overcome their conflicts. Simple conflict paradigms would suffice to bring home these lessons to students. If possible, students would move on to more complex research of an experimental and laboratory nature, with emphasis on conceptualizing their problems, seeing the link between the conceptualizations and the empirical evidence, and developing alternative ways of viewing the data. This rigor would presumably teach students to observe carefully and to develop hypotheses that are testable at all turns, not simply expositions that have an "intuitive appeal," although the latter might be a satisfactory way to begin conceptualizing, given that it submits to sufficient rigor later. These projects would have to be written up in standard research formats and presented in seminars emulating presentations at professional meetings to be engaged in later in the student's professional course and development.

Following work on animals, the fledgling clinician should work with children, perhaps in preschool setting, in day-care centers, and the like. Here careful observations of one child for (say) a whole day, or for several days, in the manner of Barker (1965) and Barker and Wright (1951) would be advisable. The child's behavior could be recorded as a function of the interpersonal interactions current during the observational time, and so on. Testing children might have some relevance, but the general observational posture would, at first at least, be the more important training consideration. Fledgling clinicians would learn in this format to relate the child's behavior to the observable circumstances rather than performing exercises where they guess what the child is thinking; if there is a question about this, let the child be asked or more carefully observed; or let other avenues of validation be followed; the clinician should not be permitted to stop with, and crystallize, his hypotheses, but should submit them to testing. In a setting of this type, the fledgling clinician could move into a very wide array of research and observational areas, involving teachers, parents, peers, and issues related to subject matter, social and other skills, and so on. One could hardly envision a more productive laboratory for training. All the while, the tyro clinician is learning to be an observer, which is of first and foremost importance; second, to "take data," that is, record events pertinent to some question that is being studied; third, to analyze the data and to see how limited (and limiting) are many hypotheses that move us to studies we initially think might be productive (it is unlikely that more than a few studies out of 100 hit "pay dirt," and the clinician/researcher, the scientist/practitioner needs to learn that research is hard work but holds many rewards) (Bachrach, 1972). Most clinicians do not learn even to count the occurrence of the "facts" they allege are important in what they do.

Finally, then, the budding clinician will move into work with adolescents and adults, having been trained, now, to observe carefully and to formulate hypotheses with perspicacity and parsimony. Although testing in the usual psychometric sense will be part of this portion of the clinician's training, it will be used sparingly and an emphasis will arise on fashioning new observational and testing procedures to fit the situation rather than calling on the plethora of instruments and tests we have just because we have them!

While the more rigorous part of training is going on for these (mainly) 4 years of clinical preparation (prior to internship), classroom and seminar work will center around the historical development of the major concepts and/or theories of relevance to psychology *generally* as well as clinically, with proper emphasis on social and developmental psychology and on burgeoning fields such as neuropsychology, the ways computers can handle data economically and how they perhaps simulate human thinking, and other intriguing issues. Systems of psychology can be seen as trends that have developed while confronting the major questions of psychology as a science, its social responsibilities, how research problems and methods have been articulated and changed over time, how fusion and friction have generated new problems, and how one can, standing before this array of fascinating events, move a little bit forward in the direction of acquiring new knowledge. If one is not intrigued by these questions and how one can enter the stream of activity, one should not be in a scientific field – clinical psychology or otherwise –

and one should probably change his or her profession to some area more devoted to practice and immediate social reinforcement (said not to belittle these motivational complexes, but to differentiate science from other constructive enteprises involving the study of human behavior). Summarizing this discussion all too briefly, we may characterize it as follows:

| Clinical selection, training from the outset that fails to emphasize research; only service. | The mix and meld methods now current purporting to develop a scientist-practitioner model which is really a PRACTITIONER-science mode of doubtful value to either. | A truly scientific emphasis by rearranging the future clinician's experience from selection, through training, to profession SCIENTIFIC activity where research is always uppermost. |

Some would argue that if we train clinicians this way we shall have only scientists, researchers, and theoreticians, and not clinicians. Although this reply may have some validity, we do not really know how much better clinicians we would develop if we took a different route to this goal. My observation is that the best observers are both the best researchers and the best clinicians in the larger sense of the term. I would personally rather put my life in the hands of a research-minded physician or psychologist than a run-of-the-mill practitioner who has a limited viewpoint to espouse (and to live and earn by) and is interested in me only as a specimen for his or her theory. A modicum of charisma, smiling, handshaking, empathy, and commiseration are doubtless needed; but much, much more than agreeableness has to be built into the relationship. The public will gradually learn that substance is more important than style, that charisma is often misleading, and that some people are interested in, and need, the steak, not just the "sizzle"!

Criteria for Short-Term Therapy Cases. It is interesting that among the "dynamic" short-term psychotherapists there is much said about criteria for inclusion in brief psychotherapy (Davanloo, 1978; Flegenheimer, 1982; Mann, 1973; Mann & Goldman, 1982; Sifneos, 1972; Wells, 1982). The list of "ideal" characteristics for effective short-term psychodynamic treatment is fairly long, and the contra-indications are likewise numerous. When one surveys the list of have and have-not characteristics in prospective short-term psychodynamic candidates, one wonders what happens to patients/clients who are left after the severe dichotomous classification is employed (many must be referred out?). On the one hand the "haves" appear not to need treatment and are certainly not good candidates for all the dynamic content, including Oedipal strivings and resistance and transference matters; they could well be treated, as they are in other settings, rather straightforwardly in a very short span of time, probably under 10 sessions, if we are to take national averages seriously. On the other hand, the "have nots" appear so unlikely and unattractive to the psychodynamic clinician that they don't "deserve" consideration; they get "referred," or they go-it-on-their-own or, perhaps in some instance, enter long-term therapy (although with their lagging motivation and lack of "psychological mindedness" they would appear as poor candidates for the rigor of long-term psychodynamic treatment; hence they are selected out either by the therapist or by themselves, and likely get no help).

Since none of these psychodynamic clinicians do research on their classifications on who leaves therapy "prematurely," and on outcome from the selected-in and selected-out patients, we are still at a loss for the validity of the selective criteria. At best we have to take the dynamic short-term viewpoint on faith insofar as research backup is concerned; at worst, we have to say that this viewpoint is scarcely ever favorable to the mental health consumer and, as such, fits poorly with other data on mental health needs among the populace (Guttentag, Salasin, & Belle, 1980; Veroff, Kulka, & Douvan, 1981).

Data from the first chapters of this book contest the findings of the short-term psychodynamic therapists. First of all, the attritional flow of cases is described as a highly stable curve, deviation from which thus far appears to be based on unusual selectivity (although unsubstantiated), and probably represents relatively poor data collection since the criteria of selection are largely in the hands of clinicians and are not the product of objective assessments, discernible cut-off points, and the like. Since we have little data on outcome findings from the highly selected clients for the dynamic short-term methods, we have no confidence in their alleged relevance or superiority. The issue here may be shown to be as follows:

Highly selected cases based on unverified criteria, unrelated to outcome.	Some selection that intuitively occurs as to who gets beyond intake in any short-term therapy system.	Moving to explicit study as herein appraised as to who gets what benefits from any amount of short-term therapy from intake-only onward, based on research.

The only defensible method now available to us concerning short-term treatment of any type is to take all comers, then let the data accumulation tell us what, where, how, when, with whom, we can build effective and efficient short-term models for psychotherapy. Given the described nature of the attritional matters, anything short of this openness to research and practice is folly; moreover, it is research-blind, unscientific, and certainly an affront to the public and to the population of mental health consumers.

The Self-Help Movement. Possibly the newest and sketchiest topic discussed in this chapter in relationship to the social matrix of psychological help relates to grassroots, self-help or support groups. These groups, often spontaneous, informal, made up of people in close social and work approximation with each other, have arisen for a variety of reasons (Dodson, 1976; Gottlieb, 1981; MacMurray, Cunningham, Cater, Swenson, & Bellin, 1976; Maguire, 1983; Stokes, 1981). Formal help for psychological and psychotherapeutic problems as addressed by community mental health clinics, private practice mental health persons, and the ministry is not sufficient to meet the need. Often these relatively accessible systems of help are too formal for many people and connote "illness," "craziness," and other condemnatory terms, as well as implying a coercive element ("You *ought* to be in an asylum," or "You *better* get help," and so on). In speaking with persons who make up self-help groups in church, school, and community settings, one gains the impression (although not researched) that the groups are very loose: arising seemingly spontaneously, they try to meet a need not met by formal systems of therapy, and they cost little or nothing. They are open — people come and go at will — and the participants are accessible to one another on informal bases at any time whatsoever. One young college girl broke up with her fiancé and in the midst of her emotional reaction asked a girlfriend in a state hundreds of miles away to come to her rescue. The distant friend came at once, bag and baggage, moved in with the distressed one, and was still present in her home 2 months later when the young lady came in for formal psychotherapeutic help. Although the formal psychological help appeared necessary for the distressed young woman, the immediate and unconditional availability of the friend was remarkable in unconditional responsiveness and in steadfastness, although her skills were severely limited. Perhaps mental health experts need to learn something from these kinds of self-help initiations — to be less formal, to respond sooner, to know that support is uppermost although not wholly sufficient, and so on.

In contrast to the grassroots, self-help groups that seem to arise and decline spontaneously, there are more formal helping systems that society has seen fit to erect to meet, mainly, the needs of dischargees from mental hospital systems. These persons have presented refractory problems for decades (Budman, 1981; Felner & Jason, 1983; Gottlieb, 1981; and the Psychosocial Rehabilitation Journal, Vol. 1, 1978). Many publications give testimony to the avenues society has provided for rehabilitating former hospital inmates to community living in hopes not only of keeping them out of hospitals in the future, but of providing more skillful help in current adjustment to society, work, and family living. Not too many of these former patients get into formal psychological or psychiatric help of a psychotherapeutic nature, but many may be "maintained" on drugs. Day-care facilities are commonly the mainstay of these former patients' adjustments to current social living, and often they are a far better alternative to hospitalization than most people realize.

Two broad reasons may be advanced for the growth of the more or less formal intermediate ("halfway") settings on the one hand and the self-help, grassroots movement on the other. One reason is that traditional help has not been either direct or efficient enough to meet the widely felt needs of disturbed people and their families; the treatment record is not good; hence alternatives must be sought, especially those that might reduce recidivism. A second reason is that more people, especially among the less needy and less chronic, are realizing that they can take matters into their own hands; professional help is not needed most of the time and even when it is engaged it may be far from satisfactory (Phillips, 1982). Just as in health and nutritional matters, self-help is becoming more popular, more economical, and perhaps more pertinent to most people's lives. The mental health movement involving self-help is a prime example of this approach (Veroff, Kulka, & Douvan, 1981).

The broad range of self-help movements and the somewhat more formal intermediate attempts at solutions to passing or even chronic and acute psychological problems are taking us more and more into the social matrix. There is less of an attempt to isolate the psychologically needy person from his or her natural orbit, and more reliance on common support measures that can be provided by a few peers, often spontaneously. Surely this kind of movement is evident in the crisis intervention and "hotlines" resources in communities (Ewing, 1978), which are another kind of help, somewhat social-matrix-involved and very responsive, although less personal than face-to-face contact.

The earlier notion that what we loosely call mental health was wholly an individual matter, located in the "psyche," has been giving way consistently to the notion that psychological well-being is socially anchored (Phillips, 1978). If people did not intuitively, or from a commonsense standpoint, see that psychological integrity and adjustment are fundamentally a social matter, little in the way of self-help and intermediate sources of treatment would have ever arisen — or been helpful. The populace is wiser than the experts in this respect. Just as holistic health/medicine is making important inroads in our thinking and self-care (Pelletier, 1979), so is all manner of psychological assistance.

One could conceptualize these trends as follows:

The "mind" as an isolated entity seemingly mysterious and unrelated to the rest of the person, or to social living.	Yielding some in relation to psychosomatic relationships and their stress-related characteristics.	Advent of intermediate "halfway" helping institutions for emotional problems.	Rise of fully self-help/emergency and informal psycho/social care and support systems with informal systems seen more as integral to the social matrix.

BEHAVIORAL DEFICITS IN PSYCHOTHERAPY

The usual account of a person's emotional or personality difficulties alleges the person not loved as a child, or accepted, and so forth. The present clinically observed deficits are hypothesized to come from earlier deficits. However, deficits may arise from excesses as well and this matter is usually overlooked clinically and in personality theory. It makes a lot of difference if our concern in psychotherapy and behavior change relates to problem solving that helps set more attainable goals, with more commensurate means, rather than a focus on the past or the unconscious. If we say that the deficit one experienced emotionally at the hands of adults and parents is the cause of the present difficulty and we, as clinicians, offer this as "the explanations", how can we remediate this condition in any direct way? It seems impossible. Although acceptance of one's fate or plight is found everywhere on the road to wisdom and generally makes for more efficient and satisfying living, that attitude applies to any kind of discrepancy in one's life, not alone to loss early on.

The other way to view present deficits (leaving out deficits arising from poor education, low ability, various handicaps, all objectively assessable) is to regard them as springing from earlier excesses in one's expectations (to use this far overworked word). If a child is overly indulged, given in to on demand, overly praised, adulated to unrealistic degrees, it is not surprising that later on in the world at large this person will anticipate similar treatment by others. A resulting selfish attitude is bound to create severe conflicts for the person and perhaps send him or her to therapy. The person, in therapy, will report that others don't like or love or support or regard him or her, and the person will go around with a heavy emotional burden thus created. The easier, more honest, direct and productive therapeutic approach is to point out that one's expectations go a long way toward defining one's receipts, emotionally and socially speaking. Our culture promotes many notions that are excessive; we hear and read about these in the advertising of products, in high school and college commencement addresses, in stereotyped versions and prescriptions about how one is to deal with one's burdens, and so on. Exhortations of the sort, "set your goals high," "hitch your wagon to a star," "there's plenty of room at the top," and so on, ad infinitum and ad nauseam, pound our ears and color our vision interminably. We go around empty-handed, so to speak, expecting our palms to be filled with bounty; if they are not, we contend we are getting a "raw deal" and other reactions. We are engaged in a conflictful battle between expectations and realizations that surrounds and engulfs us.

Therapeutically speaking, we do not have to agree with the client in regard to these complaints, but we have to take them seriously enough to engage the client in progressive change. The frequent report of "awfulizing" that Ellis has pointed up so saliently arises from the same conflictual base. "Isn't it awful that I am not appreciated, loved, adored by?" and so on, the patient is repeatedly saying. In conflict terms the negative aspects, the avoidance gradient, must be lowered as the approach (aspirational) gradient is also lowered; the conflict must come to rest at less intense levels. (We all have some conflicts along these expectation-realization lines most of the time, but we abide them without too much struggle and with no great deficit resulting in our general performance.)

It is in the interest of therapeutic economy, also, that we tackle the deficit problem as one based on overexpectations, on excesses, not on inherited social/emotional deficits. Horney realized this clearly, as have some other therapists, but the "cultural approval system" is overly sympathetic and empathetic to the individual pronouncing to the world his deficits that are based on what others have done *to* him or her. There is, of course, lots of evil and unfairness in the world, but since none of us is alleged to have been promised a rose garden — we really were so promised (by implication) in the excess version of what is being said — we need not get up each morning expecting to relish the beauty of the roses.

This is not to say that fairness, honesty, humility and loving support characterize parents, families, schools, institutions, corporations, and governments; they are all faulted to a lesser or greater degree. But most of these humilities and unfairnesses are taken in stride by most of us most of the time; we are not usually very neurotic about these discrepancies in our lives. What we agonize over is the strong belief that we have come to expect unquestioningly that we have been neglected, not loved, and so forth, and that all this history is now coming back to haunt us in our adolescent and adult years. This is a very unrealistic, unlikely, highly biased version of what makes the need for therapy, what caused our psychopathologies, and what we need to do to ameliorate conditions. Some ways in which better alignment of the micro and macro considerations, based on the conflict notions espoused here, add up to a different summary of one's difficulties as follows:

Belief in early deficit, profound loss, not loved, victimized.	Seeing parents as human and subject to limitations as are all people.	Seeing one's difficulties more open to change despite one's history, and as related to one's present conflicts irrespective of origins.	Assertive approaches to emotional relief and problem solving, seeing one's self as a particular in a general society that helps set artificial goals and promote empty and unrealizable motivations, both levels — individual and social — calling for more realism.

The Japanese have something to say to us in the Western world in this respect. Reynolds, in his interesting book *Naikan Therapy* (1983) points out the following: "It [Naikan therapy] is . . . about the way of life and view of life upon which the therapy is based . . . that emphasizes how much each of us has received from others, how little we have returned to them, and how much trouble and worry we have caused our loved ones from as far back as we can recall" (p. 1). This is a viewpoint startlingly opposite to what we have been taught in the Western world, from the Freudian legacy onward, especially in the United States. I have yet to meet a therapy case that came anywhere close to believing in any of the three propositions of Naikan therapy (or seeking help on such a basis), yet I know some of it must be true in the lives of many American neurotics, especially among adolescents and youth who do not yet have the maturity to balance debts and credits properly in their social and emotional lives. I have yet to encounter a therapist who even comes close to believing and following what Reynolds has described as the tenets of Naikan Therapy; yet I know that most therapists have sooner or later to come up with some such notions as they discuss with clients other responsibilities for correcting evils, past and present, in their lives. We have an unusually narrow cultural outlook on therapy in the Western world, especially in the United States, and we are now emerging into a field of inquiry and on to a more sensitive terrain where we might well pause and think, as therapists, far more often about what we do and how and why and the larger meaning of it all. Naikan therapy, although not socially oriented in the ways espoused in this book, nonetheless has a strong social (familial) reference, even though the therapeutic modus operandi is to stress the "inner" meanings and issues of the patient in this Japanese therapy modality ("nai" means inner and "kan" means observation; hence self/inner observation). The Japanese at least use this "inner" pivot to emerge into social sensitivities and responsibilities, a bit of a leg up on society in the larger context.

It is apparent from these and other themes in regard to psychotherapy that it is more of a guild than it is an art or a science. It is riddled with viewpoints that are poorly supported, if at all, and tattered with internal inconsistencies that render its overall view somewhat impotent. Psychotherapy is now having to give way to a content-free conceptualization based on more hard-rock macro-level data, forcing a growth toward a more socially oriented theory and practice. As these measures at the macro level gain momentum and are well-supported with research, what we now consider psychotherapy will have to be written in a new key, played on somewhat different instruments, and by different players. The role of the traditional expert will come to be seen more as the *architect of change*—the designer of systems of care. These systems will become more integral to the social matrix (and, of course, feedback remedial and corrective changes to be taken up by society at large). Less need will exist for one-on-one therapists. Supplanting the proliferation of individual psychotherapies will be inventories of new systems of help at both micro and macro levels, utilizing more fully the solidity of behavioral knowledge from the laboratory integrated within the social matrix. We shall then have both a truly scientific and a useful—socially responsive and responsible—psychotherapy.

IMPLICATIONS

Where, now, are the traditional problems of psychotherapy prediction, research, practice, theory development? If the present perspective is even partially correct, we will have ushered in a new era in the quest for knowledge concerning psychotherapy, behavior change, the role of the individual and the social matrix, not to mention a host of problems related to evaluation, training, cost effective delivery systems, and so forth. The implications of this viewpoint are more far-reaching than just psychotherapy, important as the issue is. The implications are also seen in the development of more efficient and effective analogue intervention/research possibilities as well. The ramifications go even farther: They apply to all manner of health service delivery systems, from the treatment of minor medical problems out to following the patient with terminal illness through his or her course. The literature on patient (medical) compliance is a burgeoning literature and one resembling the present discussions of psychotherapy to a considerable extent (Eisenberg, 1977; Engel, 1968, 1975, 1977a, 1977b; DiMatteo & DiNicola,

1982; Friedman & DiMatteo, 1982). This literature fails to show any discernible flow of cases or attritional characteristics since present researchers are not looking at, or reporting, data in this way (Bassuk & Gerson, 1980; Becker & Maiman, 1975; Brown, 1978; Deykin, Weissman, Tanner et al., 1975; DiMatteo & DiNicola, 1982; Ewalt, Cohen, & Harmatz, 1972; Fiester, Mahrer, Giambra, & Ormiston, 1974; Friedman & DiMatteo, 1982; Gillum & Barsky, 1974; Hurtado, Greenlick, & Colombo, 1973; Marston, 1970; Mechanic, 1978; Orford, 1974; Raynes & Patch, 1973; Rosenberg, Davidson, & Patch, 1972; Shelton & Levy, 1981; Stone, 1979; Veroff, 1981; Watts, 1972). If the clinic data could be accumulated in the manner testing the attrition curve phenomenon, just as a starter, data in the medical/patient compliance field would submit readily to the systematic organization of how the delivery systems operate, across types of patients, diagnoses, out-/in-patient settings, length of treatment and related variables. Thus far, data have been accumulated in terms of dichotomous variable differences: sex, age, seriousness of disability, and so on; and these have been arranged according to diagnosis. Diagnosis may be far more important in the case of medical compliance, and the course of treatment may be more ably specified and structured, compared to psychotherapy. Comparing medical treatment as derived from a formal system with psychotherapy (both walk-in and analogue treatment) may prove to be very heuristic. It may be that *psychotherapeutic* intervention, as well as medical intervention, may prove economical in the study of attrition and the flow of cases among medical patients (Cummings & Follette, 1976). The intermingling of data on attrition may be very beneficial for the understanding of how formal medical and psychological delivery systems operate, as well as showing how they can substitute for one another in some ways. Medical psychology (or behavioral medicine) could, then, take on some new features *at the delivery system level* that may or may not be posited on diagnosis and the like; the social relevance of the therapist/patient contact may turn out to be the principal determiner of "satisfaction" in both medical and psychological help with technical competence and the presence of a scientific armamentarium of techniques and instruments reduced in importance except for the most profoundly needy cases (Freidman & DiMatteo, 1982, esp. pp. 3–6 and 9–14). There is no necessary prologue to therapy in the individual historical sense. The context that arouses opportunity for change is the only viable prerequisite.

11 Overview

This book has had the purpose of presenting some new developments in the study of psychotherapy and behavior change. The main thrust and the one around which other problems, questions and data have been assembled is the *attrition curve*. When data on the number of cases coming for intake and various numbers of interviews are plotted in relation to the number of cases remaining after each session, the resulting curve is a negatively accelerating, declining ("decay") curve, resembling a Poisson distribution. This distribution is characterized, in turn, by approximately equal means and standard deviations, an important finding in its own right, as it applies to the conduct of delivering psychotherapeutic services to clients in outpatient settings. The observation of the attrition curve arose in connection with plotting the number of sessions clients (students) had over a year's time at a university counseling center. Once this observation had been made (for 1980–1981 originally), it became an intriguing quest to see if it would obtain the same setting for other years and possibly in other outpatient, mental health delivery systems. The curve has been found yearly since 1980–81, in the counseling center and in a number of other settings, whether these settings specialized in one type of patient (e.g., alcoholic patients), in time-limited (or unlimited) setting (a Health Maintenance Organization service in an urban community), and in community mental health clinics.

FROM DROPPING OUT TO ATTRITION

Pursuing the standard literature for references to attrition revealed scant concern with this problem. Although several outstanding reviews of "dropping out" from psychotherapy were found, these studies concerned themselves primarily with demographic variables on patients/clients who left therapy "prematurely" (clinicians reported); there were no cases in which data were aggregated in a way that would show the negatively accelerating, declining attrition curve. The pursuit of the curve became a strong drive for the senior author and those associated with him. This book reports on this trail over the past 3 to 4 years.

Despite the fact that reviews of "dropping out" of psychotherapy did not show the attrition curve, one frequently encountered tables in published research that allowed the replotting of data from the figures given, mostly by arranging a column in a table that represented the crucial arrangement: "percent remaining after each numbered session" in the delivery of services, and also showing this curve graphically. In many studies allowing the rearrangement of data, a curve of the same attritional type was found. This strengthened the belief that delivery of psychotherapy services followed this curve wherever data allowed a test of this notion. In most instances, however, data on the distribution means and standard deviations were not available, so the close proximity of these two statistics was not readily confirmed in most published research, although the search went as far back as 40 to 50 years; yet some of the older data were confirmatory of the attrition curve.

The attrition curve applied to walk-in, self-initiated clientele found in outpatient mental health units and in university counseling centers. What would be the case with analogue studies where clients were invited, conscripted, and so forth? The publication in the past few years of numerous accounts of analogue studies, mostly of a short-term duration and some in relation to meta-analysis research, was an inviting literature to pursue in the quest for attritional data. Attritional data there were, but not arrangeable in the manner possible for walk-in clientele served in outpatient clinics. It was necessary to put together the attritional data from analogue studies by what was called the "flow of cases" through the course of treatment. Similar to the intake process in outpatient, self-initiated services, analogue studies began with the collection of potential clients by several means, their subsequent selection down to proper candidate status in the light of the analogue study objective (reducing performance anxiety, overcoming shyness, achieving improvement, learning social skills and/or assertiveness), and following these cases through to the termination (and follow-up) of the analogue study format. We observed several junctures in this flow of cases through the system and found, indeed, that attrition was present, although it was alleged in meta-analysis reports not to be present or to be of very minor consideration. Despite a number of differences in clientele among outpatient psychotherapy cases and the more likely invited or conscripted analogue clients, they bore considerable resemblance in attritional matters. Several suggestions followed from the initial study of analogue/meta-analysis research on psychotherapy and behavior change, an important one being that of building questionnaires covering presenting complaints so they could be placed in critical tandem with behavior change/intervention efforts leading to refinements of each and a potentially higher effect size as a result. This suggestion—not yet tried out—could be a stimulus for research that would present more economical efforts toward analogue type of intervention and possibly parallel various empirical efforts to make regular therapy delivery systems more effective.

One important characteristic of the attrition curve is the steepness of the drop following intake (or the first therapy session). The literature reports means and standard deviations on study populations when two or more contrasting therapy groups are examined with questions concerning the relative change between two or more treatment regimens, but there was no literature found that noted the steepness of the attritional drop after intake save for tangential references in some reviews of "dropping out," indicating the percentage of clients that did not return after the first contact. The attritional phenomenon was not, therefore, described in detail as has been attempted here.

Why is the intake so important? We studied several aspects of this question and found that dropping out was not simply that, alone; and it was not negative; attrition did not connote psychotherapeutic failure, necessarily; in fact, most people left for good and ample reasons, according to their replies to inquiries. The intake began to loom as not only the modal description point of psychotherapy service delivery feature; it became a decisive choice point. The study of the intake was then submitted to examination in several ways, as reported herein.

Once the notion of dropping out was weakened, the influence of the attrition curve as an overall, objective description of service delivery characteristics began to occur more and more often—as we examined the literature—and began to suggest that "that's the way clinics operate." The attrition curve characteristics were found to exist despite all other features we could examine: diagnosis, age, sex, presenting complaint(s), ethnic features, time-limited or not treatment, and the nature of the time-limiting effort (e.g., 10 or 20 sessions). It appeared strongly that the attrition curve was the most important descriptive way of examining and studying psychotherapy service delivery efforts (or systems), that all other problems related to psychotherapy came after the study of the attrition curve.

NEW RESEARCH QUESTIONS

Many new features of research began to appear, faster than could possibly be accommodated. One question that arose early on was related to people having second admission to some psychotherapy delivery systems. We were able to get data from an alcoholic outpatient clinic on this subject, and except for smaller means and standard deviations, the attrition curve remained about the same among the second admission cases as it had with the first admission group. In time we were able to get data on people in a given geographic area pursuing therapy in different clinics; it was shown that people consulted different clinics in the same descriptive manner that people as a total population utilized services in a given clinic in terms of the number of visits utilized. That is, a greater number of people, proportionally, had zero or only one previous visit to a given clinic in a limited geographical area; far fewer had two, and so on down to seven or eight visits along the asymptote, when the inquiry covered a 2½ year span.

The attrition curve shows the asymptote of the distribution. This observation is important because it tells how the system extends cases beyond what one might assume to be the natural limits of the distribution — say about three standard deviations beyond the mean. What of clinics that extend cases out to seven or eight standard deviations beyond the mean? Are they inefficient? Do they have an unusual clientele? Do only some therapists hold patients/clients for much longer times? And so on.

Clearly in view now is the attrition curve. It raised a number of questions about the mean and standard deviations of the distributions, the length of the asymptote, and a host of questions about clientele served, efficiently or not, and so on. A leg up on the delivery system was obvious. The relevance of the attritional curve for all manner of psychotherapy research and practice questions was illuminated. How can one do research on psychotherapy outcome, on comparing different therapy regimens, on differences in cases, and so forth, without referring to the baseline of the attrition curve? Again, the curve seemed to come before anything else one might do in research and practical ways to study and/or improve upon psychotherapy.

With this much of a platform to stand on, it became convincing that a host of other problems were at hand. How about client and therapist ratings of therapy? Of the intake? Outcome? If therapists had not known heretofore of the attrition curve, what difference did that make? Did therapists go on the assumption that most therapy would (ideally) be long-term? Or that short-term therapy was a kind of Band-Aid? Would therapists agree to different policies that influenced delivery of services without feeling that their contributions, as independent workers, were being vitiated in some important way? Would clients despite various interventions continue to behave in accordance with the attrition curve? If so, what influence should that have on our delivery system efforts? There was — and is — no apparent end to the number of intriguing questions that could be asked. Therapy was now becoming something far different from what we had all been taught to believe. If the attrition curve was valid, what about all the espoused differences among and between therapies? Were they much more the same than very different? If they were different, was that in relationship to the attrition curve? Or outside it? Or what?

How can we have theories of therapy if all data submit to the attrition curve (Reda & Mahoney, 1984)? Possibly in terms of the nature of the slope — whether the drop comes at intake, or a little bit later? The mean number of sessions and the standard deviation? But these questions have never been raised nor explored before. Most data show the national norm means fall between four and six or seven sessions for outpatient psychotherapy cases. Does that mean we should all get in line and offer an up-front, incisive, active, problem-solving therapy and forget about theoretical differences? Probably so, but we cannot prove it at this juncture. Much more research is indicated, but it may mean that psychotherapy is, whether we like it or not, content-free at the outset. That is, no particular content need guide our theories; clients need supportive interaction with the therapist and some problem solving. But as to the particulars of theories of psychotherapy, we have no way now of showing they make a great deal of difference.

Apropos of the last point, client satisfaction and problem solving seemed to account for most of the variance in the client replies to follow-up questionnaires. But some humility is needed here. Most systems of psychotherapy probably do not follow up well on more than a fifth or sixth of their original psychotherapy clientele (what was called "ostensible therapy cases"), starting from the intake as the first session in the operation of the delivery system. Our data show we can get about 35%–40% replies from those who come back for one or more sessions following intake. Are other data bases much better? Do theorists of psychotherapy really do better — if at all — in their follow-up efforts? Do they take account of attritional loss all along the way, or do they just throw out such cases as immediately irrelevant? Is any psychotherapy theory really buttressed by good data based on the fundamentals of the attrition curve? It is highly doubtful.

PROGRAMMATIC, COOPERATIVE RESEARCH

So many new problems arose it was difficult to keep up with them even from a nominal standpoint. There is enough research suggested herein to keep a multitude of therapists/theorists/researchers busy for a long time and we should now promote cooperative programmatic research. The problems opened up here are too vast for one or a few clinics, and the importance of problems related to the psychotherapies delivery system must submit to new research questions and technique, holding in clear view the attritional curve baseline.

THE FLOW OF CASES

We moved from the notion of dropping out from therapy to attrition. The next move, descriptively speaking, was the study of the flow of cases. We seem to assume, although we know of no one who has made the matter explicit, that cases flow throughout the year in a fairly even way from one point to the next. In the university setting it is obvious that things start up in September and die down in May or June; thus low and high variations are inevitable. We do not know how other delivery systems — say those connected with hospitals, those serving communities, or those specializing in a given, limited clientele — operate, but we know that in the university setting not only is the flow uneven month to month, the sex breakdown is different at different times of the year (we know of no reason why), and that the leaner intake times lead to longer mean numbers of therapy sessions, irrespective of "need." Many policy problems and issues reside in these and other data related to the flow of cases through the system.

Not only is the flow of cases through the system important, the flow *into* the system has come under scrutiny. We found no consistent literature on pre-intake attrition to guide us, but we noted that there were three classes of pre-intake attrition: those that failed to show up at the appointed time, those that had made appointments but called to cancel, and those that made appointments, cancelled, and then rescheduled and entered the formal system, as such. This finding over 2 years showed that the community probably contains a number of potential clients who are somewhat ambivalent about entering the formal system for therapeutic help. Some, of course, enter only temporarily, as with intake-only clients, but others enter hesitantly and continue on for a while. At the far end of the distribution, we know only that extended cases are quite different statistically in the number of sessions they have, compared to controls seen by the same therapists, but we do not have evidence they are generally much different from the general run of cases in the system. And we do not know how many continue on to other therapy experiences, formal or informal, after leaving one system, although our data show that about one third of our fairly young and economically advantaged clients have had previous therapy of some formal type.

Thus we have lengthened and enlarged our understanding of psychotherapy — we moved from the invidious term, "dropout," to the study of the attrition curve as an unusually stable, interesting, and research-provoking phenomenon, on to the study of the flow of cases as it is shown in pre-intake data at least; but there is also a suggestion of important research at the tail end — the asymptote and beyond — in the service delivery system (see Fig. 10.1).

Figure 10.1 is an attempt to synthesize some of the major aspects of this set of research findings and theoretical issues. We have seen how the initial notion of "dropout" has had to yield to the description of how psychotherapy service delivery follows the attrition curve, a Poisson distribution with approximately equal means and standard deviations. This figure speaks to that end, but it adds on the third point, viz., the flow of cases from the social setting to pre-intake, through the formal system (the clinic), and beyond the asymptote into the post-treatment return of the client to the natural community and social support system (or into other formal systems). We see the complexity of the problem in broader view. We have barely scratched the surface of these problems and respectfully suggest the reader with investigative interests delve ever more into the many junctures in this help-seeking enterprise that cry out for research. Insofar as Fig. 10.1 is concerned, the help-seeking and the flow of cases through the system are probably not much different in the analogue intervention modality than that described for self-initiated, walk-in cases. However, exploring the similarities and differences between the two service delivery systems (and moving on to medical/patient compliance/adherence, as well) is strongly indicated, for no matter which way the data take us, it will be instructive.

What is now called for—it bears repeating—in the study of psychotherapy and behavior change—is not only following up on the many research areas delineated here but the organizing of cooperative, programmatic, planned research that will unite the efforts of a number of researchers to work on these problems. With the coming about of this prospect, psychotherapy and behavior change will have been put on a thoroughly scientific, socially oriented, and consumer conscious basis. This is about all we can ask for in the present state of development of our scientific and practical efforts.

HELP-SEEKING BEHAVIOR

We are now obliged to move on to another conceptualization of the psychotherapy matter—that of help-seeking behavior. This comes about in several ways and enlarges even more our notions about psychotherapy and what the whole process is about, and how far wide of the mark much research, theory and practice have been in view of these enlargements. We noted that clients in a given geographic community went from one clinic to another and that when these data are aggregated, they show a curve of the negatively accelerating, declining ("decay") type, the same that describes the flow of cases from intake to asymptote within a given clinic. Help-seeking, it is suggested, must be a fairly describable and stable set of social phenomena, if we are to allow some extrapolation from the data. Moreover, clients who are kept track of as they move from one facility to another can also be shown to follow the same negatively accelerating, declining curve. In the instances of extending the attrition curve to flow of cases and to help-seeking, we find that a community of people being served by a number of clinics shows this characteristic curve; and that individuals, when traced from one facility to another, also follow this same distribution. The baselines, then, for the study of the delivery of psychotherapy services are about the same in three widely spaced settings: the individual clinic, the use of a collection of clinics in a given geographic area by the total clientele, and the use of clinical facilities by individuals as they are traced or followed from one setting to another. They are an unusually stable set of baselines, apparently of much more importance than the usual sorts of data afforded us by the research community, as its members have pursued a host of questions about how the clients perceive the intake, therapy, and so on. We have to begin our therapy in a new key (Cheifetz & Salloway, 1984; Levy, 1984; Widiger & Rorer, 1984).

Throughout this book every more or less traditional research problem in psychotherapy is forced into a new mold; a whole host of new research problems are brought forward, such that the uses of the traditional problems appear smaller and smaller and will have to present new approaches if they are to survive as viable matters for research, knowledge, training of therapists, policies of clinics and serving the consuming public in economical and productive ways.

In essence, the delivery system studied and reported on here is far more than a delivery system in the usual sense of the term. It is the testing ground for psychotherapy research, practice, theory, and training. Institutional functioning may say more about behavior than does study of the behavior in its micro (individual) aspects; the study of psychotherapy is a good example of the limitations of individual study, dyadic interactions, and/or small groups, because each of them fails to some extent to take the community into consideration. The only way the individal, dyadic and small group variables can be profitably combined into a useful composite is through the delivery system acting to align these three features in terms of the primary data—the number of sessions—and the secondary data—the quality of service—plus the efficacy of the whole product vis-à-vis societal criteria.

References

Acosta, F. X., Yamamoto, J., & Evans, L. A. (1982). *Effective psychotherapy for low income and minority patients.* New York: Plenum.

Affleck, D. C., & Medwick, S. A. (1959). The use of the Rorschach Test in the production of the abrupt terminator in individual psychotherapy. *Journal of Counseling Psychology, 23,* 125–128.

Ajzen, I., & Fishbein, M. (1980). *Understanding attitudes and predicting social behavior.* Englewood Cliffs, NJ: Prentice-Hall.

Albers, R. J., & Scrivner, L. L. (1977). The structure of attrition during appraisal. *Community Mental Health Journal, 13,* 325–331.

Altman, H., Evenson, R., & Cho, D. W. (1978). Predicting length of stay by patients hospitalized for alcoholism or drug dependence. *Journal of Studies on Alcohol, 39*(1), 197–201.

Anderson, O. D., & Parmenter, R. (1939). *A long-term study of the experimental neurosis in the sheep and dog.* Psychosomatic Medicine Monographs, Vol. II, Nos. III & IV. Menasha, WI: Banta.

Andrews, G., Hewson, D., & Vaillant, G. (1978). Life event stress, social support, coping style, and risk of psychological impairment. *Journal of Nervous and Mental Disease, 166,* 307–316.

Avnet, H. H. (1965a). How effective is short-term psychotherapy? In L. R. Wolberg (Ed.), *Short-term psychotherapy.* New York: Grune & Stratton.

Avnet, H. H. (1965b). Short-term treatment under auspices of a medical insurance plan. *American Journal of Psychiatry, 122,* 147–151.

Bachrach, A. J. (1972). *Psychological research: An introduction.* New York: Random House (3rd ed.).

Baekeland, F., & Lundwall, L. (1975). Dropping out of treatment: A critical review. *Psychological Bulletin, 82,* 738–783.

Baekeland, F., Lundwall, L., & Shanahan, T. (1973). Correlates of patient attrition in the outpatient treatment of alcoholism. *The Journal of Nervous and Mental Disease, 157*(2), 99–107.

Balch, P., Ireland, J. F., McWilliams, S. A., & Lewis, S. B. (1977). Client evaluation of community mental health services: relation to demographic and treatment variables. *American Journal of Community Psychology, 5,* 243–247.

Baldwin, B. (1978). A paradigm for the classification of emotional crisis: Implications for crisis intervention. *American Journal of Orthopsychiatry, 43,* 538-551.

Barker, R. G. (1965). Explorations in ecological psychology. *American Psychologist, 20,* 1-14.

Barker, R. G, & Wright, H. F. (1951). *One boy's day.* New York: Harper & Row.

Barlow, D. H., Hayes, S. C., & Nelson, R. O. (1984). *The scientist practitioner.* New York: Pergamon.

Barnett, M. H. (1981). The effect of client preparation upon involvement and continuation in psychotherapy. (Doctoral dissertation, University of Florida). *Dissertation Abstracts International, 42*(5): 2040-B. (University Microfilms No. 8124411)

Barten, H. H. (1971). *Brief therapies.* New York: Behavioral Publications.

Bassuk, E., & Gerson, S. (1980). Chronic crisis patients: A discreet clinical group. *American Journal of Psychiatry, 137*(12), 1513-1516.

Beck, A. T. (1976). *Cognitive therapy and emotional disorders.* New York: International University Press.

Becker, M. H., Maiman, L. A. (1975). Sociobehavioral determinants of compliance with health and medical care recommendations. *Medical Care, 13*(1), 10-24.

Bellack, A. S., & Hersen, M. (Eds.). (1979). Research and practice in social skills training. New York: Plenum.

Bennett, M. J., & Wisneski, M. J. (1979). Continuous psychotherapy within an HMO. *American Journal of Psychiatry, 136,* 1283-1287.

Bergin, A. E., & Lambert, J. J. (1978). The evaluation of therapeutic outcome. In S. L. Garfield & A. E. Bergin (Eds.), *Handbook of psychotherapy and behavior change: An empirical analysis* (2nd ed.). New York: Wiley.

Bergman, A. B., & Werner, A. J. (1963). Failure of children to receive penicillin by mouth. *New England Journal of Medicine, 268,* 1334-1338.

Berzins, J. I., Bednar, R. L., & Severy, L. J. (1975). The problem of intersource consensus in measuring therapeutic outcome. *Journal of Abnormal Psychology, 84,* 10-19.

Betz, N., & Shullman, S. (1979). Factors related to client return rate following intake. *Journal of Counseling Psychology, 26*(6), 542-545.

Beuter, L. E., Johnson, D. T., Newell, C. W., Warburn, S. N., & Elkins, D. (1973). The A-B theory type distinction in psychotherapy. *Journal of Abnormal Psychology, 82,* 273-277.

Blocher, D. H., & Biggs, D. A. (1983). *Counseling psychology in community settings.* New York: Springer.

Bloom, B. L. (1980). Social and community interactions. *Annual Review of Psychology, 31,* 111-142.

Bloom, B. L. (1981). Focused single-session therapy: Initial development and evaluation. In S. H. Budman (Ed.), *Forms of brief therapy.* New York: Guilford.

Bowen, W., Tremlow, S., & Stuart, W. (1978). Locus of Control and treatment dropout in an alcoholic population. *British Journal of Addiction, 73*(1), 51-54.

Brammer, L. M., & Shostrom, E. L. (1982). *Therapeutic Psychology.* Englewood Cliffs, NJ: Prentice-Hall. 4th Ed.

Brandt, L. W. (1964). The rejection of psychotherapy. The discovery of unexpected numbers of pseudo rejectors. *Archives of General Psychiatry, 10,* 310-312.

Brandt, L. W. (1965). Studies of "dropout" patients in psychotherapy: A review of findings. *Psychotherapy: Theory, research and practice, 2,* 2-13.

Brosch, P. H. (1980). Systematic preparation for individual psychotherapy: its effect on client anxiety, attrition and response to treatment. (Doctoral dissertation, American University, 1980). *Dissertation Abstracts International, 41*(2): 683-B. (University Microfilms No. 8017672)

Brown, B. B. (1978). Social and psychological correlates of help-seeking behavior among urban adults. *American Journal of Community Psychology, 6*(5), 425-439.

Brown, J. S. (1948). Gradients of approach and avoidance responses and their relations to level of motivation. *Journal of Comparative & Physiological Psychology, 41,* 450–465.

Budman, S. H. (Ed.). (1981a). *Forms of brief therapy.* New York: Guilford.

Budman, S. H. (1981b). Looking toward the future. In S. H. Budman (Ed.), *Forms of brief therapy.* New York: Guilford.

Burisch, M. (1984). Approaches to personality inventory construction. *American Psychologist, 39,* 214–227.

Burnham, C. A. (1951). *Reliability and validity of psychologists' evaluating therapy readiness.* Doctoral dissertation, New York University.

Burton, A. (1975). Therapist satisfaction. *American Journal of Psychoanalysis, 35,* 115–122.

Butcher, J. N., & Koss, M. P. (1978). Research on brief and crisis-oriented therapies. In S. A. Garfield & A. E. Bergin (Eds.). *Handbook of psychotherapy and behavior change: An empirical analysis* (2nd ed.) New York: Wiley.

Byers, J. A. (1982). *Everyman's database primer.* Culver City, CA: Ashton-Tate.

Caggiano, R. A. (1981). Factors related to premature termination and customer satisfaction of mental health services in a community mental health center. (Doctoral dissertation, Boston University, 1980). *Dissertation Abstracts International, 41*(12): 4654-B. (University Microfilms No. 8112234).

Carkhuff, R. R., & Truax, C. B. (1965). Lay mental health counseling: The effects of lay group counseling. *Journal of Consulting Psychology, 29,* 426–431.

Cheifetz, D. I., & Salloway, J. C. (1984). Patterns of mental health services provided by HMOs. *American Psychologist, 39,* 495–502.

Colby, K. M., & Spar, J. E. (1983). *The fundamental crisis in psychiatry: Unreliability of diagnoses.* Springfield, IL: Charles C. Thomas.

Collins, A., & Pancost, D. (1976). *Natural helping networks.* Washington, DC: National Association of Social Workers.

Cooley, E. J., & Lejoy, R. (1980). Therapeutic relationship and improvement as perceived by clients and therapists. *Journal of Clinical Psychology, 30,* 562–570.

Corrigan, J. D., Dell, D. M., Lewis, K. N., & Schmidt, L. D. (1980). Counseling as a social influence process: A review. *Journal of Counseling Psychology, 27,* 395–441.

Corsini, R. J. (Ed.). (1981). *Handbook of innovative psychotherapies.* New York: Wiley.

Counseling Psychologist (1982). *Counseling psychology: The next decade, Vol. 10,* No. 2, whole issue.

Covi, L., Lipman, R. S., & Drogatis, L. R. (1974). Drugs and group psychotherapy in neurotic depression. *American Journal of Psychiatry, 131,* 191–198.

Cowen, E. L. (1973). Social and community intervention. In P. H. Mussen & M. R. Rosenzweig (Eds.), *Annual review of psychology.* Palo Alto, CA: Annual Reviews, Inc.

Cummings, N. A. (1977). Prolonged (ideal) vs. short-term (realistic) psychotherapy. *Professional Psychology, 8,* 491–501.

Cummings, N. A., & Follette, W. T. (1976). Brief therapy and medical utilization: An eight-year follow-up. In Dorken, *Professional psychology today.* San Francisco: Jossey Bass.

Cummings, N. A., & Vandenbos, F. (1979). The general practice of psychology. *Professional Psychology, 10,* 430–440.

Curran, J. P., & Monti, P. M. (Eds.). (1982). *Social skills training.* New York: Guilford.

Davanloo, H. (Ed.). (1978). *Basic principles and techniques in short-term dynamic psychotherapy.* New York: Spectrum.

Dawes, R. M., Landman, J., & Williams, M. (1984). Reply to Kurosawa (Comment). *American Psychologist, 38,* 74–75.

Deykin, E., Weissman, M., Tanner, J., & Prusoff, B. (1975). Participation in therapy. A study of attendance patterns in depressed outpatients. *Journal of Nervous Mental Diseases, 160*(1), 42–48.

Di Loreto, A. O. (1971). *Comparative psychotherapy: An experimental analysis.* Chicago: Aldine-Atherton.

DiMatteo, M. R., & DiNicola, D. D. (1982). *Achieving patient compliance.* New York: Pergamon.

Dodson, F. (1976). *The you that could be.* Chicago: Follett.

Dowds, B. N., & Fontana, A. F. (1977). Patients' and therapists' expectations and evaluations of hospital treatment: Satisfactions and disappointments. *Comprehensive Psychiatry, 18*(3), 295–300.

Durlak, J. A. (1979). Comparative effectiveness of paraprofessional and professional helpers. *Psychological Bulletin, 86*(1), 80–92.

Eastaugh, S. R., & Hatcher, M. E. (1982). Improving compliance among hypertensive: A triage criterion with cost-benefit implications. *Medical Care, 20,* 1001–1017.

Edwards, D. W., Yarvis, R. M., Mueller, D. P., & Langsley, D. G. (1978). Does patient satisfaction correlate with success? *Hospital and Community Psychiatry, 29,* 188–190.

Eiduson, B. T. (1968). Two classes of information in psychiatry. *Archives of General Psychiatry, 18,* 405–419.

Eisenberg, L. (1977). The search for care. *Daedalus, 106,* 235–246.

Ellis, A. (1962). *Reason and emotion in psychotherapy.* New York: Lyle Stuart.

Emmelkamp, P. M. G. (1982). *Phobic and obsessive-compulsive disorders: Theory, research and practice.* New York: Plenum.

Emrick, C. D., & Lassen, C. L., (1977). The nonprofessional therapeutic agent. In A. S. Gurman & A. M. Razin (Eds.), *The effective psychotherapist: A handbook.* New York: Pergamon.

Emrick, C. D., Lassen, C. L., & Edwards, M. T. (1978). Nonprofessional peers as therapeutic agents. In A. Gurman & A. Razin (Eds.), *Effective psychotherapy: A handbook of research.* New York: Pergamon.

Engel, G. L. (1968). A life setting conducive to illness: The givingup-given-up complex. *Annals of Internal Medicine, 69,* 293–300.

Engel, G. L., (1975). A unified concept of health and disease. In T. Millon (Ed.), *Medical behavioral science.* Philadelphia: W. B. Saunders.

Engel, G. L., (1977a). The care of the patient: Art or science/ *Johns Hopkins Medical Journal, 140,* 222–232.

Engel, G. L., (1977b). The need for a new medical model: A challenge for biomedicine. *Science, 196,* 129–136.

Epperson, D. (1981). Counselor gender and early premature terminations from counseling: A replication and extension. *Journal of Counseling Psychology, 28*(4), 349–356.

Epperson, D. L., Bushway, D. J., & Warman, R. E. (1983). Client self-terminations after one counseling session: Effects of problem recognition, counselor gender and counselor experience. *Journal of Counseling Psychology, 30,* 307–315.

Ewalt, P. L., Cohen, M., & Harmatz, J. S. (1972). *Prediction of treatment acceptance by child guidance clinic applicants: An easily applied instrument. American Journal of Orthopsychiatry, 32*(5), 857–864.

Ewing, C. P. (1978). *Crisis intervention as psychotherapy.* New York: Oxford University Press.

Eysenck, H. J. (1952). The effects of psychotherapy: An evaluation, *Journal of Consulting Psychology, 16,* 319–324.

Eysenck, H. J. (1960). *Handbook of Abnormal Psychology.* London: Pitman.

Eysenck, H. J. (1965). The effects of psychotherapy. *International Journal of Psychiatry, 1,* 97–178.

Eysenck, H. J. (1966). *The effects of psychotherapy.* New York: International Science Press.

Eysenck, H. J. (1967). New ways in psychotherapy. *Psychology Today, 1,* 39–47.

Fagan, P. J. (1982a). *A comparison of rejectors, dropouts and remainers at a university counseling center.* Unpublished manuscript.

Felner, R. D., & Jason, L. A. (Eds.). (1983). *Preventive psychology: Theory, research and practice.* New York: Pergamon.

Fiester, A. R. (1977). Client's perceptions of therapists with high attrition rates. *Journal of Consulting and Clinical Psychology, 45*(5), 954–955.

Fiester, A. R., Mahrer, A. R., Giambra, L. M., & Ormiston, D. W. (1974). Shaping a clinic population: the dropout problem reconsidered. *Community Mental Health Journal, 10*(2), 173–179.

Fiester, A. R., & Rudestam, K. E. (1975). A multivariate analysis of the early dropout process. *Journal of Consulting and Clinical Psychology, 43,* 528–535.

Fiske, D. W., Cartwright, D. G., & Kirtner, W. L. (1964). Are psychotherapeutic changes predictable? *Journal of Abnormal and Social Psychology, 69,* 418–426.

Flegenheimer, W. V. (1982). *Techniques of brief psychotherapy.* New York: Jason Aronson.

Flynn, T. C., Balch, P., Lewis, S. D., & Katz, B. (1981). Predicting client improvement from satisfaction with community mental health center services. *American Journal of Community Psychology, 9,* 339–346.

Follette, W. T., & Cummings, N. A. (1967). Psychiatric services and medical utilization in a prepaid health plan setting. *Medical Care, 5,* 25–35.

Frank, J. D. (1973). *Persuasion and Healing, 2nd ed.* Baltimore: Johns Hopkins University Press.

Frank, J. D. (1974). Therapeutic components of psychotherapy. *Journal of Nervous and Mental Disease, 159,* 325–342.

Frank, J. D. (1979). The present status of outcome studies. *Journal of Consulting & Clinical Psychology, 47,* 310–316.

Frank, J. D., Gliedman, L. H., Imber, S. D., Nash, E. P., & Stone, A. R. (1957). Why patients leave psychotherapy. *Archives of Neurology and Psychiatry, 77,* 283–299.

Frank, J. D., Gliedman, L. H., Imber, S. D., Stone, A. R., & Nash, E. P. (1959). Patients' experiences and relearning as factors determining improvement in psychotherapy. *American Journal of Psychiatry, 115,* 961–968.

Friedman, H. S., & DiMatteo, M. R. (Eds.). (1982). *Interpersonal issues in health care.* New York: Academic.

Gallo, P. S., Jr. (1978). Meta-analysis—A mixed meta-phor? (Comment). *American Psychologist, 33,* 515–517.

Gantt, W. H. (1944). *Experimental basis for neurotic behavior.* New York: Paul B. Hoeber.

Garfield, S. A. (1978). Research on client variables in psychotherapy. In S. A. Garfield & A. E. Bergin (Eds.), *Handbook of psychotherapy and behavior change: An empirical analysis* (2nd ed.). New York: Wiley.

Garfield, S. A. (1980). *Psychotherapy: An eclectic approach.* New York: Wiley.

Garfield, S. A. (1981). Psychotherapy: A 40-year appraisal. *American Psychologist, 36,* 174–183.

Garfield, S. A., & Affleck, D. C. (1959). An appraisal of stay in outpatient psychotherapy. *Journal of Nervous and Mental Disease, 129,* 492–498.

Garfield, S. A., & Bergin, A. E. (1978). *Handbook of psychotherapy and behavior change: An empirical analysis,* (2nd ed.). New York: Wiley.

Garfield, S. A., & Kurz, M. (1952). Evaluating treatment and related procedures in 1216 cases referred to a mental hygiene clinic. *Psychiatric Quarterly, 26,* 414–424.

Gates, S. J., & Colborn, D. K. (1976). Lowering appointment failures in a neighborhood health center. *Medical Care, 14,* 268–273.

Gelso, C. J. (1979). Research in counseling: Methodology and professional issues. *The Counseling Psychologist, 8,* 7–35.

Gelso, C. J., & Johnson, D. W. (1983). *Explorations in time-limited counseling and psychotherapy.* New York: Teachers College Press.

Gelso, C. J., Spiegel, S. B., & Mills, D. H. (1983). Clients' and counselors' reactions to time-limited and time-unlimited counseling. In C. J. Gelso & D. H. Johnson, *Explorations in counseling and psychotherapy.* New York: Teachers College Press.

Gillum, R. F., & Barsky, A. J. (1974). Diagnosis and management of patient noncompliance. *Journal of the American Medical Association, 228*(12), 1563-7.

Glasscote, R. M. (1980). *Preventing mental illness.* Washington, DC: American Psychiatric Association.

Goldring, J. (1980). *Quick response therapy: A time-limited treatment approach.* New York: Human Sciences Press.

Gomes-Schwartz, B. (1978). Effective ingredients in psychotherapy: Prediction of outcome from process variables. *Journal of Clinical Psychology, 46,* 1023-1035.

Gottlieb, B. H. (Ed.). (1981). *Social networks and social support.* Beverly Hills, CA: Sage.

Gottschalk, L. A., Mayerson, P., & Gottlieb, A. A. (1967). Prediction and evaluation of outcome in an emergency brief psychotherapy clinic. *Journal of Nervous and Mental Disease, 144,* 77-96.

Gottschalk, L. A., Winget, C. N., & Glaser, G. D. (1969). *Manual of instructions for using the Gottschalk-Glaser Content Analysis Scale.* Berkeley: University of California Press.

Grayson, H. (Ed.). (1979). *Short-term approaches to psychotherapy.* New York: Human Sciences Press.

Green, P. E. (1978). *Analyzing Multivariate Data.* Hinsdale, IL: Dryden.

Gruver, G. G. (1971). College students as therapeutic agents. *Psychological Bulletin, 76,* 111-127.

Gundlach, R. H., & Geller, M. (1958). The problem of early termination: Is it really the terminee? *Journal of Consulting Psychology, 22,* 410.

Gurman, A. S., & Razin, A. M. (1977). *Effective psychotherapy: A handbook of research.* New York: Pergamon.

Gustafson, J. P. (1981). The complex secret of brief psychotherapy in the works of Malan and Balint. In S. H. Budman (Ed.), *Forms of brief therapy.* New York: Guilford.

Guthrie, E. R. (1938). *The psychology of human conflict.* New York: Harpers.

Guttentag, M., Salasin, S., & Belle, D. *The mental health of women.* New York: Academic.

Hahn, J., & King, K. (1982). Client and environmental correlates of patient attrition from an inpatient alcoholism treatment center. *Journal of Drug Education, 12*(1), 75-86.

Hamburg, D. A., Bibring, G. L., Fisher, C., Stanton, A. H., Wallerstein, R. S., Weinstock, H. I., & Haggard, E. (1967). Committee on central fact gathering data of the American Psychoanalytic Association. *Journal of the American Psychoanalytic Association, 15,* 841-861.

Hargie, O., Sanders, C., & Dickson, D. (1981). *Social skills in interpersonal communication.* London: Croom Helm.

Haring, N. G., & Phillips, E. L. (1962). *Educating emotionally disturbed children.* Englewood Cliffs, NJ: McGraw-Hill.

Haring, N. G., & Phillips, E. L. (1972). *Analysis and modification of classroom behavior.* Englewood Cliffs, NJ: Prentice-Hall.

Heilbrun, A. B. (1972). Effects of briefing upon client satisfaction with the initial counseling contact. *Journal of Consulting and Clinical Psychology, 38,* 50-56.

Herink, R. (1980). *The psychotherapy handbook.* New York: New American Library.

Hiler, E. W. (1958). An analysis of patient-therapist compatibility. *Journal of Consulting Psychologist, 22,* 341-347.

Holliday, P. B. (1979). Effects of preparation for therapy on client expectations and participation. (Doctoral dissertation, University of Georgia, 1978). *Dissertation Abstracts International, 39,*(7): 3517-B. (University Microfilms No. 7901646)

Hollon, S. D., & Beck, A. A. (1978). Psychotherapy and drug therapy: Comparisons and combinations. In S. L. Garfield & A. P. Bergin (Eds.), *Handbook of psychotherapy and behavior change: An empirical analysis,* (2nd ed.). New York: Pergamon.

Hovland, C. I., & Sears, R. R. (1938). Experiments on motor conflict: I types of conflict and their modes of resolution. *Journal of Experimental Psychology, 23,* 477–493.

Huberty, C. J. (1984). Issues in the use and interpretation of discriminant analysis. *Psychological Bulletin, 95,* 156–171.

Hull, C. L., (1943). *Principles of behavior.* New York: Appleton-Century-Crofts.

Hurtado, A. V., Greenlick, M. R., & Colombo, T. J. (1973). Determinants of medical care utilization. Failure to keep appointments. *Medical Care, 11*(6), 189–98.

Insel, P. M. (1980). *Environmental variables and the prevention of mental illness.* Lexington, MA: Lexington.

Iscoe, I., & Harris, L. D. (1984). Social and community intervention. In M. R. Rosenzweig and L. W. Poeter (Eds.), *Annual review of psychology.* Palo Alto, CA: Annual Reviews, Inc.

Jacobson, G. F., Wilner, D. M., Morely, W. E., Schneider, S., Strickler, M., & Sommer, G. J. (1971). The scope and practice of an early-access brief treatment psychiatric center. In H. H. Barten (Ed.) *Brief therapies.* New York: Behavioral Publications.

Janis, I. L. (Ed.) (1982). *Counseling on personal decisions.* New Haven: Yale University Press.

Johnson, C. A. & Katz, R. C. (1973). Using parents as change agents for their children: A review. *Journal of Child Psychology and Psychiatry, 4,* 181–200.

Jones, E. E. (1980). Multidimensional change in psychotherapy. *Journal of Clinical Psychology, 36*(2), 544–547.

Jones, E. E. (1982). Psychotherapists' impressions of treatment outcome as a function of race. *Journal of Clinical Psychology, 38*(4), 722–731.

Journal of Counseling and Clinical Psychology (1983), Vol. 51, whole issue.

Kadushin, C. (1969). *Why people go to psychiatrists.* New York: Atherton.

Kaiser, H. F. (1959). The application of electronic computers to factor analysis. *Symposium on the application of computers to psychological problems,* American Psychological Association.

Kaiser, M. B. (1982). *The use of demographic factors and drinking history as predictors of attrition in outpatient alcoholic treatment.* Unpublished Second Year Research Project. The George Washington University.

Kalish, H. I. (1981). *From behavioral science to behavior modification.* New York: McGraw-Hill.

Karasu, T. B., Stein, S. P., & Charles, E. S. (1979). Age factors in patient-therapist relationship. *Journal of Nervous and Mental Disease, 167*(2), 100–104.

Kazdin, A. E. (1982). Evaluating the generality of findings in analogue therapy research. *Journal of Consulting and Clinical Psychology, 46,* 686–693.

Kazdin, A. E. (1978). Evaluating the generality of findings in analogue therapy research. *Journal of Consulting and Clinical Psychology, 46,* 673–686.

Kazdin, A. E. (1978). *History of behavior modification.* Baltimore: University Park Press.

Keithly, L. J., Samples, S. J., & Strupp, H. H. (1980). Patient motivation as a predictor of process and outcome in psychotherapy. *Psychotherapy and Pyschosomatics, 33*(1–2), 87–97.

Kelly, E. L., Goldberg, L. R., Fiske, D. W., & Kilkowski, J. M. (1978). Twenty-five years later: A follow-up study of the V.A. selection research project. *American Psychologist, 33,* 746–755.

Kendler, H. H. (1981). *Psychology: A science in conflict.* New York: Oxford University Press.

Kerlinger, F. N. (1973). *Foundations of behavioral research* (2nd. ed.). New York: Holt, Reinhart & Winston.

Kernberg, O. F., Berstein, E. D., Coyne, L., Appelbaum, A., Horwitz, L., & Voth, H. (1972). Psychotherapy and psychoanalysis. Final report of the Menninger Foundation Psychotherapy Research Project. *Bulletin of the Menninger Clinic, 30, Nos. 1 and 2.*

Kilbourne, B., & Richardson, J. T. (1984). Psychotherapy and new religions in a pluralistic society. *American Psychologist, 39,* 237–251.

Kissell, S. (1974). Mothers and therapists evaluate long-term and short-term child therapy. *Journal of Clinical Psychology, 30,* 296–299.

Klein, D. C. (1960). Some concepts concerning the mental health of the individual. *Journal of Consulting Psychology, 24,* 288–293.

Klerman, G. L., Di Mascio, A., Weissman, M. M., Prusoff, B., & Paykel, E. S. (1974). Treatment of depression by drugs and psychotherapy. *American Journal of Psychiatry, 131,* 186–191.

Knapp, P. H., Lavin, S., McCarter, R. H., Wermer, H., & Zetzel, E. (1960). Suitability for psychoanalysis. *Psychoanalytic Quarterly, 29,* 459–477.

Knight, R. P. (1941). Evaluation of the results of psychoanalytic therapy. *American Journal of Psychiatry, 98,* 434–446.

Kogan, L. S. (1957). The short-term case in a family agency: Part I, the study plan. *Social Casework, 38,* 231–238.

Koss, M. P. (1979). Length of psychotherapy for clients seen in private practice. *Journal of Consulting and Clinical Psychology, 47,* 210–212.

Krasner, L. (1971). Behavior therapy. In P. H. Mussen (Ed.), *Annual Review of Psychology.* Palo Alto, CA: American Review.

Krasnoff, A. (1977). Failure of MMPI scales to predict treatment completion. *Journal of Studies on Alcohol, 38*(7), 1440–1442.

Kurland, A. A. (1956). The drug placebo — its psychodynamic and conditioned-reflex action. *Behavioral Science, 2,* 101–110.

Kurosawa, K. (1984). Meta-Analysis and selective publication bias. (Comment). *American Psychologist, 33,* 73–74.

Lambert, M. J., Christensen, E. R., & DeJulio, S. S. (Eds.). (1983). *The assessment of psychotherapy outcome.* New York: Wiley.

Lambert, M. J., DeJulio, S. S., & Stein, D. M. (1978). Therapist interpersonal skills: Process, outcome, methodological considerations, and recommendations for future research. *Psychological Bulletin, 85*(3), 467–489.

Landman, J. T., & Dawes, R. M. (1982). Psychotherapy outcome: Smith and Glass' conclusions stand up under scrutiny. *American Psychologist, 37,* 504–516.

Landman, J. T., & Dawes, R. M. (1984). Reply to Orwin and Cordray (Comment). *American Psychologist, 38,* 72–73.

Lazare, A., Cohen, F., Jacobson, A. M., Williams, M. D., Mignone, R. J., & Zisook, S. (1972). The walk-in patient as a "customer." *American Journal of Orthopsychiatry, 42,* 872–883.

Lazare, A., Sherman, I., & Wasserman, L. (1975). The customer approach to patienthood. *Archives of General Psychiatry, 32,* 553–558.

Lenrow, P., & Cowden, P. (1980). Human services, professionals, and the paradox of institutional reform. *American Journal of Community Psychology, 8*(4), 463–484.

Leve, R. M. (1974). A comment on Garfield, Prager and Bergin's evaluation of outcome in psychotherapy. *Journal of Consulting and Clinical Psychology, 42,* 293–295.

Leventhal, A. M. (1964). Prediction of number of counseling interviews. *Psychological Reports, 15,* 106.

Levitt, E. E., & Fisher, W. P. (1981). The effects of an expectancy state on the fate of applications and psychotherapy in an outpatient setting. *Journal of Clinical Psychiatry, 42*(46), 234–237.

Levy, E. I. (1963). Psychologist serving as intake interviewer. *Journal of Consulting Psychology, 10,* 97–98.

Levy, L. H. (1984). The metamorphosis of clinical psychology. *American Psychologist, 39,* 486–494.

Linn, M. (1978). Attrition of older alcoholics from treatment. *Addictive Disease, 3*(3), 437–447.

Luborsky, L., Auerbach, A. H., Chandler, M., Cohen, J., & Bachrach, H. M. (1971). Factors influencing the outcome of psychotherapy: A review of quantitative research. *Psychological Bulletin, 75,* 145–185.

Luborsky, L., Singer, B., & Luborsky, L. (1975). Comparative studies of psychotherapy. *Archives of General Psychiatry, 32,* 995–1008.

Luborsky, L., & Spence, D. P. (1978). Quantitative research on psychoanalytic therapy. In S. L. Garfield & A. E. Bergin (Eds.), *Handbook of psychotherapy and behavior change: An empirical analysis.* New York: Wiley.

MacMurray, V. D., Cunningham, P. H., Cater, P. B., Swenson, N., & Bellin, S. S. (1976). *Citizen evaluation of mental health services: A guidebook for accountability.* New York: Human Sciences Press.

Maguire, L. (1983). *Understanding social networks.* Beverly Hills, CA: Sage.

Maier, N. R. F. (1939). *Studies of abnormal behavior in the rat.* New York: Harpers.

Malan, D. H. (1963). *A study of brief psychotherapy.* New York: Lippincott.

Malan, D. H. (1973). The outcome problem in psychotherapy research: A historical review. *Archives of General Psychiatry, 29,* 719–729.

Malan, D. H. (1976). *Frontiers of brief psychotherapy.* New York: Plenum.

Mandel, H. P. (1981). *Short-term psychotherapy and brief treatment techniques.* New York: Plenum.

Mann, J. (1973). *Time-limited psychotherapy.* Cambridge, MA: Harvard University Press.

Mann, J., & Goldman, R. (1982). *A casebook in time-limited psychotherapy.* New York: McGraw-Hill.

Marcus, A. C., Reeder, L. G., Jordan, L. A., & Seeman, T. E. (1980). Monitoring health status, access to health care and compliance behavior in a large urban community. *Medical Care, 28,* 253–265.

Marston, M. V. (1970). Compliance with medical regimens: A review of the literature. *Nursing Research, 19,* 312–323.

Martin, P. J., Moore, J. E., Sterne, A. L., & Larue, D. (1977). Therapists as prophets: Their expectancies and treatment outcome. *Psychotherapy: Theory, Research and Practice, 14*(2), 188–195.

Martin, P. J., Moore, J. E., Sterne, A. L., & McNairy, R. M. (1977). Therapists prophesy. *Journal of Clinical Psychology, 33*(2), 502–510.

Martini, J. L. (1978). *Patient-therapist value congruence and rating of client improvement.* Dissertation Abstracts International 38 (9-B) 4469. Abstract No. 09188. University of Western Ontario, London, Canada.

Masserman, J. H. (1943). *Behavior and neurosis.* Chicago: University of Chicago Press.

McNair, D. M., Lorr, M., & Callahan, D. M. (1963). Patient and therapist influences on quitting psychotherapy. *Journal of Consulting Psychology, 27,* 10–23.

McWilliams, J., & Brown, C. (1977). Treatment termination variables, MMPI scores and frequency of relapse in alcoholics. *Journal of Studies on Alcohol, 38,* 477–486.

Mead, G. H. (1934). *Mind, self, and society: From the standpoint of a social behaviorist.* Chicago: University of Chicago Press.

Mead, G. H. (1938). *The philosophy of the act.* Chicago: University of Chicago Press.

Mechanic, D. (1978). Effects of psychological distress on perceptions of physical health and use of medical and psychiatric facilities. *Journal of Human Stress, 4*(4), 26–32.

Meehl, P. E. (1978). Theoretical risks and tabular asterisks: Sir Karl, Sir Ronald, and the slow progress of soft psychology. *Journal of Consulting and Clinical Psychology, 46,* 506–534.

Miller, N. E. (1971). *Selected papers on conflict, displacement, learned drives and theory.* Chicago: Aldine-Atherton.

Miller, N. E., & Dollard, J. (1950). *Personality and psychotherapy: An analysis in terms of learning, thinking and culture.* New York: McGraw-Hill.

Mintz, J., Luborsky, L., & Christoph, P. (1979). Measuring the outcomes of psychotherapy:

Finding of the Pennsylvania Psychotherapy Project. *Journal of Consulting and Clinical Psychology, 47,* 319–334.

Myers, J. K., & Auld, F. (1955). Some variables related to outcome in psychotherapy. *Journal of Clinical Psychology, 11,* 51–54.

National Center for Health Statistics. (1966). *Characteristics of patients of selected types of medical specialists and practitioners.: USA, July 1963–June 1964.* Washington, DC: USPHS Publication No. 1000, Series 10, No. 28.

O'Leary, M., Calsyn, D., Chaney, E., & Freeman, C. (1977). Predicting alcohol treatment program dropouts. *Journal of Diseases of the Nervous System, 38*(12), 993–995.

O'Leary, M., Robsenow, D., & Chaney, E. (1979). The use of multivariate personality strategies in predicting attrition from alcoholism treatment. *Journal of Clinical Psychiatry, 40*(4), 190–193.

Orford, J. (1974). Simplistic thinking about other people as a predictor of early dropout at an alcoholism halfway house. *British Journal of Medical Psychology, 47*(1), 53–62.

Orwin, R. G., & Cordray, D. S. (1984). Smith and Glass' psychotherapy conclusions need further probing: In Landman and Dawes' reanalysis (Comment). *American Psychologist, 38,* 71–72.

Pardes, H., & Pincus, H. A. (1981). Brief therapy in the context of mental health issues. In S. H. Budman (Ed.), *Forms of Brief Therapy.* New York: Guilford.

Parloff, M. B., Waskow, I. E., & Wolfe, B. E. (1978). Research on therapist variables in relation to process and outcome. In S. L. Garfield & A. E. Bergin (Eds.), *Handbook of psychotherapy and behavior change: An empirical analysis.* New York: Wiley.

Patterson, C. H. (1966). *Theories of counseling and psychotherapy.* New York: Harper & Row.

Patterson, C. H. (1980). *Theories of counseling and psychotherapy* (3rd ed.). New York: Harper & Row.

Patterson, V., & Heilbron, D. (1978). Therapist personality and treatment outcome: A test of the interaction hypothesis using the Campbell A-B Scale. *Psychiatric Quarterly, 50*(4), 320–332.

Paul, G. L. (1966). *Insight and desensitization in psychotherapy.* Stanford, CA: Stanford University Press.

Peake, T. H. (1979). Therapist-patient agreement and outcome in group therapy. *Journal of Clinical Psychology, 35*(3), 637–646.

Pelletier, K. R. (1979). *Holistic medicine: From stress to optimum health.* New York: Delacorte.

Pfouts, J., Wallach, M. S., & Jenkins, J. W. (1963). An outcome study of referrals to a psychiatric clinic. *Social Work, 8,* 79–86.

Phillips, E. L. (1960). Parent-child psychotherapy: a follow-up study comparing two techniques. *Journal of Psychology, 49,* 195–202.

Phillips, E. L. (1978). *Social skills basis of psychopathology.* New York: Grune & Stratton.

Phillips, E. L. (1982). *Stress, health and psychological problems in the major professions.* Lanham, MD: University Press of America.

Phillips, E. L. (in press). *Social skills: History and prospect.*

Phillips, E. L., & DePalma, D. M. (1983, August). *Attrition from A to Z: Preintake, intake and early therapy factors.* Paper presented at meeting of American Psychological Association, Los Angeles.

Phillips, E. L., & Fagan, P. J. (1982a, July). *Long-term results from time-limited psychotherapy.* Paper presented at 20th Congress of International Association of Applied Psychologists, Edinburgh, Scotland.

Phillips, E. L., & Fagan, P. J. (1982b, August). *Focus on the intake and first therapy interview.* Paper presented at American Psychological Association, Washington, DC.

Phillips, E. L., & Johnston, M. S. H. (1954). Theoretical and clinical aspects of short-term parent-child psychotherapy. *Psychiatry, 17,* 267–275.

Phillips, E. L., Kaiser, M. B., Heavner, T. (1983, December). *How the study of attrition relates to evaluation of psychotherapy.* Paper presented at 17th Annual AABT meeting, Washington, DC.

Phillips, E. L., Raiford, A. W., & Batrawi, S. A. (1965). The Q-sort reevaluated. *Journal of Consulting Psychology, 29,* 422–425.

Phillips, E. L., & Wiener, D. N. (1966). *Short-term psychotherapy and structured behavior change.* New York: McGraw-Hill.

Poser, E. (1966). The effects of therapist's training on group therapeutic outcome. *Journal of Consulting Psychology, 30,* 1283–1289.

Posin. J. I. (1963). Approaches to brief psychotherapy in a university health service. *Seminars in Psychiatry, 1,* 399–404.

Pothier, P. E. (1975). *Patient compliance in therapy.* NIMH.

The Psychosocial Rehabilitation Journal, Vol. 1 (1978).

Rachman, S. J. (1971). *The effects of psychotherapy* (2nd ed.) Oxford: Pergamon.

Rachman, S. J., & Wilson, G. T. (1980). *The effects of psychological therapy.* New York: Pergamon.

Raynes, A. E., & Patch, V. D. (1973). Attrition at referral among heroin addicts. *International Journal of Addiction, 8*(5), 839–46.

Reda, M. A., & Mahoney, M. J. (1984). *Cognitive psychotherapies: Recent developments in theory, research, and practice.* Cambridge, MA: Ballinger.

Reder, P., & Tyson, R. L. (1980). Patient dropout from individual psychotherapy. *Bulletin of the Menninger Clinic, 44,* 229–252.

Reynolds, D. K. (1976). *Morita psychotherapy.* Berkeley: University of California Press.

Reynolds, D. K. (1980). *The quiet therapies: Japanese pathways to personal growth.* Honolulu: University of Hawaii Press.

Reynolds, D. K. (1983). *Naikan psychotherapy.* Honolulu: University of Hawaii Press.

Rodolfa, E. R., Rappaport, R., & Lee, V. E. (1982). Variables related to premature termination in a university counseling service. *Journal of Counseling Psychology, 30,* 87–90.

Rogers, C. P. (1951). *Client-centered therapy.* Boston: Houghton-Mifflin.

Rogers, C. R., & Dymond, R. (1954). *Psychotherapy and personality change.* Chicago: University of Chicago Press.

Rogers, C. R., Gendlin, E. T., Kiesler, D., & Truax, C. B. (1967). *The therapeutic relationship and its impact.* Madison: University of Wisconsin Press.

Rosenberg, M., Davidson, G. E., Patch, V. D. (1972). Patterns of dropouts from a methadone program for narcotic addicts. *International Journal of Addiction, 7*(3), 415–425.

Rosenstein, M. J., & Milazzo-Sayer, L. J. (1981). Characteristics of admissions to selected mental Health facilities, 1975. Rockville, MD: USDHHS.

Rosenstock, I. M. (1974). The Health Belief Model and preventive health behavior. *Health Education Monographs, 2,* 354–386.

Rosenthal, R. (1979). The "file drawer" problem and tolerance for null results. *Psychological Bulletin, 86,* 638–641.

Rossi, P. H., Freeman, H. E. (1982). *Evaluation: A systematic approach* (2nd ed.). Beverly Hills: Sage.

Sadoka, J. M., Cohen, B. H., & Beall, G. (1954). Test significance for a series of statistical tests. *Psychological Bulletin, 51,* 172–173.

Sarvis, M. A., Dewees, M. S., & Johnson, R. F. (1958). A concept of ego-oriented psychotherapy. *Psychiatry, 22,* 277–287.

Sashin, J., Eldred, S., & Van Amerongen, S. (1975). A search for predictive factors in institute supervised cases. *International Journal of Psychoanalysis, 56,* 343–359.

Schofield, L. (1978). Internal-external locus of control and withdrawal AMA from an alcohol rehabilitation program. *Journal of Clinical Psychology, 34*(2), 571–573.

Seligman, M. E. P. (1975). *Helplessness: On depression, development and death.* San Francisco: Freeman.

Selya, H. (1974). *Stress without distress.* Philadelphia: Lippincott.

Shapiro, D. A., & Shapiro, D. (1983). Comparative therapy outcome research: Methodological implications of meta-a-nalysis. *Journal of Consulting and Clinical Psychology, 51,* 42–53.

Shelton, J. L., Levy, R. L. (1981). *Behavioral assignments and treatment compliance.* Champaign, IL: Research Press.

Shepard, D. C., & Moseley, T. A. E. (1976). Mailed versus telephoned appointment reminders to reduce broken appointments in a hospital outpatient department. *Medical Care, 14,* 268–273.

Shostrom, E. L. (1966). *Three approaches to psychotherapy. Films of Rogers, Pers and Ellis.* Santa Ana, CA: Psychological Films.

Shuelman, S. A., Gelso, C. J., Mindus, L., Hunt, B., & Stevenson, J. (1980). Client satisfaction with intake: Is the waiting list all that matters? *Journal of College Student Personnel, 11,* 114–121.

Siegel, J. M. (1973). Mental health volunteers as change agents. *American Journal of Community Psychology, 1,* 138–158.

Sifneos, P. E. (1972). *Short-term psychotherapy and emotional crisis.* Cambridge, MA: Harvard University Press.

Sifneos, P. E. (1979). *Short-term dynamic psychotherapy: Evaluation and technique.* New York: Plenum.

Silverman, W. H., & Beech, R. P. (1979). Are dropouts, dropouts? *Journal of Community Psychology, 7,* 236–242.

Singleton, W. T., Spurgeon, P., & Stammers, R. B. (1980). *The analysis of social skills.* New York: Plenum.

Sinnett, E. R., & Danskin, D. G. (1967). Intake and walk-in procedure in a college counseling setting. *Personnel and Guidance Journal, 45,* 445–451.

Sloane, R. B., Staples, F. R., Cristol, A. H., Yorkston, N. J., & Whipple, K. (1975). *Short-term analytically oriented psychotherapy versus behavior change.* Cambridge: Harvard University Press.

Small, L. (1971). *The briefer therapies.* New York: Brunner/Mazel.

Smart, R., & Gray, G. (1978). Multiple predictors of dropout from alcoholism treatment. *Archives of General Psychiatry, 35,* 363–367.

Smith, M. L., & Glass, E. G. (1977). Meta-analysis of psychotherapy outcome studies. *American Psychologist, 32,* 552–560.

Smith, M. L., Glass, G. V., & Miller, T. I. (1980). *The benefits of psychotherapy.* Baltimore: Johns Hopkins University Press.

Snyder, W. U. (1947). "Warmth" in nondirective counseling. *Journal of Abnormal and Social Psychology, 41,* 491–495.

Solomon, R. L. (1964). Punishment. *American Psychologist, 19,* 239–253.

Stieper, D. R., Wiener, D. N. (1965). *Dimensions of psychotherapy.* Chicago: Aldine.

Stokes, B. (1981). *Helping ourselves: Local solutions to global problems.* New York: Norton.

Stone, C. (1979). Patient compliance and the role of the expert. *Journal of Social Issues, 35,* 34–59.

Straker, M. (1968). Brief psychotherapy in an outpatient clinic: Evolution and evaluation. *American Journal of Psychiatry, 124,* 39–45.

Strong, S. R. (1968). Counseling: An interpersonal influence process. *Journal of Counseling Psychology, 15,* 215–224.

Strupp, H. H. (1978). Psychotherapy research and practice: An overview. In S. L. Garfield & A. E. Bergin (Eds.), *Handbook of psychotherapy and behavior change: An empirical anaysis.* New York: Wiley.

Strupp, H. H. (1981). Theoretical issues in forms of brief therapy. In S. H. Budman (Ed.), *Forms of brief therapy.* New York: Guilford.

Strupp, H. H., & Bloxom, A. (1973). Preparing lower-class patients for group psychotherapy: Development and evaluation of a role- induction film. *Journal of Consulting and Clinical Psychology, 41,* 373-384.

Strupp, H. H., Fox, R. E., & Lessler, K. (1969). *Patients view their psychotherapy.* Baltimore: Johns Hopkins University Press.

Strupp, H. H., & Hadley, S. W. (1979). Specific vs. nonspecific factors in psychotherapy: A controlled study of outcome. *Archives of General Psychiatry, 36,* 1125-1136.

Strupp, H. H., Hadley, S. W., & Gomes-Schwartz, B. (1977). *Psychotherapy for better or worse: An analysis of the problem of negative effects.* New York: Jason Aronson.

Tantam, D., & Klerman, G. (1979). Patient transfer from one clinician to another and dropping out of outpatient treatment. *Social Psychiatry, 14*(3), 107-113.

Terkel, S. (1974). *Working.* New York: Avon Books.

Trower, P., Bryant, B., & Argyle, M. (1978). *Social skills and mental health.* London: Methuen.

Ursano, R. J., & Dressler, D. M. (1974). Brief versus long-term psychotherapy: A treatment decision. *Journal of Nervous and Mental Diseases, 159,* 164-171.

Veroff, J. B. (1981). The dynamics of help-seeking in men and women: A national survey. *Psychiatry, 44,* 189-200.

Veroff, J., Kulka, R. A., & Douvan E. (1981). *Mental health in America: Patterns of help-seeking from 1957 to 1976.* New York: Basic Books.

Wallach, M. A., & Wallach, L. (1983). *Psychology's sanction for selfishness: The error of egoism in theory and therapy.* San Francisco: Freeman.

Wallerstein, R., Robbins, L., Sargent, H., & Luborsky, L. (1956). The psychotherapy research project of the Menninger Foundation. *Bulletin of the Menninger Clinic, 20,* 221-280.

Watts, T. E. (1972). The regularity of attendance of male tuberculosis patients diagnosed at Mulago Hospital between January and July in 1968 and in 1970. *Tubercle, 53*(3), 174-181.

Weeks, G. R., & L'Abate, L. (1982). Paradoxical psychotherapy. New York: Brunner/Mazel.

Weissman, M. M., Geanakoplos, E., & Prusoff, B. (1973). Social class and attrition in depressed outpatients. *Social Casework, 54,* 162-170.

Wells, R. A. (1982). *Planned short-term treatment.* New York: Free Press.

Widiger, T. A., & Rorer, L. G. (1984). The responsible psychotherapist. *American Psychologist, 39,* 503-515.

Wilkinson, A., Prado, W., Williams, W., & Schnadt, F. (1971). Psychological test characteristics and length of stay in alcoholism treatment. *Quarterly Journal of Studies on Alcohol, 32,* 60-65.

Wilson, G. T. (1981). Behavior therapy as a short-term therapeutic approach. In S. H. Budman (Ed.), *Forms of brief therapy.* New York: Guilford.

Windle, C. (1983). *Provisional data on federally funded mental health centers,* 1978-1979. Survey and Reports Branch, NIMH.

Wine, J. D., & Smye, M. D. (1981). *Social competence.* New York: Guilford.

Wolberg, L. R. (1980). *Handbook of short-term psychotherapy.* New York: Thieme-Stratton.

Zamostny, K. P., Corrigan, J. D., & Eggert, M. A. (1981). Replication and extension of social influence process in counseling: A field study. *Journal of Counseling Psychology, 28,* 481-489.

Zamostny, K. P., Corrigan, J. D., & Eggert, M. A. (1982, August). *Prediction of client satisfaction with intake and attrition following intake using social influence variables.* Paper presented at meeting of American Psychological Association, Washington, DC.

Zax, M., & Klein, A. (1960). Measurement of personality and behavior change following psychotherapy. *Psychological Bulletin, 57,* 435-448.

Zilbergeld, B. (1983). *The shrinking of America.* Boston: Little, Brown.

Author Index

Subject Index